TOP CAREERS
FOR
HISTORY
GRADUATES

Also available
Top Careers for Art Graduates
Top Careers for Business Graduates
Top Careers for Communications Graduates
Top Careers for Economics Graduates
Top Careers for Liberal Arts Graduates

History
Graduates

Checkmark Books®
An imprint of Facts On File, Inc.

Checkmark Books
An imprint of Facts On File, Inc.
132 West 31st Street
New York NY 10001

Library of Congress Cataloging-in-Publication Data

Top careers for history graduates.
    p. cm.
    Includes index.
    Summary: Provides guidance for the student considering a career in
history or a related field, discussing such things as what jobs are
available, which college major is the best preparation for each, and
which high school courses provide a good foundation.
    ISBN 0-8160-5567-X (pbk: alk. paper)
    1. History—Vocational guidance—United States—Juvenile literature.
[1. History—Vocational guidance. 2. Vocational guidance.]
    D13.5.U6T67 2004
    902′.3′73—dc22   2003020409

Checkmark Books are available at special discounts when purchased in bulk quantities for businesses, associations, institutions, or sales promotions. Please call our Special Sales Department in New York at (212) 967-8800 or (800) 322-8755.

You can find Facts On File on the World Wide Web at http://www.factsonfile.com

Text design by David Strelecky

Cover design by Cathy Rincon

Printed in the United States of America

MP Hermitage 10 9 8 7 6 5 4 3 2 1

This book is printed on acid-free paper.

CONTENTS

SECTION I

WHY DO YOU NEED A COLLEGE DEGREE?

More people are receiving college degrees than ever before. In 2000, more than 1 million students earned their bachelor's degrees. By 2001, 58 percent of all individuals between the ages of 25 and 29 had completed some part of a college education. The National Center for Education Statistics reports that 29 percent of this same age group held at least a bachelor's degree.

With a larger number of college graduates entering the workforce, many employers now require a college degree for jobs that previously had lower educational requirements. This "educational upgrading" has occurred primarily in occupations that are considered desirable and are high paying.

Employers want workers with good communication, teamwork, and problem-solving skills. They want workers who are able to learn quickly, workers who can adapt and adjust to workplace challenges, and workers who have the desire to excel and achieve. Above all, they want college graduates.

However, this book does more than tout the importance of a college degree. Also included is information on how to define and evaluate your skills and interests, how to choose a major, how to make the most of your college program, and how to turn your college degree into a satisfying job.

This book, in particular, focuses on students interested in studying history. The following sections describe the contents.

SECTION I

Introduction: Meet the History Major provides an overview of history education. It also provides basic information on colleges and universities, suggested courses, necessary skills, potential employers, starting salaries, and further avenues for exploration.

Chapter 1: Your High School Years will help you select a major and prepare for college study while you are still in high school. You will read about suggested courses, assessment tests, methods of exploring the history major, and choosing a college.

Chapter 2: Making the Most of Your Experience as a History Major will help you make the best use of your college years—even if you are not sure of a major upon entering school. Topics include typical history curricula, the benefits of pursuing a minor, methods of exploring careers, and preparing for the workforce.

Chapter 3: Taking Your History Degree to Work offers tips on finding your life direction after graduation, job searching, improving your resume, applying for jobs online, successful interviewing, and the benefits of a graduate degree.

Section I also features informative interviews with college professors and workers in the field who will provide further insight on the history major and its career options.

SECTION II

The second half of the book features profiles of 35 careers in the field of history. Each article discusses the occupation in detail.

The **Quick Facts** section provides a brief summary of the career, including recommended school subjects, personal skills, work environment, minimum educational requirements, salary ranges, certification or licensing requirements, and employment outlook. This section also provides acronyms and identification numbers for the following government classification indexes: the *Dictionary of Occupational Titles* (DOT), the Guide to Occupational Exploration (GOE), the National Occupational Classification (NOC) Index, and the Occupational Information Network (O*NET)-Standard Occupational Classification System (SOC) index. The DOT, GOE, and O*NET-SOC indexes have been created by the U.S. government; the NOC index is Canada's career-classification system. Readers can use the identification numbers listed in the Quick Facts section to access further information on a career. Print editions of the DOT (*Dictionary of Occupational Titles*. Indianapolis, Ind.: JIST Works, 1991) and GOE (*The Complete Guide for Occupational Exploration*. Indianapolis, Ind.: JIST Works, 1993) are available from libraries, and electronic versions of the NOC (http://www23. hrdc-drhc.gc.ca/2001/e/generic/welcome.shtml) and O*NET-SOC (http://online.onetcenter.org) are available on the World Wide Web. When no DOT, GOE, NOC, or O*NET-SOC numbers are present, this means that the U.S. Department of Labor or the Human Resources Development Canada have not created a numerical designation for this career. In this instance, you will see the acronym "N/A," or not available.

The **Overview** section is a brief introductory description of the duties and responsibilities involved in this career. Oftentimes, a career may have a variety of job titles. When this is the case, alternative career titles are presented in this section.

The **History** section describes the history of the particular job as it relates to the overall development of its industry or field.

The Job describes in detail the primary and secondary duties of the job.

Requirements discusses high school and postsecondary education and training requirements, certification or licensing, if necessary, and any other personal requirements for success in the job. The majority of the careers in *Top Careers for History Graduates* require a minimum of a bachelor's degree, but we also included are a few careers that may have a minimum educational requirement of a graduate degree. For example, the careers of anthropologist, archaeologist, college professor, ethnoscientist, lawyer, librarian, and political scientist require a master's or doctorate degree. Conversely, the book includes a few careers that require less than a college degree (such as genealogist and tour guide); however, some college-level business courses are highly recommended for these positions.

Exploring offers suggestions on how to gain some experience in or knowledge of the particular job before making a firm educational and financial commitment. While in high school or the early years of college, you can learn about clubs and other activities, for example, that will give you a better understanding of the job.

The **Employers** section gives an overview of typical places of employment for the job and may also include specific employment numbers from the U.S. Department of Labor.

Starting Out discusses the best ways to land that first job, be it through a college placement office, newspaper ads, or personal contacts.

The **Advancement** section describes what kind of career path to expect from the job and how to get there.

Earnings lists salary ranges and describes the typical fringe benefits.

The **Work Environment** section describes the typical surroundings and conditions of employment—whether indoors or outdoors, noisy or quiet, social or independent, and so on. Also discussed are typical hours worked, any seasonal fluctuations, and the stresses and strains of the job.

The **Outlook** section summarizes the job in terms of the general economy and industry projections. For the most part, Outlook information is obtained from the Bureau of Labor Statistics and is supplemented by information taken from professional associations. Job growth terms follow those used in the *Occupational Outlook Handbook*:

- Growth described as "much faster than the average" means an increase of 36 percent or more.
- Growth described as "faster than the average" means an increase of 21–35 percent.
- Growth described as "about as fast as the average" means an increase of 10–20 percent.
- Growth described as "more slowly than the average" means an increase of 3–9 percent.
- Growth described as having "little or no change" means an increase of 0–2 percent.
- "Decline" means a decrease of 1 percent or more.

Each career article concludes with **For More Information,** which lists organizations that can provide career information on training, education, internships, scholarships, and job placement.

Throughout the book you will also find sidebars that provide further information about issues in the history field. The book concludes with a glossary of history terms used throughout the career articles, as well as a list of books for further reading.

Whether you are a high school student unsure of a college major, a college student interested in learning more about careers, or an adult thinking about returning to school, this book will help you learn more about the history major and the career options available to those with this background.

MEET THE HISTORY MAJOR

WHAT IS HISTORY?

History is the social science concerned with the study of the social, cultural, political, and economic events of our past. The history department is usually part of the school of liberal arts at most colleges and universities. Related liberal arts majors include anthropology, economics, English, fine arts, languages/linguistics, political science/government, religious studies, philosophy, and sociology.

The study of history is usually divided into ancient, medieval, and modern segments and subdivided into many specialties and concentrations.

According to the U.S. Department of Education, 25,247 students graduated with an undergraduate degree in history in 2000. Another 2,573 graduated with a master's degree and 984 graduated with a doctorate.

History has long been a popular college major. In fact, the number of students majoring in history at the undergraduate level has been increasing in recent years. In the 2001–02 academic year, history majors increased by 6.1 percent from 2000–01, according to the American Historical Association.

WHY STUDY HISTORY?

Many people think that history is simply the study and memorization of dates and famous people, but there is a lot more to the study of history than remembering facts such as when the Magna Carta was issued (1215 A.D., if you're curious), especially at the college level. We study the events, people, and movements of the past to help us understand the world we live in and to plan the world of the future. In a practical sense, the study of history is a great foundation for almost any career field. The study of history is not just for aspiring historians and teachers; it can be applied to any type of career that requires you to think critically and creatively, assess and evaluate information, and hone your writing and speaking skills.

WILL I GET A JOB IF I MAJOR IN HISTORY?

Many people feel that a history major, and most liberal arts majors, for that matter, is an inadequate preparation for the world of work. Oftentimes people feel that a college degree should be a gateway to a specific job track, such as computer science, accounting, or nursing. Although some people might favor a specialized major, you can take heart: Majoring in history will prepare you for the challenges of the workplace and provide you with some advantages over non-liberal arts majors. Many of today's employers value graduates with general-knowledge degrees such as history, as these graduates possess the communication, problem-solving, and organizational skills that are universally important. If you plan carefully and make good use of your college years, using that time to determine your strengths and weaknesses and likes and dislikes, majoring in history will help you build an educational and skill foundation that will prepare you for success in almost any field.

WHAT COURSES WILL I TAKE?

During your freshman and sophomore years—no matter what subject you major in—you'll need to complete your college's core curriculum. These introductory classes in science, English, sociology, writing, mathematics, psychology, and other areas will help you learn more about your interests.

As a history major, you'll study a wide variety of topics, events, and people. All history majors take introductory courses, such as introduction to ancient history, introduction to western civilization, introduction to modern civilization (you get the idea), that provide a general overview of major areas of historical study. Taking these classes will help you choose a specific area of study or concentration within the major. Concentrations focus on geographical regions, themes, time periods, or a combination of these areas. Since history majors do a lot of research and writing, you will probably be required to take one or more classes that are specifically designed to help you develop these skills.

WHAT WILL I LEARN?

Besides engaging with the rich story of human history, the study of history will teach you how to

- write and speak effectively
- analyze ideas and information
- develop strong research skills
- think about and solve problems and issues in a variety of ways
- communicate effectively with a diverse group of people
- develop an appreciation and respect for other cultural traditions

WHERE WILL I WORK
AND HOW MUCH WILL I EARN?

Although most people assume that history majors go on to become historians, only a small percentage of history graduates pursue careers in this area. Many history majors work as teachers; others work as archivists, curators, and directors at museums and historical societies. Other history graduates may pursue careers in writing and editing, advertising and marketing, or business. Some students pursue an undergraduate major in history as preparation for advanced studies in law, religion, library science, political science, finance, government, education, journalism, business, or other subject areas.

In short, you can do almost anything you want with a history major. A history major opens many professional doors, and with additional education, the sky's the limit.

The National Association of Colleges and Employers reports that history majors earned average starting salaries of $32,108 in summer 2003.

You can learn more about history by visiting the following websites:

American Association for State and Local History
http://www.aaslh.org

The American Historical Association
http://www.theaha.org

Best of History Websites
http://www.besthistorysites.net

The Center for History and New Media
http://chnm.gmu.edu

EDSITEment
http://edsitement.neh.gov

History Matters: The U.S. Survey on the Web
http://www.historymatters.gmu.edu

The History Net
http://www.thehistorynet.com

The History Place
http://www.historyplace.com

National Council for History Education
http://www.history.org/nche

Organization of American Historians
http://www.oah.org

Princeton Review: Find a Major
http://www.princetonreview.com/college/research/majors

Yahoo! Resources for History
http://dir.yahoo.com/Arts/Humanities/History/Organizations

INTERVIEW: Clarence Wyatt

Dr. Clarence Wyatt is the chairperson of the history department at Centre College in Danville, Kentucky. He is also the author of Paper Soldiers: The American Press and the Vietnam War *(University of Chicago Press, 1993). Dr. Wyatt discussed the history major and opportunities in the field with the editors of* Top Careers for History Graduates.

Q. For what types of careers does a history major prepare students?

A. The standard, but patently false, assumption is that a history major only prepares one to teach history or lead a life of self-indulgent poverty. Actually, a history major is great preparation for MANY careers. Any activity (including the study of history) that puts a premium on the ability to make sense of incomplete or conflicting information; to make sound judgments; to assess character; to write and speak clearly and with grace; to deal with ideas, policies, or people; and that is grounded in an understanding of social groups, is a wonderful training ground.

Q. What are the most important personal and professional qualities for history majors?

A. The first is a deep appreciation of and curiosity about people. You can't love history if you don't have these two qualities. Every good historian is a bit of a voyeur. You also need to have a quick mind and a quick eye—to catch the little nuance in a piece of evidence, to make the connections between events and ideas, in other words, to be a bit of a detective. Also, strong writing skills—or the willingness to put in the work to develop them—are a must.

Q. Do new history students in your program have any expectations about what the study of history will entail?

A. We have strong students at Centre, but even well-prepared students are a bit surprised by the level of critical thinking that we demand—the questioning of assumptions, of face value, the emphasis on the why, not just the who, what, when, and where, that we ask for. Also, we assign a great deal of reading and writing.

Q. What type of internships are available to history students at Centre College?

A. At Centre, we make a strong effort to connect the strengths of the liberal arts to the wider world, and internships are clearly a key part of that. We have a very strong alumni network that we use quite effectively, and we have developed good connections with the political, nonprofit, and corporate communities in Kentucky and across the nation—particularly in Washington and New York. Let me give you some examples of the internships that I've sponsored in the last two or three years.

Positions

- with six of the eight members of Kentucky's Congressional delegation
- with the executive director of the 2001 Presidential Inaugural Committee
- with a variety of public and private attorneys
- with one of the leading public relations firms in the Southeast
- with the leading U.S. Civil War preservation project in the country
- with two U.S. district judges
- with the Kentucky Department of Homeland Security (this young woman helped to direct the assessment of threat to Kentucky's infrastructure—roads, bridges, dams, etc.)

- with the Kentucky History Center
- with the 2000 vice presidential debate held here at Centre, for which I served as co-chair

I could provide more examples, but I think these give you a sense of how well the skills of a history major translate to a variety of endeavors, and how aggressive and creative we try to be in making that point clear.

Q. Should students pursue a graduate degree in history?

A. That would depend on where they want to go with that graduate work. If they are interested in study and teaching at the college/university level, I first try to talk them out of it—educating them about the long haul, the crap-shoot that job placement becomes, etc. I'm trying to test just how badly they want to do this. If students still have the fire after all my attempts at discouragement, I advise them to find the person in their particular area of interest who best combines an outstanding record as a scholar and a teacher, and worry less about the name of the institution. I also encourage them to get teaching experience as early and extensively as they can.

Q. What advice would you offer history majors as they graduate and look for jobs?

A. I would advise being creative in terms of how you present yourself. Don't talk so much about your major or your classes—an employer worth his or her salt is interested in what you've done as much as what you can do; focus on the skills and attributes that you've developed and market the dickens out of them—they are very valuable.

CHAPTER 1

YOUR HIGH SCHOOL YEARS

As a high school student, you might think you're too young to begin thinking about a career. But even if you're only a sophomore or junior, college is just around the corner. You need to begin thinking about what you will major in and what you will do with the rest of your life. If you're reading this book, you probably have an interest in history. But in addition to studying history, you should use your high school years to explore your interest in related majors such as geography, philosophy, sociology, government, political science, religious studies, anthropology, archaeology, economics, art history, and even subject areas that have nothing to do with history. You might be surprised at where your journey takes you.

This chapter will help you learn more about yourself, about history, and about choosing a college.

SUGGESTED COURSES

Take a wide variety of college preparatory classes in high school to help you determine what subjects you like and dislike. Take English, speech, geography, philosophy, social studies, government, sociology, mathematics, business, and science. Of course, take as many history classes as you can. You should also take a foreign language, since many colleges require that their students, and especially history majors, be proficient in a language other than their own. While computer science might not be the first subject that comes to mind when you think of history, computer classes will help you hone your research, word-processing, and Internet skills—skills that you'll use in college and the world of work regardless of your major. You might even use these skills to apply to colleges online.

Ask your guidance counselor to suggest classes that will help prepare you to study history in college.

ASSESSMENT TESTS

There are other ways to decide which major is right for you. Personal assessment tests will focus on your values, interests, academic strengths, and personality and help you evaluate your college and career options. It is best to take one or more of these tests while in high school. They will help you focus on a major and even pick a college that is well known for its education in the major you choose. The following are some of the more popular tests available (Note that some of these tests require a fee. Talk to your high school guidance counselor or adviser for more details.):

- Scholastic Aptitude Test (SAT): The SAT is a three-hour test measuring verbal and mathematical reasoning skills. Many colleges and universities use the SAT as an indicator of academic performance in combination with grades, class rank, extracurricular activities, the personal essay, and teacher recommendations. Visit http://www.collegeboard.com for more information.

- American College Testing Program (ACT): Similar to the SAT, the ACT is designed to assess high school students' academic abilities and estimate their college performance. The test covers four basic areas: English, math, reading comprehension, and scientific reasoning. For details, visit http://www.act.org.

- Kuder Career Planning System: The Kuder test helps individuals evaluate their interests, skills, and values. Suggested college majors and careers are ranked based on survey responses. For sample tests and more information, visit http://www.kuder.com.

- Myers-Briggs Type Indicator: This assessment test identifies an individual's personality type using four general, but opposite, dispositions: extraversion/introversion, sensate/intuitive, thinking/feeling, or judging/perceiving. Based on responses to test questions, the individual is characterized as one of 16 personality types. Visit http://www.cpp-db.com for details.

- Career Key: Developed by Lawrence K. Jones, a college professor specializing in career counseling and development, this website hosts a quick and easy assessment to help you explore jobs that fit your career type, such as artistic or enterprising. After answering questions about your interests and skills, the Career Key develops a list of appropriate jobs that fit your responses. Visit http://www.careerkey.org to take your own assessment test.

- Armed Services Vocational Aptitude Battery (ASVAB): The ASVAB, administered by the U.S. Department of Defense, is a multi-aptitude test available at over 14,000 high schools nationwide. The tests evaluate students' vocabulary skills, reading comprehension, math skills, math reasoning, general science knowledge, shop and technical skills, mechanical knowledge, and knowledge of electronics. Scores are combined to reveal three general scores for verbal, math, and academic ability. See http://asvabprogram.com for more information.

- Princeton Review Career Quiz: This quick and easy multiple-choice survey will help you determine your worker "type" (such as careful/orderly or quick/random) and your main work interests (such as artistic/creative or mechanical/technical). To try it out, visit http://www.princetonreview.com/cte/quiz.

INTERVIEW: Natasha Gray

Natasha Gray is an Assistant Professor of History at Lawrence University in Appleton, Wisconsin. She spoke with the editors of Top Careers for History Graduates *about the major.*

Q. What type of careers are available to students who earn a history degree?

A. Any job that requires the ability to analyze complex information. Students face a job market where they will in all probability have to change careers several times . . . . In choosing a major, student should ask themselves if they will learn skills that could be applied to a wide variety of jobs. As a history major, you will learn to read documents closely, analyze statistical information, and find meaning in a wide variety of cultural products from film to car design. You also learn how to "put yourself in the shoes" of people who are very different from you: dictators and do-gooders, popes and peasants, warriors and mystics.

The ability to understand different worldviews—no matter how strange or even repugnant they may seem—is a critical skill in our era of globalization. In the new information economy, these are the skills that will empower college graduates to succeed.

Q. What are the most important personal and professional qualities for history majors?

A. The ability to see the world from another person's perspective. History is based on the premise that people understand each other regardless of differences. Anyone can write the history of anyone else. To do this, you have to have three qualities: commitment to gather and analyze all available information to the best of your ability, a willingness to constantly examine how your own beliefs and life experience are shaping your emerging understanding of events, and, finally, imagination. Someone who has a commitment to understanding the perspectives of others, to fostering imagination, and to continual improvement through critical self-examination will be well equipped to solve problems in both the study of history and life.

Q. When the average student enters your program, what are their expectations? Are they prepared or unprepared for the curriculum?

A. That is hard to say. High school history programs vary in their quality. Some students are very well prepared and others are not. Many students became interested in history through studying World War II. Some of these budding military historians are frustrated to discover that they are expected to learn all sorts of "soft social history." Other students believe that they can get by as a history major through memorization. This strategy can get you Bs at the introductory level, but stops working well after that.

Q. What is your advice to students regarding the pursuit of graduate degree in history?

A. I advise students who are interested in becoming history professors to do a serious analysis of the academic job market before choosing a field of study. Look through the last few years of *Perspectives: Newsmagazine of the American Historical Association* (http://www. theaha.org/perspectives) and read the articles on the job market and look at advertisements for positions. You will find that the job market for American and European history is much more competitive than it is for Asia, Latin America, the Middle East, or Africa.

EXPLORE AND LEARN MORE

Besides assessment tests, there are many other ways to explore your interest in history while you're in high school.

Join a Club

Join your school's history or foreign language club. Clubs are great places to meet like-minded people and explore your interest in history. Extracurricular activities also look great on your college application.

Contribute to a Newspaper/Literary Magazine

Get involved with your school's student newspaper or literary magazine. You'll learn how to perform research, interview people, analyze and assess information, follow directions, meet deadlines, and work with others—skills that you will need if you are interested in studying history. If your school doesn't have a newspaper or literary magazine, start one.

Write and Submit History Essays/Papers for Review

If you like to write about history, you should consider submitting your work to *The Concord Review,* a quarterly journal that has published history papers of over 500 high school students since 1987. Essays may be on any historical topic (ancient or modern, domestic or foreign) and must be approximately 5,000 words, with endnotes and bibliography. An application fee is required for each essay, but applicants receive a one-year subscription to the publication. For more information, contact *The Concord Review (TCR),* 730 Boston Post Road, Suite 24, Sudbury, MA 01776. Visit the TCR website, http://www.tcr.org, to read sample essays.

The National Writing Board, an affiliate of *The Concord Review,* also offers independent assessment of high school history papers in of either 2,000 words or 5,000 words (the two categories are judged separately) with endnotes and bibliography. An application fee is required for each essay submission. If you submit your paper, the Board will send you a three-page report critiquing your work, which you can send to college admissions offices or simply use as feedback. For more information, contact the National Writing Board, 730 Boston Post Road, Suite 24, Sudbury, Mass. 01776, http://www.tcr.org/nwb.

Participate in Student Government

The study of government is an important aspect of almost any history program. Get involved with student government to learn more about our system of government and to meet people who share similar interests. Participating in student government will help you to develop your critical thinking, leadership, organization, and information- and people-management skills. College admissions officers also like to see participation in activities such as student government on college applications.

If you aren't elected to student government, you can still learn about the political process by volunteering on a political campaign or by visiting your local city council to watch politicians at work. You can also check out the Youth Leadership Initiative (http://www9. youthleadership.net/youthleadership), a program sponsored by The University of Virginia Center for Politics, which helps middle- and high-school students learn more about our political process.

Join a Professional Association as a Student Member

Many professional history organizations offer student membership to high school and college students. This membership often allows you to access newsletters and other resources from the organization. For example, student members of the American Association for State and Local History (http://www.aaslh.org) receive *Dispatch,* a national monthly newsletter that reports on the history field, professional development opportunities, and resources for history professionals. Student members of the National Council on Public History (http://www.ncph.org) receive *The Public Historian* and *Public History News,* quarterly journals that provide more information for those interested in public history.

Volunteer

Community service is a great way to help others, meet new people, learn applicable skills, and test your interest in a field. Volunteering at a museum, historical society, cultural center, or other historical organization will expose you to all kinds of historical issues and allow you to meet historians, archivists, organization directors, researchers, writers, archaeologists, anthropologists, and other professionals who have a history-related background. It will also help you to develop leadership, organizational, interpersonal, and other skills that you will need to be successful in any field.

Get a Job

A summer or part-time job, whether it's working as a sales clerk in a department store, as a food service worker in a fast food restaurant, or as a delivery person for a pharmacy, will teach you time-management skills, responsibility, and how to get along with others. It might also help you save money toward college tuition and related costs. An ideal entry-level position would be with a history-related employer, such as a museum, historical society, or nonprofit historical preservation agency. In such positions you'll get the chance to meet people who are interested in history, and you might even make such a great impression that you'll be considered for positions in the future. College admissions officials will be impressed by the fact that you excelled at your studies while holding down a job.

Talk to the Experts

Ask your guidance counselor or history teacher (another expert resource for information on this field) to set up an information interview with a historian or another worker in a history-related field. Compile a list of questions before the interview to ensure that you will make good use of the worker's valuable time. Suggested questions include: What are the pros and cons of your job? Can you describe a typical day on the job? What other fields can I work in with a history degree?

Use Books and Television

Countless books offer detailed information on history majors and careers. One excellent publication is *Careers for Students of History*, published by the American Historical Association (AHA), the National Council on Public History (NCPH), and the Public History Program at the University of South Carolina. To learn more about this book, visit the websites of the AHA (http://www.theaha.org) or the NCPH (http://www.ncph.org).

Another way to learn more about history is to watch documentaries and other programs on the History Channel, The Discovery Channel, or the Public Broadcasting Service.

CHOOSING A COLLEGE

What criteria are most important to you when you think about choosing a college? Academic programs? Size? Admissions requirements? Cost? Extracurricular activities? Location? A combination of all these factors? If you've already decided to major in history, you'll need to choose a college that has a reputation for having a good history program.

Selecting a college is one of the most important decisions you will make in your life. Choosing the right college will provide you with the tools for academic and career success. You'll receive a good education, meet professors who can serve as mentors as you enter a career, and form friendships that you may keep your entire life. Picking the wrong school is not the end of the world (plenty of people have switched schools after their freshman or sophomore years without facing disaster), but having to switch schools later in your college years may delay your education and make you frustrated or unhappy. So, how do you learn more about colleges so you can make a good decision? Try the following resources for information on choosing a college.

Guidance Counselors

Your guidance counselor can provide you with comprehensive information on academic programs, financial aid, application deadlines, and other facts about colleges and universities. Criteria to consider when choosing a college include academic programs offered, reputation or ranking, atmosphere (e.g., small or large college, private or public, diversity of student body), student-to-teacher ratio (the number of students for every teacher), location (local or out of state), costs (tuition, housing, books), graduation rates, and extracurricular activities (clubs, sports, intramural organizations, or Greek organizations).

Schedule a meeting with your guidance counselor to discuss your college plans. Before the meeting, make a list of the criteria that are most important to you for choosing a school. Save this list, and refer back to it as you narrow your list of choices. Create a college search folder so that you can find the appropriate information when needed.

Some guidance counselors track recent high school graduates and may be able to provide you with the names and contact information of students at schools in which you have an interest.

If college seems out of reach financially, talk to your guidance counselor about financial aid packages. There are a multitude of scholarships, grants, and loans available to aspiring college students.

College Recruiters

Most high schools invite college recruiters to visit their schools to talk with students. Recruiters give students details about their institutions' academic programs, location, student life, faculty, extracurricular activities, and other features. Sign up for as many college visits as you think fit your interests. Prepare a list of questions to ask the recruiter. Visit the school's website beforehand to learn more general information about the institution. That way, you won't waste time on basic questions. If a college that you are interested in does not visit your school, ask your guidance counselor to help you schedule a meeting with a representative.

College Fairs

College fairs are an excellent way to learn more about college. A college fair is an organized gathering of college and university admissions representatives at a hotel, exhibition hall, and sometimes even your school. Each representative sets up a booth that features information about his or her college. Some college fairs even specialize in a specific academic discipline, such as history. When you attend these fairs, you'll visit these booths and talk to representatives about academic programs, admissions, financial aid, campus life, and other topics that will help you narrow your list of choices.

To prepare for a college fair, make a list of what you are looking for in a school (see the "Guidance Counselors" section in this chapter) as well as a list of questions to ask the representative. Some suggested questions are

- What are the two or three most popular majors at your school?
- Can you tell me about the history major at your school?
- What is the reputation of your history department?
- What first-year courses would I take if I were to major in history?
- What is the student-to-faculty ratio at your school?
- What percentage of students receives financial aid?
- What kinds of extracurricular activities does your college offer?

Be sure to bring a pen and paper so that you can record representatives' responses and your own thoughts on each college. When you get home from the fair, be sure that the pile of brochures you collected doesn't end up forgotten in a corner of your bedroom. Sit down and carefully read through each brochure while at the same time referring to your notes. You'll soon discover that some colleges aren't what they seemed, while others seem even more appealing. Fill out the information cards for the most appealing colleges to get more information. If you have additional questions, you might want to contact the admissions department directly for more information.

For a list of college fairs, visit http://www.nacac.com/fairs_ncf. html.

Contact Colleges Yourself

If guidance counselors, recruiters, and college fair representatives can't answer all your questions, you can contact college admissions offices directly to obtain their catalogs. You can also view catalogs and other information on colleges at their websites. Visit CollegeSource Online (http://www.collegesource.org) to view over 25,000 college catalogs in complete, original page format.

To view a list of colleges offering bachelor's degree history programs in the United States, visit universities.com (http://www. universities.com). The American Historical Association also offers a *Directory of History Departments and Organizations in the United States and Canada*. A limited online edition of this print directory is available at http://www.theaha.org/pubs/directory. Visit http://ncph. org/degree.html for a list of universities that offer public history degree programs.

You can find a list of schools offering master's degrees and Ph.D.'s in history at gradschools.com (http://www.gradschools.com).

Campus Visits: Giving Schools a Test Drive

Visiting a college is probably the best way to gather information. Since you will be spending your (and perhaps your parents') time and money visiting campuses, it is important to come to campus visits prepared. Consider the following points before you make your first campus visit:

- Find out as much as you can about the college before you visit. Visit its website and read print publications to learn more about the school. Talk to your friends, teachers, and parents about the school. Some colleges even have programs in which you can talk to currently enrolled students or alumni about their experiences.

- Make a list of things you would like to learn about during your visit. These might include academics, financial aid, student housing, the library, the school newspaper, and extracurricular activities.

- Schedule a campus tour with the admissions office ahead of time. Setting up a formal tour lets the admissions department know that you are interested in the school. This might even lead to a short interview with an admissions counselor during your visit. Again, be prepared with a list of questions for the counselor. You might also want to schedule a meeting with a financial aid officer to discuss your financial aid options.

- Try to spend at least 24 hours on campus, and take your tour when school is in session. This will give you a chance to try the meals, visit the library, stay in a dorm, sit in on a history class, and experience other real aspects of the college lifestyle. You'll also get a chance to meet students with similar interests who can offer you another perspective on campus life. Be sure to bring a map of the school. You don't want to waste precious time trying to find the admissions office or other important places on campus.

- You won't possibly be able to remember all of your questions and thoughts on each college, so be sure to bring a notebook and pen to take notes with during your visit. You might even want to bring a camera to snap photos of important sites on campus as a way to jog your memory once you return home.

- Approach campus visits with an open mind, but remember that no college or university would employ a guide who hated the school. Each college aims to present itself in the best possible light to encourage interest. Be sure to balance what you learn on your campus tour with information from other resources, such as college guidebooks, fellow students, guidance counselors, your parents, and your own observations.

If you are unable to visit colleges, you might consider visiting CampusTours.com (http://www.campustours.com), a website that offers virtual campus tours of over 850 colleges and universities.

LAST, BUT NOT LEAST
Remember to ask your parents, guardians, relatives, and teachers for input on your college decision. They might even know someone who attended the colleges on your list. Take their advice seriously, but be sure that the final decision is your own.

For more information on choosing the right college, visit

Adventures in Education (See "Find the Right School" in the "High School" section)
http://www.adventuresineducation.org

College Board
http://www.collegeboard.com

College Is Possible
http://www.collegeispossible.org

CollegeNet
http://www.collegenet.com

colleges.com
http://www.colleges.com

CollegeLink
http://www.collegelink.com

CollegeNews
http://www.collegenews.org

Princeton Review
http://www.princetonreview.com

INTERVIEW: Melissa Mannon

Melissa Mannon is the owner of Archives and Information Consulting Services in Londonderry, New Hampshire. She spoke with the editors of Top Careers for History Graduates *about her career.*

Q. Please describe your primary and secondary job duties.

A. As an archives consultant, I assist institutions with managing their historical information and records. I generally perform surveys (inventories) of their holdings and make recommendations about how they can best care for their materials based on my findings. I make recommendations regarding the arrangement and preservation of their records. I also make suggestions as how to facilitate access to historical information. I create long and short range plans to reach goals regarding the care of records, and I help create standard archives management documents such as collection development policies. I am also often brought in as a facilitator to help towns coordinate the care of records among various institutions in the town. Such work involves promoting outreach to town citizens so that they understand the importance of the care of historical records and support archives management efforts. I ensure that towns are in compliance with local laws regarding the care of public records. Finally, another important part of my work is training the nonarchivists (historical society volunteers, town clerks, etc.) within a town who often handle historical records to properly care for materials using archival standards.

When I worked as an archivist in a particular institution, rather than as a consultant, I managed records for the institution through the creation of policies and procedures. I cared for records by arranging, describing, and preserving them. I encouraged appropriate new donations to the collections. I performed outreach to get people interested in our collections by advertising collections and creating exhibits. I provided reference services to archives' visitors. In addition to encouraging outside donations to our collections, I worked to preserve the history of our institution by collecting records created by institutional employees. As an archivist in a small institution, I implemented retention schedules, which ensured that outdated records were discarded. In a larger institution, this job would be performed by a records manager who would work with the archivist.

Q. What type of training did you receive to prepare for work in this field?

A. My undergraduate degree is in art history. I spent some time as a curatorial intern in the university art gallery. In this capacity, I put together an exhibit of the photographic work of three German photographers operating during the mid-20th century. I spent a lot of time researching for the exhibit in area archives. This got me interested in archives work. I went on to pursue a degree in library science with a specialty in archives management. In addition to classes, I pursued internships in area archives to get the hands-on experience necessary for a career in this field.

There are only two accepted graduate fields of study for archives work. These include the master of library science (also known as the master of library and information science) with a specialty in archives or an M.A. in history with an archives specialty. People can enter the field by working in an archives and "moving up," but this is the exception and not the rule and is frowned upon by many archivists. Some institutions may accept people with graduate degrees in American studies, history, or another history-related field, but again, this is not the norm. People pursue many different undergraduate majors before pursuing an archives degree. I feel that mine prepared me well for this career.

My graduate degree is in library science with a specialty in archives management. I pursued internships in conjunction with classroom study. After graduation, I worked as a temporary archival assistant to gain additional experience. I also continued volunteering as an intern until I found a permanent archives position a year after graduation.

Q. What are the most important personal and professional qualities for archivists?

A. Most importantly, an archivist must enjoy organizing things. A love of history is definitely a plus. Contrary to the popular belief of those outside the profession, an archivist must be a good communicator to properly perform outreach and reference duties. It is helpful for an archivist to be a good planner. He or she must be an abstract thinker, yet also be able to pay attention to detail. Knowledge of computers and advanced technologies is becoming more and more important in this field.

Q. What advice would you give to college students as they graduate and look for jobs in this field?

A. It is highly recommended that you pursue a course of graduate study in the field. Many positions these days are also requiring a second graduate degree for archivists. Do not expect to become the head archivist at an institution immediately upon graduation. You may need to volunteer at an institution to gain additional experience after you have gotten your graduate degree. Some students are able to parlay internships into paid positions upon graduation. Archives is an extremely competitive field.

Q. What is the future employment outlook for archivists?

A. The demand for archivists is expected to grow in our information-based society. The outlook for archivists with technology experience is especially good. However, this is a field where we often have to convince others of the value of history and the value of organizing and caring for information. Many do not understand why it is important to maintain our history, and thus we will never likely be as valued as many other fields where benefits of the work performed is immediate and obvious to the general public. It is important to be flexible and willing to pursue work in adjunct fields. For example, an archivist may find work as a records manager or information specialist performing a variety of duties related to information management.

CHAPTER 2

MAKING THE MOST OF YOUR EXPERIENCE AS A HISTORY MAJOR

You've been accepted to college, moved into your dorm, met your roommate, walked the quad, and checked out the library and other campus resources. Now you anxiously await the beginning of classes. But how do you feel about your academic goals? Sure, you've picked your classes for your first semester, but what about after that? Are you any closer to deciding a major than you were a few months ago?

If not, you can relax. There's plenty of time to explore your interests before you have to choose a major. Most colleges don't require students to pick a major until the end of their sophomore year (and some students even switch their majors after that). Use your freshman and sophomore years to explore your interests and satisfy your college's general education requirements (sometimes known as prerequisites) that every student, whatever his or her major, must fulfill before graduation. These introductory classes will help you identify the fields you excel in and enjoy, which is a good indicator of a potential college major.

SUGGESTED COURSES

History is a very broad field, and since all college history programs are a bit different, there is no way to list definitively all the courses that you will take as a history major. Most students interested in history enter college unsure of what they want to study. As freshmen and sophomores, they take their college's general education requirements, which include introductory classes in psychology, sociology, philosophy, fine arts, business, science, mathematics, English, computer science, speech, and foreign language, as well as history courses such as western civilization, American history, medieval history, and ancient civilization. By the time most students complete their prerequisites, they have a better idea of what they would like to study. Most history majors choose (or design) a concentration that allows them to study specific geographical regions, themes, or time periods, or a combination of these areas. For example, Princeton University, one of the top colleges in the nation for history majors, offers the following history concentrations: Africa; Ancient Greece and Rome; Asian History; Europe since 1700; history of science and technology; intellectual and cultural history; Latin America; Medieval and Renaissance Europe; modern imperialism and colonialism; Near East; Russia; United Kingdom; U.S. History; war, revolution, and the state; and women and gender. Other history departments might offer concentrations that focus on Jewish history, the Middle East, comparative empires and cultures, or thematic subjects treated comparatively such as work, war, and revolution; popular culture; or family history.

To complement your specific concentration, you will take courses that focus on the history of specific countries, continents, and geographical regions (e.g., the American Southwest, the Middle East, and the Far East), as well as religions, historical movements (e.g., American Civil Rights, the charismatic movement, feminism), historical figures, and many other subject areas.

Finally, some colleges will require you to take one or more classes that develop your research and writing skills.

DON'T FORGET A MINOR

A minor is the study of an academic concentration involving fewer classes than what is required for a major. You do not need a minor to earn a bachelor's degree. Pursuing a minor will make you a much more marketable job candidate, especially if you would like to work in a field that is not history related. For example, minoring in business might provide you with enough experience to get an entry-level management position. Or a minor in art history might give you enough experience to work as an editor at a magazine that specializes in historical art issues. A history major who minors in computer science could have the background to work as a consultant for a computer company that is redesigning the History Channel's website. Other typical minors include English, foreign language, geography, government, philosophy, political science, and sociology.

CONSIDER A DOUBLE MAJOR

You can also prepare for nonhistory careers by pursuing a double major. A double major is the simultaneous pursuit of two distinct majors. Students who complete the requirements of a double major receive one bachelor's degree that states that they majored in two disciplines.

Majoring in one discipline is hard enough, so before you double major, be sure to do the following:

- Ask your academic counselors for advice on pursuing a double major. They may be able to recommend complementary majors, such as history and political science, and steer you clear of double majors, such as history and engineering, that might not be as marketable as other combinations.
- Research your school's requirements for completing a double major.
- Talk to fellow students who are currently pursuing a double major.

Consider the following pros and cons before you decide to pursue a double major.

Benefits of a double major are as follows:

- allows you to explore two distinct majors while most of your classmates only explore one major
- makes you a more marketable job candidate (only, of course, if you maintain a high GPA)
- improves your chances of getting into graduate school

Drawbacks of a double major are as follows:

- It is very difficult to study two subjects at once. Your social life might suffer as a result of the extra work you need to do to maintain your grades.
- While you can complete some double majors in four years, others will require an extra semester, or even another year, to complete the course work. Of course, pursuing a double major will require that you spend more money and time than you would if you just pursued a single major.
- Double majoring will reduce the number of credits you have available to explore other subject areas.

EXPLORE AND
GET YOUR FOOT IN THE DOOR

There are also many ways to expand your horizons outside the classroom. The following suggestions will allow you to explore and discover career possibilities, provide you with challenges not found in the classroom, and give you experiences that will complement your schoolwork in ways that will make you a more attractive job candidate.

- Learn about different cultures by joining campus organizations or attending on-campus cultural events.

- Read *A Student's Guide to History*. ISI Guides to the Major Disciplines (Wilmington, Del.: Intercollegiate Studies Institute, 2000); *Historical Thinking and Other Unnatural Acts: Charting the Future of Teaching the Past*. Critical Perspectives on the Past. (Philadelphia: Temple University Press, 2001); and *From Reliable Sources: An Introduction to Historical Methods*. (Ithaca, N.Y.: Cornell University Press, 2001).

- Read all you can about history, including magazines such as *History Today* (http://www.historytoday.com), *History Magazine* (http://www.history-magazine.com), *Smithsonian* (http://www.smithsonianmag.com), *The Public Historian* (http://www.ucpress.edu/journals/tph), *Public History News* (http://ncph.org/onlinenewsletter.html), and *Perspectives Online* (http://www.theaha.org/perspectives).

- Visit local historic sites.

- Conduct an oral history project in your community.

- Join Phi Alpha Theta (http://www.phialphatheta.org), the international honor society for history undergraduate and graduate students. The society has chapters at 820 colleges and universities.

- Work or volunteer as a tour guide at a local museum, historical society, or historical site.

- Work or volunteer in the archives department of a library, historical society, or museum.

- Become a student member of the Organization of American Historians (http://www.oah.org) or other professional organizations.

- Contact the chair of your history department to see if any of the professors hire student assistants. You could help with photocopying or even assist with a research project.
- Get an internship at a historical society, a museum, the History Channel, or the National Park Service. Join a history, geography, religious studies, philosophy, government, or sociology club on campus.
- Spend a semester or summer abroad studying history.

INTERVIEW: Michael Santos

Dr. Michael Santos is a professor of history and the director of the center for history and culture of central virginia at Lynchburg College, an independent liberal arts college located in Lynchburg, Virginia. Dr. Santos spoke with the editors of Top Careers for History Graduates *about the history major and the field in general.*

Q. For what types of jobs does a history major prepare students?

A. A history major can prepare a student for any career that he or she wants to pursue because it teaches the student how to do research, write and speak effectively, analyze data, and think critically about a host of topics and issues.

Q. What are the most important personal and professional qualities for history majors?

A. Intellectual curiosity and honesty and a critical mind. An historian needs to be willing to dig for the truth to find answers, to question accepted assumptions, and draw his or her own conclusions.

Q. When students enter your program, what are their expectations? Are they prepared or unprepared for the curriculum?

A. A lot of students have been taught that history is nothing more than memorization of dates and facts that have no relevance to their lives or to issues in contemporary society. I have to spend the first semester of our freshman history course in world civilization getting students to appreciate the relevance of the past for today. We focus on legacies of the past and how these have shaped not only the society in which we live, but the values and attitudes that our students take for granted. Getting students to see history as a discipline requiring critical thought and analysis is our biggest challenge.

Q. Are there any misconceptions about this major that you'd like to address?

A. The biggest misconceptions are that history is irrelevant and the only thing you can do with a history major is teach. As I've indicated, these are inaccurate assumptions because taught correctly, history is both relevant and preparatory for any career.

Q. What internship opportunities are available to students in your program?

A. Students have the opportunity to work at area museums and historical sites, such as Poplar Forest, the Lynchburg Museum System, and Point of Honor. They may also work through the Center for the History and Culture of Central Virginia that I direct to do research for public presentations in a variety of different contexts.

Q. What areas of your field have been promising in recent years?

A. Public history is a growing field. Americans visit museums and watch the History Channel in record numbers, so there's clearly a market for venues that interpret the past. Unfortunately, academic history has not kept up with the public interest.

Q. What is your advice to students regarding the pursuit of graduate degrees in history?

A. Go for it. If you have the talent and the desire, you can find a job when the time comes. Your training as an undergraduate and a graduate student will open possibilities you cannot even imagine right now.

Q. What advice would you offer history majors as they graduate and look for jobs?

A. Follow your heart and your instincts. Pursue a career that you find personally challenging and rewarding. Don't worry about how much money you'll make—do something you want to do with your life and you'll never regret it. And know that your major has prepared you to succeed in any venue.

PREPARING FOR THE WORKFORCE

As you enter your junior and senior years, you need to be concerned with more than just getting good grades: You'll need to begin preparing yourself to enter the workforce. Use this time to broaden your experiences, make professional contacts, develop skills not taught in the classroom, and connect your degree to the world of work. Doing this will give you an advantage over those who put off thinking about life after school until their senior years. The following are some recommendations to prepare yourself for the workforce.

Use Your Connections

Ask your college professors and advisers for advice on the types of jobs that are available to history majors. They might even be able to share a few job leads or industry contacts. More importantly, they can provide you with letters of recommendation for a potential employer. Be sure to approach a professor or adviser with whom you have a good rapport and who teaches or advises in an area of history that you are most interested in studying.

Get an Internship

An internship is one of the best ways to prepare for a career. An internship is a structured learning relationship with a business, government agency, nonprofit company, or other organization. Internships can be paid or unpaid, full or part time. Participating in an internship will help you gain valuable professional and personal skills, learn about a specific industry or field, and make valuable connections with potential employers. A good internship will involve much more than filing or answering phones. As an intern with a history background, you might write copy for press releases, interview people for a historical study, or sit in on planning meetings for the launch of a new history website. An internship, especially one with a well-respected employer, will give you an advantage over other job applicants who have not gained real-world experience.

Most colleges have established internship programs with businesses and government agencies. Many students participate in an internship as part of their studies. Museums, historic research organizations, state and national archives, government agencies, historic preservation groups, living history programs, and nonprofit organizations offer history-related internships. The following historical organizations offer lists of internships for history majors at their websites:

- National Council on Public History (http://ncph.org/jobs_intern.html)
- PreserveNet (http://www.preservenet.cornell.edu/employ.html)

If you have trouble getting a job after you graduate, consider getting an additional internship with a history-related employer. It might lead to a full-time job, and if nothing else, it will provide additional valuable experience.

Check out the following books for more information on internships: *The History Internship Book* (Winston-Salem, N.C.: Career Education Institutes, 2002); *Peterson's Internships 2003* (Lawrenceville, N.J.: Peterson's, 2002); and *The Internship Bible* (New York: Princeton Review, 2004).

The following websites can teach you more about internships:

InternshipPrograms.com
http://internships.wetfeet.com

Internships.com
http://www.internships.com

InternWeb.com
http://www.internweb.com

Rising Star Internships
http://www.rsinternships.com

Attend Job Fairs and Talk with Recruiters

Another good way to learn more about employers and possibly land a job is by meeting recruiters at job fairs, which may be held at your college or a local exhibition hall or hotel. Check with your college career center for lists of employers and dates of job fairs.

Prepare for a job fair in the same manner that you would prepare for a job interview. You won't be meeting just one potential employer, but many. Be sure to dress conservatively (no jeans and sweatshirts) and be well groomed. Get to the job fair as early as possible. Recruiters will be fresher and more enthusiastic about discussing job opportunities with you. Bring the following items to the job fair:

- Resume. Bring 15–20 copies of your resume to distribute to companies that seem interesting to you.

- Note-taking materials. Bring a pen and paper so that you can take notes on your conversations and contacts.
- Letters of recommendation. Make enough copies of your two or three best letters of recommendation to pass out to prospective employers.
- Portfolio. A portfolio will help you hold your resumes, letters of recommendation, notes, and other examples of your work.
- Briefcase. Use this to hold all of the aforementioned materials, as well as pamphlets, booklets, and business cards that you receive from potential employers. Walking around with a briefcase will also make you look more professional than the typical attendee clutching a plastic bag bulging with materials.

Use the limited time you have with each recruiter wisely. Be assertive, but not pushy. Present an overview of your qualifications and how they fit the company or position. When you make an especially promising contact, ask for the recruiter's business card. Make a note of conversations with these contacts. That way, you can explore their company or organization further as well as remain in contact for future job possibilities. If you are lucky enough to land an interview, be sure to send a thank-you note to the recruiter and convey your excitement at the opportunity that you've been given.

For more information on job fairs, visit the following websites:

American Job Fairs
http://www.americanjobfairs.com

CareerFairs.com
http://careerfairs.com

CollegeGrad.com
http://www.collegegrad.com

TheJobFair.com
http://www.thejobfair.com

JobWeb Online Career Fair
http://www.jobweb.com/employ/fairs

Schedule an Information Interview

Information interviews are different from traditional job interviews in that your goal is to gather information, not interview for a specific position. Information interviews are informal conversations with working professionals and are conducted solely for your benefit. By meeting workers and discussing their jobs and work environment, you can get firsthand information on a variety of careers. In addition to meeting new people on a professional level, information interviews can also provide you with the opportunity to sharpen your interview skills and be better prepared for actual job interviews.

Just like anything else in life, there is a right way and a wrong way to conduct an information interview. Consider the following dos and don'ts before you schedule your first information interview.

Do

- Get as much information as possible about the person's career, field, and company beforehand. That way, you won't waste time asking basic questions.
- Have a list of questions ready to ask the individual (see list of questions in this section).
- Listen attentively without interrupting the individual.
- Bring along a notepad and pen so that you will be able to take notes during the interview.
- Dress professionally. Although an information interview is more informal than a traditional job interview, it is not an excuse to show up dressed as if you're going to a ballgame or out to dinner with your friends. Dress and act as if you are going to an actual job interview.
- Ask for references or other assistance so that you can continue your research.
- Thank the interviewee for his or her time at the completion of the interview.
- Send a written thank-you note to acknowledge the person's time and assistance.
- Follow up if the person has asked you to keep him or her apprised of your progress.

Don't

- Arrive at the interview late, unprepared, or dressed inappropriately.
- Interrupt a person while he or she is speaking.

- Press the interview subject if he or she chooses not to answer a question.
- Ignore time constraints established by the interviewee.
- Push your resume or ask for a job.

Asking the right questions is the most important part of an information interview. Before you set up an information interview, prepare a list of questions to ask the interviewee. Some worthwhile questions are

- I have done some research about this position, and _____ is what I've found. Can you tell me more about what sort of work is done here?
- Can you describe your typical workday?
- Why did you decide to work for this organization?
- Who are your major clients? Major competitors?
- What are the most rewarding aspects of your job? Most challenging?
- How have you been able to balance the demands of the office with your personal life? Do you often find yourself bringing home additional work that you didn't finish at the office?
- How can you advance in your job?
- When you hire new employees, what skills do you look for in candidates?
- Has your company hired history graduates in the past?
- How do you suggest that students find jobs in this field?
- What additional training or education should I pursue to enhance my chances of finding a position within this field?
- What is the future employment outlook for your career?
- Who else can I talk to for more information on this career/field?

For more tips on information interviews, visit the following websites:

About.com: Information Interviewing
http://jobsearch.about.com/cs/infointerviews

Career Key: Information Interviewing
http://www.careerkey.org/english/you/
information_interviewing.html

Monster.com: The Hows of Informational Interviewing
http://campus.netscape.monster.com/articles/jobhunt/infohow

Quintessential Careers: Informational Interviewing Tutorial
http://www.quintcareers.com/informational_interviewing.html

INTERVIEW: Dan Paterson

Dan Paterson is a book conservator employed in the conservation department of a major library. He was kind enough to speak to the editors of Top Careers for History Graduates *about his background and experiences in the field.*

Q. What are your main responsibilities as a book conservator?

A. My main responsibilities are preparing rare books for digitization so that they can be included in digital library projects. The books have been previously selected and then examined to determine if they need conservation treatment. I take the book and perform all the written and photo documentation so that there is a record of the condition of the book prior to treatment and upon completion. The treatment sometimes involves taking the book apart, washing it, and rebinding it in a manner that is sympathetic to the original. Other times, it might just be reattaching the outside boards or mending tears in the pages. The treatment of each item is different based on its individual needs. Typically, I have a few projects to work on at the same time. Treatments can take anywhere from a few hours to several weeks to complete, depending on the amount of work involved and the complexity of the treatment.

Q. What was your educational background? Did this education prepare you for your career or what you do things differently if you could start over?

A. I received a bachelor's degree in history from Kenyon College in Ohio and a master of library and information science degree and a certificate in conservation from the University of Texas at Austin. I think that the history major prepared me well because I learned the value of original source material. In retrospect, however, I would probably add a major in chemistry if I could do it all over again.

Conservation is a multi-disciplinary field and having a stronger background in materials science and studio art would have better prepared me for entering the field.

Q. What type of internships have you participated in?

A. I had several internships prior to graduate school. These consisted of working in different conservation labs performing basic techniques and learning the principles of conservation. I also had internships throughout graduate school. Learning conservation techniques requires a lot of practice and repetition, and internships are a part of that.

Q. Are you a member of any professional associations relating to your field?

A. Yes, I belong to the American Institute for the Conservation of Historic and Artistic Works and the International Institute for Conservation of Historic and Artistic Works. Both hold annual meetings, publish journals, and have established the standards and principles that conservators in the United States and abroad adhere to when performing conservation treatments.

Q. What professional qualities does a book conservator need to be successful?

A. I think you have to be detail-oriented and like working with your hands. You have to be good at solving three-dimensional problems. You have to really respect the items that you are working on and keep in mind that there may only be a few copies of them in existence, and it is your responsibility to see that they are treated properly. In addition, you have to be aware of the history and provenance of an item and understand how conservation treatment will affect these aspects of the material now and in the future.

Q. What advice would you give college students who are interested in book conversation?

A. I would say getting related experience is helpful, such as an internship in conservation lab or a job in a research library.

Q. What is the future employment outlook for book conservators? Will book conservation change in the future due to technological innovations or other factors?

A. More digital technology is being used in the documentation stage, and this will continue to be the trend. The actual hands-on conservation part will not change. There will always be a need for people who specialize in the preservation of art and historical artifacts. The question is whether libraries and museums will continue to support them. Libraries and museums normally operate on very tight budgets and conservation has, in the past, suffered because of the expensive nature of treatment. The field in general will change because new areas of expertise are developing, such as people who are trained to specialize in the preservation of electronic media.

Q. Do you foresee any changes in the educational/skill requirements for this career?

A. I think the general trend at this time is to hire conservators with master's degrees. Fifteen or 20 years ago, most book conservators were trained as apprentices and this is now a more difficult avenue to pursue and gain entrance into the field. There is some discussion about certifying conservators within the AIC, but this is probably several years from becoming a reality. I think the ability to learn how to use digital technology for documentation purposes will continue to grow and be a requirement for anyone entering the field.

CHAPTER 3

TAKING YOUR HISTORY DEGREE TO WORK

Graduation day was one of the best days of your life. You received your diploma, celebrated with your classmates, and accepted congratulations from your friends and family. The world was your oyster. And then came the morning after: If you hadn't started already, now you absolutely needed to start looking for a job. Unlike accounting, engineering, or nursing majors, who have a clearly defined career path, history majors often have to do a bit more work when it comes to determining their direction after graduation. A history degree does not usually prepare you for a specific career unless you intend to become a historian or a history teacher, and even then you may still need to acquire additional training or certification. However, the history degree does provide you with polished communication, research, and problem-solving skills that will be invaluable in many different careers. Your task now is to determine your strongest skills, the types of jobs that interest you, and what types of organizations and companies you should think of joining.

Before you tackle these issues, do a self-assessment. You may have taken this type of test before in high school or college, whether it was the Myers-Briggs or another such formal assessment, to decide what classes to take or what major to choose. This time you need to focus on your future career. Keeping your history major in mind, write down specific interests and skills that have been proven in your previous schoolwork and work experience. Then, think about jobs that will best utilize these strengths and preferences. Are you stronger in research and analysis, or are you better at writing? Perhaps it's a combination of both, or something else entirely.

After writing down and evaluating your skills and interests, ask yourself the following questions:

- Do I enjoy working independently (like an archivist, genealogist, or writer does), or as part of a team (like demographers, Foreign Service officers, museum directors or curators)?

- Am I a self-starter, or do I need more interaction and supervision to stay motivated and focused?
- Are financial rewards (i.e., a higher salary) important, either out of either necessity or desire? Or am I more concerned with finding a job that is fulfilling—regardless of the size of the paycheck?
- Does the location of a job matter? Do I want to stay close to family and/or friends? Would I rather work in a city, suburb, or rural environment? Would I rather work in an office (as a book editor, research assistant, or writer), in a classroom (as a college professor, elementary school teacher, or secondary school teacher), in another country (as an archaeologist, cultural adviser, ethnoscientist, or foreign correspondent), in a laboratory (as a book conservator), or in a museum (as an education director, curator, teacher, or tour guide)?
- Do I need or want a flexible working schedule? Am I willing to work occasional long or irregular hours or on weekends (as a FBI agent, government official, or newspaper editor)?
- Continue to think of more narrowly focused questions, and read through the careers in this book to see which ones match your interests. Your answers and career research should help you decide what you want to do with your life. The key is to keep in mind your strengths and skills—and find a job and work environment that fits.

JUMP-START YOUR JOB SEARCH

Once you choose a career path, your next step is to focus on finding employers interested in hiring you. Considering U.S. economic conditions over the past several years, this may be easier said than done. History and other liberal arts graduates may have a particularly hard time in a weak economy, since some employers have misconceptions about the skills and abilities that these graduates can bring to a job. You will need to show employers how your skills and college experiences match up with the responsibilities of the position. Jobs are available, and keep in mind that history graduates possess many skills that other applicants lack. The following job search methods will help you land your first job.

Networking

Networking is a great way to find out about job openings. Contact your former professors, classmates, academic advisers, internship and summer job bosses, and even your friends and family, to let them know that you are looking for a job.

You can also use your college's alumni association to locate job leads. Contact its director for a list of recent graduates in your area. Some graduates, especially in big cities, organize themselves into social and professional clubs. Find out if there is such a club in your area and, if so, get involved. You'll meet new people who may already be working in your chosen field, and they might even know of available jobs.

Try the Liberal Arts CareerNETWORK

If your school is a member of the Liberal Arts CareerNETWORK, finding job leads will be even easier. The CareerNETWORK works like this: employers of liberal arts graduates submit information on internships and full-time and summer jobs to one of the colleges in the consortium, and then these listings are forwarded via the Internet to the career services offices of all the other consortium schools. Students at participating schools can review the opportunities and submit their resumes when they find promising positions.

Members of the Liberal Arts CareerNETWORK include Amherst College (Mass.), Bates College (Maine), Bowdoin College (Maine), Brandeis University (Mass.), Carleton College (Minn.), Clark University (Mass.), Colby College (Maine), Colgate University (N.Y.), College of the Holy Cross (Mass.), College of Wooster (Ohio), Connecticut College (Conn.), Hamilton College (N.Y.), Hartwick College (N.Y.), Hobart and William Smith Colleges (N.Y.), Hope College (Mich.), Macalester College (Minn.), Middlebury College (Vt.), Mount Holyoke College (Mass.), Oberlin College (Ohio), St. Lawrence University (N.Y.), Skidmore College (N.Y.), Smith College (Mass.), Trinity College (Conn.), Union College (N.Y.), Vassar College (N.Y.), Washington and Lee University (Va.), Wellesley College (Mass.), and Wesleyan University (Conn.). For more information, visit http://www.lacn-group.org/barter.html.

Look for History Jobs on the Web

The World Wide Web is a great place to search for history-related jobs. Visit the following websites to start your job search:

American Historical Association's *Perspectives* magazine
(available to association members only)
http://www.theaha.org/perspectives

Chronicle of Higher Education: Career Network
http://chronicle.com/jobs

H-Net Job Guide for the Humanities and Social Sciences
http://oldwww.matrix.msu.edu/jobs

National Council on Public History: Job Listings
http://ncph.org/jobs.html

Museum Employment Resource Center
http://www.museum-employment.com

MuseumStuff.com (lists of museums throughout the United
States)
http://www.museumstuff.com/links/history

USAJOBS (official job site of the U.S. Federal Government)
http://www.usajobs.opm.gov

INTERVIEW: Molly McKenna

Molly McKenna is a law librarian in Chicago, Illinois. She spoke with the editors of Top Careers for History Graduates *about her career.*

Q. What are your primary and secondary job duties?

A. My primary job duty as a law librarian is to handle research requests. This can vary from a simple case pull to a 50-state survey of lemon laws. A lot of the research that comes through the reference desk is business in nature: SEC filings, corporate affiliations, news article searches. Law librarians do legislative histories on both the state and federal levels. My secondary job duties could include any of the following on any given day: acquisitions, budgets, cataloging, book processing, providing tutorials on how to use the library and online sources, interlibrary loans, and circulation.

Q. What was your college major?

A. My college major was history. I had a student job at the law library. This training helped, but probably was not necessary. I have my master's in library science. In that program, I took specific courses geared towards law libraries and legal research. Hands on experience is really the only way to learn to be a law librarian.

Q. Was your history degree useful preparation for this career or would you recommend another undergraduate major to aspiring law librarians?

A. A history major helped to prepare me for this career in the sense that I had to spend a lot of time in libraries doing research for papers. Any degree could be beneficial depending on what specialty you decide to pursue in the library field. For example, if you want to work in a hospital or medical library, you would need to be more familiar with medical terminology and, therefore, a science degree might be more beneficial.

Q. What personality traits do successful law librarians need to have?

A. Law librarians need to have personalities that lend themselves to constant interaction with demanding patrons. They need to be professional, patient, intelligent, assertive, and well rounded. Professionally, law librarians need to be willing to be flexible with their time and schedules. Law librarians often are asked to stay late to finish a project for an attorney. They also need to be able to work well under pressure. It is not unusual to have a request from the middle of a meeting where the attorneys are now waiting for you to find the information they want immediately and deliver it to them within minutes. Law librarians need to be able to multi-task. It would be very rare that you would be able to devote all of your time to just one request. Librarians find themselves working on several requests at one time.

Q. What type of library science job can a person get with just a bachelor's degree in history?

A. If someone graduates with a bachelor's degree in history and wants to get into the law library field, they would only really be able to get a technical service or clerk job. It would be a good place to start to get into the field and then, after observing librarians, they could decide if this would be a career they want to pursue.

Q. What is the future employment outlook for law librarians?

A. Future employment outlooks vary quite a bit depending on who you talk to. Law firms, like most other sectors of the economy, are not expanding right now. Unfortunately, library budgets are generally one of the first things to get cut. Firms are also merging more frequently and that often means at least one librarian losing his or her job. The library world is changing dramatically. The real trend is for librarians to keep changing their role in the firm. Many libraries are now under the direction of the firm's technology department. Law librarians need to learn and excel at technology, as well as legal research. Law librarians need to be able to troubleshoot computer problems for public access terminals. They need to know how to create and maintain Intranet pages for the firm. They need to familiarize themselves with as much technology as they can. Some librarians have even begun work on document management systems for their firms. The bottom line is that librarians need to be able to market themselves and their worth to the firms. If they do this successfully, then they will have a solid career, if they don't they will vanish.

THE RESUME

Before you can start networking, utilizing the Liberal Arts CareerNETWORK, or searching for jobs on the Web, you need to be sure that your resume is in top shape. Your resume is the first thing an employer sees, so be sure that it makes a great impression. Resume-writing is considered one of the most difficult tasks in the job search process, but there is no reason to get stressed about a document that is all about you. You should know yourself by now, and a resume is really just a report about your achievements and the skills you have developed during your college years and beyond. Follow these steps to create a top-notch resume.

1. Make sure the heading is current and accurate. The heading presents your contact information and should serve as a strong starting point for prospective employers. Be sure to list current contact information in your heading. You don't want to list an address or phone number for an apartment that you are moving out of a week or two after you send your resume. Include your email address, but be sure that it sounds professional—get a new email address if your current one is something like wildman@zzz.com.

2. Develop the body. The body of your resume should include your objective/summary (the position you are applying

for), qualifications, educational experience, personal skills, academic achievements (include your GPA if it is over 3.0 on a 4.0 scale), work experience and/or internships (including responsibilities and accomplishments that best fit the job requirements), and employment history (if applicable).

3. Execute a simple but effective presentation. One-page resumes are most common, but if you have a lot of work experience, you might need a two-page resume. Do not fold your resume or staple or tape sheets together. Print your resume on matching, high-quality paper, using traditional fonts, point sizes, and other formatting. If you are applying for an artistic position, you might consider creating a slightly flashier resume. The bottom line: Your resume should quickly and concisely convey your qualifications to a prospective employer.

4. Proofread, proofread, proofread. When you have completed your resume, proofread it a number of times to check for mistakes and inconsistencies. Many human resource professionals toss resumes that have even one typo. So, proofread again and again so that your resume doesn't end up in the wastebasket. Have a trusted friend, parent, or teacher read through your materials, too. The more people who look at your resume, the less chance a mistake will slip through.

5. Tailor the resume. The most successful resumes are tailored to fit a particular position or employer, meaning that each time you apply for a new job, you need to reexamine and rewrite your resume to fit the needs of the specific employer. For example, if you are applying for an editing position at *Archaeology* magazine, you should detail your major in history, minor in archaeology, and your internship at *History Today*. This would also be a good time to reference your experience writing for your college newspaper, your work assisting a professor with historical research, and your field work at an archaeological dig in northern Italy. Citing skills such as these will give you an advantage over applicants who have less experience and less-tailored resumes.

6. Create a logical order of sections. If you're a recent college graduate, it is a good idea to move the education section to the beginning of your resume. Include classes that are relevant to the position. If you don't have relevant employment

Resume Advice from Those Who Trash Them

Companies receive resumes by the handful. Make that piles. Or perhaps tons. Especially during times of slow economic growth, the number of resumes that come across a typical hiring manager's desk can be overwhelming. Fortunately for them (but not for the job seekers), there are many glaring errors that applicants commit that send their resume right into the trash bin. According to monster.com, here's a list of the top 10 resume mistakes from the recruiters and hiring managers who see them each and every workday.

1. Problem: Spelling errors, typos, and just plain bad writing.

   Fix: Read your resume over carefully, use spell check, and have friends and family members look it over for mistakes you might have missed.

2. Problem: Too many duties, not enough explanation.

   Fix: Instead of simply listing your previous job descriptions, describe your accomplishments. Employers don't need to know exactly what you did at your last job, but instead, they want to hear about the direct results of your efforts. For example, list any improvements you brought to your previous job or department.

3. Problem: Employment dates are wrong or missing completely.

   Fix: Include time ranges in months or years for all work positions. Explain any gaps in your work history in your cover letter. Employers need dates to verify your experience and gain a sense of your overall work history.

4. Problem: You don't seem to know your name and address.

   Fix: Double-check your contact information each and every time you update your resume. The whole point of the resume is to get a phone call asking for an interview. Employers will not look you up to contact you.

5. Problem: Converted or scanned resume shows formatting errors.

   Fix: If you are emailing your resume, make sure it is saved and sent in plain text (ASCII) format. Even if you send your resume by fax or mail, use plain text because some employers scan resumes for easy browsing. Fancy fonts, boxes, or colors are unnecessary on a professional resume and will only cause problems.

(continues)

Resume Advice from Those Who Trash Them
(continued)

6. Problem: Organized your resume by function.

   Fix: Most employers prefer a chronological resume, where work and school experience is listed by date, over a functional one, where experience is listed by skills or functions performed. Month- or even year-long gaps in employment (which becomes obvious in chronological resumes) are more common now than in previous years and can be filled with volunteer work or continued education.

7. Problem: Too long.

   Fix: Highlight only your work and educational experience that is most prevalent to the job at hand. Recruiters simply don't have the time to read through long resumes.

8. Problem: Too wordy.

   Fix: Similar to #7, pare down your work, school, and other descriptions to include just the most important highlights.

9. Problem: Unqualified.

   Fix: Apply only to jobs for which you are qualified. You're not only wasting the employer's time, you're wasting your own when you apply for positions that require higher degrees or more work experience than you have.

10. Problem: Too personal.

    Fix: Include your fondness for stamp collecting if you are applying to work in the post office. Otherwise, leave it off your resume. In other words, list only information that's pertinent to the employer and the open position. Listed activities and interests should be included only if they are related to the job.

experience, you might want to create a section called "EXPERIENCE" to replace the "EMPLOYMENT" section. That way, you can list internships, class projects, independent study, and other applicable experiences.

7. Tell the truth and nothing but the truth. You may be tempted to stretch the truth regarding your work experience, employment dates, and educational background to make yourself

more appealing to employers. A word of advice: DON'T! Padding your resume with exaggerated or outright false claims is unethical and not the way to land your dream job. A growing number of large companies are performing background checks on job applicants, and you don't want to risk losing that dream job by presenting misleading information. Be confident in yourself, and present your educational and professional achievements accurately at all times.

8. Bring samples. Some employers may follow up with a request for samples of your writing or other work. Have material ready to respond to such a request. Send only your best work, and don't inundate the employer with materials—a few samples will do.

COVER LETTERS

Don't forget to include a cover letter with your resume. Use your cover letter to ask for an interview and educate potential employers about the skills and abilities you will bring to the company.

Since your cover letter is the first thing a potential employer reads, be sure that it is as sharp as your resume. Use the same paper stock as your resume to ensure uniformity. Address your cover letter to the person who is responsible for hiring. Don't use a generic greeting such as "To whom it may concern." Take the time to find out the appropriate person's name (whoever is in charge of hiring), and use it in your greeting. You can find out a person's name by calling the company or visiting the staff page of the company's website.

Organize your cover letter in the following manner: The first paragraph should state why you want to work for the company and identify the job for which you are applying. The second paragraph should highlight your experience and skills. The final paragraph should again reference your strong interest in the position and request an interview with the employer. Proofread your cover letter and ask a friend or family member to review it for typos, grammatical errors, and inconsistencies.

If you are applying for a position in academia, you will need to prepare a cover letter that is slightly different than the traditional business cover letter. Visit Academic Cover Letters (http://owl. english.purdue.edu/handouts/pw/p_covseek.html) for more information on creating this type of cover letter.

For more information on resumes and cover letters, visit the following websites:

Career-Resumes
http://www.career-resumes.com

CollegeGrad.com
http://www.collegegrad.com/resumes

JobStar: Resumes & Cover Letters
http://jobstar.org/tools/resume

JobWeb Guide to Resumes and Interviews
http://www.jobweb.com/Resumes_Interviews

Monster.com: Writing Cover Letters
http://content.monster.com/resume/samples/coverletters

Resume.com
http://www.resume.com

The Resume Place, Inc.
http://www.resume-place.com

APPLYING FOR JOBS ONLINE

Although newspaper job ads have not disappeared, the Internet is beginning to replace newspapers and other traditional sources as employers' preferred way to advertise job openings. Ninety percent of employers now prefer job applicants to respond to job listings online, according to a survey by the National Association of Colleges and Employers. Although information on creating a top resume can be found almost anywhere, many students are still left wondering how to prepare their resume for online submission. Here's a list of the things to consider before you click the "Send" button.

- If submitting your resume online, save it as "text only" to convert it into ASCII format. This is the only way to guarantee that the recipient of your resume is reading it in the manner and format in which you intended. Fonts and automatic formatting that you may have used in a word processing program may not be correctly converted when the resume reaches an employer. Sending your resume in text-only format also ensures that employers receive your information free from possible attachment viruses.

- Once you save your resume as text, clean up the body of the email, watching out for new line and section breaks. If you used bullets in your resume, replace them with asterisks (*).

If you used formatted section breaks, use dashes (——) to separate sections.

- When you prepare your email to send to the employer, write your cover letter in the body of the email, and then attach the text-only version of your resume. When the employer reads your email, your resume will actually be viewed in the body of the email, instead of as a separate attachment.

- Make sure your text-only resume is as clean and error-free as your original. Just because employers want a simple format doesn't mean they want to read typos.

THE PRESCRIPTION FOR A PERFECT INTERVIEW

If everything goes well, your carefully prepared cover letter and resume will land you an interview. What can you do to prepare for an interview? This is an especially difficult question given the wide range of interview formats in use today. Interviews can be extremely casual or ultraformal. They can last 30 minutes or two or more hours. You may interview once and be offered a position or be asked to return several times to meet with different executives. And after all this, you still may not receive a job offer. Preparing for an interview may seem overwhelming, but here are a few suggestions to make your interview a success.

- Give thought to your appearance. Conservative over trendy and/or casual is best in almost every interview situation. A dark black or blue suit is recommended for most business interviews. Make sure that you get a haircut before your interview. Don't wear tons of jewelry, too much makeup, or anything else that will diminish your presentation.

- Mind your body language. Use appropriate body language to convey your strong interest in the position. Greet the interviewer with a firm handshake, make strong eye contact, and smile and give other positive nonverbal feedback during the interview. (Don't frown, slouch, drum your fingers on the desk or chair, cross your arms, point, or make other inappropriate gestures.)

- Do your homework. Prepare for the interview by learning as much as you can about the company beforehand. Visit the organization's website (if it has one) to learn more about its history, key employees, departments, organizational structure, and products and services offered. This will increase your knowledge and allow you to ask more intelligent questions and better gauge how your skills match up with the position and the company.

- Come prepared. Bring multiple copies of your resume in case you are asked to meet with more than one interviewer. Bring pens and paper in order to take notes during the interview. You'll cover many issues during the interview, so it's best to write down main discussion topics in case you need to revisit them at a later date. It is also a good idea to bring contact information for your references (former or current teachers, guidance counselors, employers, friends, etc.) in case they are requested.

- Listen . . . then speak up. When the interviewer asks you a question, don't interrupt with what you think will be the answer. Wait for him or her to finish the question, pause to collect your thoughts, and then answer. This sounds simple, but it is often hard to do in a pressure situation such as a job interview.

- Ask questions. Listen attentively to the interviewer's description of the job and company, but be prepared when given a chance to ask questions. Come prepared with a list of at least five questions about the job and company. Some examples: How will I be trained for this job? Who will be my manager? What are the main skills required for success in this position? How many other people will I work with? Your pre-interview research at the company's website should be especially helpful as you prepare these questions. Asking questions will tell the interviewer that you are an intelligent, motivated job hunter who is excited about working for the company.

- Stress your transferable skills. History and other liberal arts graduates may be at a slight disadvantage during an interview because the skills they learned in college are not as easily quantifiable as those received by business, computer science, or engineering majors. For this reason, it is important to come to the interview prepared with a summary of your transferable skills—meaning skills you learned in college that can be applied directly to the position in question. For example, if you are interviewing for a position as a researcher/writer at a historical association, you will want to stress the research and writing skills you learned in class, the internship you had with a major news magazine, and your experience working on your school's newspaper and alumni magazine. You might also point out the strong reading comprehension, critical thinking, time-management, communication, and organizational skills you developed as a history major—skills possessed by any good researcher/writer.

- Be on time. Arrive at least a few minutes early for the interview. Being late for a job interview suggests that you lack time-management skills, and no manager wants a chronically tardy employee. Map out your travel route beforehand so that there are no surprises. Travel to the site of the interview ahead of time to gauge travel times and potential inconveniences (such as road construction, canceled train routes, etc.).

- Don't bring a friend, spouse, relative, or any other person with you to the interview. Leave your cell phone or pager at home; if you have to bring a cell phone or pager, turn it off and store it out of sight in your briefcase. Don't bring radios, food, drink, chewing gum, cigarettes, or portable headsets to the interview. Don't discuss your salary expectations unless the employer brings up the issue first. You'll have plenty of time to discuss compensation if you are called back for a second interview. (Do have a salary range in mind just in case the interviewer asks you to provide one.)

- Say thank you. At the end of the interview, thank the interviewer for his or her time. Follow up the interview with a formal handwritten thank-you or email note that reiterates your appreciation for the interview and, if appropriate, your continued interest in the position.

A NEW BREED OF INTERVIEW: THE SITUATIONAL INTERVIEW

As you prepare for interviews, be aware that some companies are using a new kind of interviewing technique called *situational interviewing*. In a situational interview, the employer will ask you to play the role of a worker (such as tour guide, editor, or teacher) and interact with an irate or troublesome "customer," "co-worker," or "student" who is actually a member of the hiring staff. Employers use situational interviews to test an interviewee's interpersonal and problem-solving skills as well as his or her ability to respond under duress. According to the *Handbook of Industrial and Organizational Psychology*, the traditional sit-down interview is only 7 percent effective in predicting an interviewee's job performance. Situational interviews, on the other hand, are accurate 54 percent of the time. There is no good way to prepare for a situational interview except to visualize possible scenarios and practice how you would correctly respond to them.

Visit the following websites for more tips on interviewing:

Ask the Interview Coach
http://www.asktheinterviewcoach.com

Collegegrad.com: Interviewing Information
http://www.collegegrad.com/intv

Job-interview.net
http://www.job-interview.net

Monster: Interview Center
http://interview.monster.com

YOU HAVE THE JOB . . . NOW WHAT?

Once you're hired, you will need to switch from student mode to worker mode. You'll spend your first months on the job getting to know your company, your co-workers, and your job duties. You will get a chance to demonstrate all the great things that you learned in college as well as learn new job skills.

If you work for a company long enough, you'll be assigned more job duties or advance to a higher position. Workers usually advance in two ways. Some move laterally to a similar position in a different department, while others move vertically to a position of higher authority or responsibility. You might also advance by moving to another employer.

THE GRADUATE FACTOR

Although your history major has provided you with excellent training and skills for success in many fields, some employers may not be willing to promote or even hire you if you have earned only a bachelor's degree. Other history graduates, as well as workers with advanced degrees in history, will also be competing with you for jobs. In addition, you may not even be eligible for the best jobs in some careers without a master's degree or Ph.D. These factors might encourage you to consider graduate school.

If you are considering graduate school, ask yourself the following questions:

- Why am I interested in grad school? Not knowing what to do with your life or waiting out a weak job market are not good reasons to invest your time and money in grad school. Grad school is an excellent option if you are committed to learning more about history or another field and are interested in increasing your marketability.

- What is the academic quality of the program? Finding the right academic fit is very important when choosing a grad school. To learn more about a program, ask yourself the following questions: What is the reputation of the history department? What are the interests/qualifications of the faculty? Do their interests match my interests? Does the department have a good reputation for developing mentoring relationships with students? Visit H-HistMajor (http://www.h-net.org/~hstmajor), a moderated Internet discussion forum by and for undergraduate history majors that features discussion on graduate school and related topics.

- Will I get into the program? Graduate programs are selective, and since graduate school application fees average $50, applying to too many schools can put a significant dent in your savings. It is better to approach the application process realistically and narrow your choices to a maximum of five graduate programs. Choose two top-rated schools, two mid-range schools, and one school that is further down the rankings. Of course, you also need to consider the academic quality, location, type of college, and other selection criteria as you narrow your list.

- What type of career do I want to pursue? Your undergraduate history degree will help you land many jobs, but some careers in this field require an advanced degree. For example, if you want to teach history (or another discipline) at the college level, you will need to earn at least a master's degree and preferably a Ph.D. If you are interested in becoming a librarian, you must earn a master's in library science. Other careers that require an advanced degree include anthropologist, archaeologist, ethnoscientist, judge, lawyer, museum director, and political scientist.

- How much will it cost? Graduate school is expensive, and if financing is an issue, you need to consider how you will pay back loans and other financial aid after you graduate. Ask yourself: How much does the graduate program cost? How will I fund my graduate education? What are average salary ranges for workers in the field who have graduate degrees? Considering these factors, will I make enough money post-graduation to make it worthwhile to pursue a graduate degree? For information on funding for history graduate students, read Grants, Fellowships, and Prizes of Interest to Historians, published by the American Historical Association (http://www.theaha.org).

- What is the current and future state of my discipline's job market? If the field you are interested in is glutted with people with master's degrees or Ph.D.'s, you might want to consider studying another field or specializing your graduate education in some way to make yourself a more appealing job candidate.

If you are really serious about graduate school, take the Graduate Record Examination (GRE). This achievement test is composed of verbal, quantitative, and analytical writing sections (not limited to any particular subject). The GRE is used to evaluate students applying for graduate school and is required by most schools. Visit http://www.gre.org to learn more.

For more information on history Ph.D. departments, read the *Directory of History Departments, Historical Organizations, and Historians,* published by the AHA (http://www.theaha.org), and *A Guide to Graduate Programs in Public History,* published by the National Council on Public History (http://ncph.org).

For more information on graduate schools, visit the following websites:

Graduate School Directory of Liberal Arts Studies: Gradschools.com
http://www.gradschools.com/listings/menus/liberal_menu.html

Graduate School Guide
http://www.graduateguide.com

The National Association of Graduate and Professional Students
http://www.nagps.org

Peterson's Graduate Schools and Programs
http://www.petersons.com/GradChannel

INTERVIEW: William Hanable

William Hanable has owned History Writer & Associates, a historical research, writing, editing, and consultation service, for 25 years. He spoke with the editors of Top Careers for History Graduates *about his career and the history major.*

Q. Please describe your primary and secondary job duties.

A. I am a self-employed consultant providing a wide range of historical services on a contract basis. These have included historical studies for the National Park Service and U.S. Air Force, editing of historical publications for private and nonprofit organizations, and management consultation for historical societies in museums. In the past, I have also been employed as a state historian, chief of a state office of history and archaeology, executive director of a state historical commission, manager of a maritime museum, and executive director of a state heritage commission.

Q. How did you train for such a wide variety of history-related careers?

A. I took a B.A. in history and an M.A.T. in history and secondary education followed by a Ph.D. in education. The history degrees provided indispensable knowledge of how to research historical data and then synthesize and evaluate it. I have also benefited greatly from short courses offered by organizations such as the American Association for State and Local History and the Smithsonian Institution on subjects such as historical interpretation and exhibit preparation. However, my experience as an employed historian in one capacity or another has been critical to my success as a self-employed consultant.

Q. Would you pursue the same educational path if you could do it all over again?

A. The course I followed gave me adequate preparation, but in retrospect, I would suggest a master's degree in history followed by a

Ph.D. in public history, assuring that the latter included some work in public administration.

Q. Did you participate in any internships while you were in college?

A. No, I didn't have that opportunity because I was working full time except during my B.A. work. However, I strongly recommend internships both as learning vehicles and as opportunities for establishing the contacts that can lead to professional employment.

Q. What are the most important personal and professional qualities for history writers?

A. As to personal qualifications, I say imagination plus the quality of being excited by history. As for professional qualifications, I say extreme competence in research methods, plus synthesis and analysis and presentation of information on a timely basis. Few people make their livings solely as history writers. For those who are not only history writers, but also history administrators of one kind or another, I would add as qualifications the ability to communicate well with others, dedication to historical concerns, and the ability to apply management techniques effectively.

Q. What advice would you give to college students who are interested in this field?

A. Be flexible. Ideal jobs are scarce. Don't expect to be successful without a graduate degree. Look for jobs that build a foundation for achieving your ideal job in the future, and realize that as you gain more experience, your perception of the ideal job will change.

Q. What is the future employment outlook for history majors?

A. There are more jobs than one would suspect, but few where people traditionally look—in colleges and universities. Most jobs are to be found in government agencies at the federal and state level, with somewhat fewer opportunities in historical societies and museums. The nongovernment jobs usually bring relatively low pay and the expectation that you will do a variety of tasks. There are also limited opportunities for employment with consulting firms, but these tend to be of short duration.

SECTION II

CAREERS

ANTHROPOLOGISTS

QUICK FACTS

School Subjects Geography History **Personal Skills** Communication/ideas Helping/teaching **Work Environment** Indoors and outdoors One location with some travel **Minimum Education Level** Doctorate degree **Salary Range** $16,000 to $38,890 to $94,788+	**Certification or Licensing** None available **Outlook** About as fast as the average **DOT** 054 **GOE** 11.03.03 **NOC** 4169 **O*NET-SOC** 19-3091.00, 19-3091.01

OVERVIEW

Anthropologists study the origin and evolution of humans from a scientific point of view, focusing on the ways of life, physical characteristics, languages, values, customs, and social patterns of people in various parts of the world. There are approximately 15,000 anthropologists actively working in the field.

HISTORY

Herodotus, a Greek historian, is generally considered the first anthropologist, having written in the early 400s B.C. about the people of the Persian Empire. His writings formed a foundation for centuries of studies to follow, as historians and other scholars researched the development of cultures and civilizations. The rise of imperialism paved the way for modern anthropology as Europeans took over foreign lands and were exposed to new cultures. In the early 19th century, amateur anthropologists formed their own societies. By the end of the 19th century, anthropologists began lecturing at colleges and universities.

Franz Boaz, through his teachings and research, helped to promote anthropology as a serious science in the 1920s. His students included Margaret Mead and Ruth Benedict, who later established their own anthropology departments. Mead conducted fieldwork, most notably among the Samoan people, that proved ground-breaking as well as controversial; for her research, she relied more on her interaction with individual groups of people than on statistics. Approaches and explanations expanded throughout the 20th century. Today, anthropologists specialize in diverse areas, focusing on geographic areas and on such subjects as education, feminism, politics, and film and photography.

THE JOB

Anthropology is the study and comparison of people in all parts of the world: their physical characteristics, customs, languages, traditions, material possessions, and social and religious beliefs and practices. Anthropologists constitute the smallest group of social scientists, yet they cover the widest range of subject matter.

Anthropological data may be applied to solving problems in human relations in fields such as industrial relations, race and ethnic relations, social work, political administration, education, public health, and programs involving transcultural or foreign relations. Anthropology can be broken down into subsets: cultural anthropology, linguistic anthropology, and physical or biological anthropology.

Cultural anthropology, the area in which the greatest number of anthropologists specialize, deals with human behavior and studies aspects of both extinct and current societies, including religion, language, politics, social structure and traditions, mythology, art, and intellectual life. *Cultural anthropologists,* also called *ethnologists* or *social anthropologists,* classify and compare cultures according to general laws of historical, cultural, and social development. To do this effectively, they often work with smaller, perhaps less diverse societies. For example, a cultural anthropologist might decide to study Gypsies of Eastern Europe, interviewing and observing Gypsies in Warsaw, Prague, and Bucharest. Or a cultural anthropologist could choose to study Appalachian families of Tennessee and, in addition to library research, talk to people in Appalachia to learn about family structure, traditions, morals, and values.

Carol Patterson Rudolph is a cultural anthropologist investigating Native American petroglyphs (carvings or inscriptions on rocks), focusing on the Southwest. "I study the culture associated with the petroglyphs," Rudolph says. "I study the myths of the cultures—the myths are the key factors in interpreting petroglyphs. The way hands, tails, body, and feet are positioned—all have meaning when matched up to myths." Her research has resulted in the books *On the Trail of Spider Woman: Petroglyphs, Pictographs, and Myths of the Southwest* (Santa Fe, N.Mex.: Ancient City, 1997) and *Petroglyphs and Pueblo Myths of the Rio Grande* (Albuquerque, N.Mex.: University of New Mexico Press, 1990). She also produced *Rock Markings*, a video on petroglyphs that aired on PBS.

"The two questions everyone wants to know," she says, "are 'How old is it?' and 'What does it mean?'" To find the answers, Rudolph works with Indian people who still know the sign language of petroglyphs, as well as other professionals. She has currently been working with an archeometrist who dates archeological material. Rudolph considers her work to be a bridge between the past and present. "Learning how people really thought comes from their original language—and that's translated on their rock."

Physical anthropologists, also called *biological anthropologists*, are concerned primarily with the biology of human groups. They study the differences between the members of past and present human societies and are particularly interested in the geographical distribution of human physical characteristics. They apply their intensive training in human anatomy to the study of human evolution and establish differences between races and groups of people. Physical anthropologists can apply their training to forensics or genetics, among other fields. Their work on the effects of heredity and environment on cultural attitudes toward health and nutrition enables medical anthropologists to help develop urban health programs.

One of the most significant contributions of physical anthropologists comes from their research on nonhuman primates. Knowledge about the social organization, dietary habits, and reproductive behavior of chimpanzees, gorillas, baboons, and other primates explains a great deal about human behavior, motivation, and origins. People working in primate studies are increasingly interested in conservation issues because the places where primates live are threatened by development and the overharvesting of forest products. The work done by Jane Goodall is a good example of this type of anthropology.

Urban anthropologists study the behavior and customs of people who live in cities.

REQUIREMENTS
High School
Follow your high school's college prep program to prepare for undergraduate and graduate programs in anthropology. You should study English composition and literature to develop your writing and interpretation skills. Foreign language skills will also help you in later research and language study. Take classes in computers and classes in sketching, simple surveying, and photography to prepare for some of the demands of fieldwork. Mathematics and science courses can help you develop the skills you'll need in analyzing information and statistics.

Postsecondary Training
You should be prepared for a long training period beyond high school. More anthropologists are finding jobs with only master's degrees, but most of the better positions in anthropology will require a doctorate, which entails about four to six years of work beyond the bachelor's degree. You'll need a doctorate in order to join the faculty of college and university anthropology programs. Before beginning graduate work, you will study such basic courses as psychology, sociology, history, geography, mathematics, logic, English composition and literature, and modern and ancient languages. The final two years of the undergraduate program will provide an opportunity for specialization not only in anthropology but in some specific phase of the discipline.

Students planning to become physical anthropologists should concentrate on the biological sciences. A wide range of interdisciplinary study in languages, history, and the social sciences, as well as the humanities, is particularly important in cultural anthropology, including the areas of linguistics and ethnology. Independent field study is also important in these areas.

In starting graduate training, you should select an institution that has a good program in the area in which you hope to specialize. This is important, not only because the training should be of a high quality, but because most graduates in anthropology will receive their first jobs through their graduate universities.

Assistantships and temporary positions may be available to holders of bachelor's or master's degrees, but are usually available only to those working toward a doctorate.

Other Requirements

You should be able to work as part of a team, as well as conduct research entirely on your own. Because much of your career will involve study and research, you should have great curiosity and a desire for knowledge.

Carol Patterson Rudolph credits a passion and dedication to her work as key to her success. "I'm fascinated with other cultures," she says. "I'm against prejudice of any kind." This respect for other cultures is extremely important, as you'll be interacting closely with people with diverse backgrounds.

EXPLORING

You can explore anthropology in a number of ways. For example, Boy Scout and Girl Scout troops participate in camping expeditions for exploration purposes. Local amateur anthropological societies may have weekly or monthly meetings and guest speakers, study developments in the field, and engage in exploration on the local level. You may begin to learn about other cultures on your own by attending local cultural festivals, music and dance performances, and cultural celebrations and religious ceremonies that are open to the public.

Trips to museums also will introduce you to the world of anthropology. Both high school and college students may work in museums on a part-time basis during the school year or during summer vacations. The Earthwatch Institute offers student expedition opportunities to a range of locations such as India, Greece, Guatemala, and England. For descriptions of programs and recent projects, see http://www.earthwatch.org.

EMPLOYERS

The American Anthropological Association (AAA) reports that there are approximately 15,000 anthropologists actively working in the profession. Traditionally, most anthropologists have worked as professors for colleges, universities, and community colleges, or as curators for museums. But these numbers are changing. The AAA estimates that while about 70 percent of their professional members still work in academia, about 30 percent work in such diverse areas as social service programs, health organizations, city planning departments, and marketing departments of corporations. Some also work as consultants. Carol Patterson Rudolph works actively as an anthropologist but supports herself with her own graphic arts and advertising business.

STARTING OUT

The most promising way to gain entry into these occupations is through graduate school. Employers might approach anthropology graduates prior to graduation. Often, professors will provide you with introductions as well as recommendations. You may have an opportunity to work as a research assistant or a teaching fellow while in graduate school, and frequently this experience is of tremendous help in qualifying for a job in another institution.

You should also be involved in internships to gain experience. These internship opportunities may be available through your graduate program, or you may have to seek them out yourself. Many organizations can benefit from the help of an anthropology student; health centers, government agencies, and environmental groups all conduct research.

ADVANCEMENT

Because of the relatively small size of this field, advancement is not likely to happen quickly, and the opportunities for advancement may be somewhat limited. Most people beginning their teaching careers in colleges or universities will start as instructors and eventually advance to assistant professor, associate professor, and possibly full professor. Researchers on the college level have an opportunity to head research areas and to gain recognition among colleagues as an expert in many areas of study.

Anthropologists employed in museums also have an opportunity to advance within the institution in terms of raises in salary or increases in responsibility and job prominence. Those anthropologists working outside academia and museums will be promoted according to the standards of the individual companies and organizations for which they work.

EARNINGS

According to the Bureau of Labor Statistics (BLS), college and university professors of anthropology earned between $45,460 and $76,730 in 2001, depending on the institution that employed them. The median salary for these professors was $58,990. A 2001–02 survey by the American Association of University Professors reported that the average salary for professors at the bachelor's level was $67,000. At the doctorate level, professors earned an average of $94,788 a year.

For those working outside of academia, the salaries vary widely. The BLS reports that the median annual salary for anthropologists and archaeologists was $38,890 in 2001. The National Association for the Practice of Anthropology (a segment of the AAA) estimates that anthropologists with bachelor's degrees will start at about $16,000 a year; with five years' experience they can make $20,000 a year. Those with doctorates will start at about $25,000, working up to $30,000 with five years' experience. Mid-career anthropologists have annual salaries of between $35,000 and $75,000. Salaries in urban areas are somewhat higher.

As faculty members, anthropologists benefit from standard academic vacation, sick leave, and retirement plans.

WORK ENVIRONMENT

The majority of anthropologists are employed by colleges and universities and, as such, have good working conditions, although field-work may require extensive travel and difficult living conditions. Educational facilities are normally clean, well lighted, and ventilated.

Anthropologists work about 40 hours a week, and the hours may be irregular. Physical strength and stamina is necessary for field-work of all types. Those working on excavations, for instance, may work during most of the daylight hours and spend the evening planning the next day's activities. Those engaged in teaching may spend many hours in laboratory research or in preparing lessons to be taught. The work is interesting, however, and those employed in the field are usually highly motivated and unconcerned about long, irregular hours or primitive living conditions.

Carol Patterson Rudolph appreciates the instant gratification of the work. "You're always working on the cutting edge," she says. "Nobody's done it before." But the constant struggle for funding can be frustrating.

OUTLOOK

Most new jobs arising in the near future will be nonteaching positions in consulting firms, research institutes, corporations, and federal, state, and local government agencies. Among the factors contributing to this growth is increased environmental, historic, and cultural preservation legislation. There is a particular demand for people with the ability to write environmental impact statements. Anthropologists will have to be creative in finding work outside of academia and convincing employers that their training in anthropology makes them uniquely qualified for the work. For these jobs, they will be competing with people from a variety of disciplines.

Although college and university teaching has been the largest area of employment for anthropologists, the demand is expected to decline in this area as a result of the steady decrease in student enrollment. Overall, the number of job applicants will be greater than the number of openings available. Competition will be great even for those with doctorates who are seeking faculty positions, and many will find only temporary or nontenured jobs. Junior college and high school teaching jobs will be very limited, and those holding a bachelor's or master's degree will have few opportunities. Positions will be available in nonacademic areas, as well as a limited number in education. The U.S. Department of Labor predicts that employment for this career will growth about as fast as the average over the next several years.

FOR MORE INFORMATION

The following organization offers valuable information about anthropological careers and student associations.
  American Anthropological Association
  2200 Wilson Boulevard, Suite 600
  Arlington, VA 22201
  Tel: 703-528-1902
  http://www.aaanet.org

To learn more about the Student Challenge Awards and the other programs available, contact
  Earthwatch Institute
  3 Clock Tower Place, Suite 100
  Box 75
  Maynard, MA 01754
  Tel: 800-776-0188
  Email: info@earthwatch.org
  http://www.earthwatch.org

The SFAA website has career listings and publications for those wanting to read more about current topics in the social sciences.
  Society for Applied Anthropology (SFAA)
  PO Box 2436
  Oklahoma City, OK 73101-2436
  Tel: 405-843-5113
  Email: info@sfaa.net
  http://www.sfaa.net

ARCHAEOLOGISTS

QUICK FACTS

School Subjects	Certification or Licensing
Art	None available
History	
	Outlook
Personal Skills	About as fast as the average
Communication/ideas	**DOT**
Technical/scientific	054
Work Environment	**GOE**
Indoors and outdoors	11.03.03
One location with some	
travel	**NOC**
	4169
Minimum Education Level	
Doctorate degree	**O*NET-SOC**
	19-3091.00, 19-3091.02
Salary Range	
$23,260 to $38,890 to	
$94,788	

OVERVIEW

Archaeologists study the origin and evolution of humans. They study the physical evidence of human culture, examining such items as tools, burial sites, buildings, religious icons, pottery, and clothing.

HISTORY

Archaeology did not become an established discipline until the 19th century. The subjects of study in the field range from fossils of humans of 4.5 million years ago to the concerns of contemporary city-dwellers. The excavation of archaeological sites has provided information about the Ice Age, the development of agriculture, the civilizations of the ancient Egyptians and the Anasazi, and other historical cultures and events. In the 1870s, Heinrich Schliemann did some early work, excavating sites in Greece and Turkey that he believed to be the city of Troy described in Homer's *Iliad*. (It was later determined that the artifacts of the area pre-dated Troy by 1,000 years.) Arguably the most famous archeological excavation involved the tomb of the Egyptian pharaoh Tutankhamen, which was discovered by British archeologist Howard Carter in 1922.

These excavations, and others before the 1960s, were large in scale. Archaeologists preferred to clear as much land as possible, hoping to uncover more artifacts. But today's archaeologists understand that much can be lost in an excavation, and they limit their studies to smaller areas. With radar, sensors, and other technologies, archaeologists can discover a great deal about a site without any actual digging.

THE JOB

Archaeology is concerned with the study and comparison of people in all parts of the world, their physical characteristics, customs, languages, traditions, material possessions, and social and religious beliefs and practices. At most universities, archaeology is considered a branch of anthropology.

Archaeologists play an important role in the areas of anthropology, especially cultural anthropology. They apply specialized techniques to construct a record of past cultures by studying, classifying, and interpreting artifacts such as pottery, clothing, tools, weapons, and ornaments, to determine cultural identity. They obtain these artifacts through excavation of sites such as buildings and cities, and they establish the chronological sequence of the development of each culture from simpler to more advanced levels. Prehistoric archaeologists study cultures that existed prior to the period of recorded history, while historical archaeologists study more recent societies. The historic period spans several thousand years in some parts of the world and a few hundred years in others. Classical archaeologists concentrate on ancient Mediterranean and Middle Eastern cultures. Through the study of the history of specific groups of peoples whose societies may be extinct, archaeologists are able to reconstruct their cultures, including the pattern of daily life.

As faculty members of colleges and universities, archaeologists lecture on the subject, work with research assistants, and publish books and articles. Those who work outside of academia, such as for corporations and government agencies, have a variety of duties and responsibilities.

Though Thomas F. King, an archaeologist in Maryland, does travel across the country to teach and consult, most of his work is focused on cultural resource management. "The cultural resource laws of this and other nations," King says, "are designed to try to make sure that 'cultural resources' such as archeological sites, historic buildings, culturally valued landscapes, and culturally valued ways of life aren't thoughtlessly destroyed in the course of modern development." This involves prescribing various kinds of planning and review processes whenever a federal agency plans to do something that might harm a resource.

As a senior archaeologist in the field, King has published the book *Cultural Resource Laws and Practice: An Introductory Guide* (Lanham, Md.: AltaMira Press, 1998). "Most of my time is spent reading and writing documents, reviewing reports, meeting with people, etc.," he says.

He also works outside of cultural resource management as the chief archaeologist on The Amelia Earhart Project of The International Group for Historic Aircraft Recovery. King explains, "It's an interdisciplinary study of the fate of the lost aviatrix, whom we think ended up on a remote South Pacific island. In this effort, we do all kinds of historical, oral-historical, archaeological, and other kinds of research."

The research involves such unique tools as robotic submersibles, ultralight aircraft, and electromagnetic resistivity meters. "But fieldwork on that project, as opposed to other kinds of research, occurs only about every two years, as we raise the money. Fundraising goes on constantly," he says.

Archaeologists often must travel extensively to perform fieldwork on the site where a culture once flourished. Site work is often slow and laborious: It can take years to uncover artifacts from an archaeological dig that produce valuable information. Another important aspect of archaeology is the cleaning, restoration, and preservation of artifacts. This work sometimes takes place on the site of discovery to minimize deterioration of textiles and mummified remains. Careful recording of the exact location and condition of artifacts is essential for further study.

REQUIREMENTS
High School

Follow your high school's college prep program to prepare for undergraduate and graduate programs in archaeology. You should study English composition and literature to develop your writing and interpretation skills. Foreign language skills will also help you

Who Employs History Majors?

Academia/Education

- Colleges and universities
- Community colleges
- Elementary schools
- Middle schools
- Secondary schools

Government

- Archives
- Bureau of the Census
- Central Intelligence Agency
- Congress
- Department of Education
- Department of Justice
- Department of State
- Department of the Interior
- Federal Bureau of Investigation
- Foreign Service
- Library of Congress
- Military services
- National Archives and Records
- National Center for Education Statistics
- National Endowment for the Humanities
- Peace Corps
- Smithsonian Institution
- Tourism bureaus
- Urban planning agencies

International Organizations

- European Union
- United Nations

(continues)

Who Employs History Majors?

(continued)

Private Sector

- Advertising agencies
- Art galleries
- Banking and financial services industry
- Corporations
- Entrepreneurships
- Genealogical services
- Historical sites
- Historical societies and associations
- Humanities and arts councils
- Internet sites
- Insurance industry
- Libraries
- Magazines
- Marketing research firms
- Museums
- Newspapers
- Nonprofit organizations
- Publishing companies
- Radio stations
- Research institutes
- Retailers
- Social service agencies
- Television stations
- Think tanks
- Tourism industry
- Zoos

in later research in other countries. Take classes in history and art to learn more about ancient and classical civilizations. Although it may seem that you'll be working mostly with fossils and ancient artifacts, you'll need computer skills to work with the many advanced technologies used in archaeological excavations. Mathematics and science courses can help you develop the skills you'll need in analyzing information and statistics.

Postsecondary Training

Most of the better positions in archaeology require a doctorate, which takes about four to six years of work beyond the bachelor's degree. Before beginning graduate work, however, you will study such basic courses as psychology, sociology, history, geography, mathematics, logic, English composition and literature, as well as modern and ancient languages. Archaeology departments are typically part of anthropology departments; few separate archaeology departments exist in U.S. colleges and universities. As a student of archaeology, you'll follow a program that involves many disciplines, including art, architecture, classics, and history.

Because most archaeology graduates receive their first jobs through their graduate work, you should select a graduate school that has a good program in the area in which you hope to specialize.

Other Requirements

To succeed in archaeology, you need to be able to work well as part of a team and on your own. You should be naturally curious and have a desire for knowledge, as these qualities will enhance your study and research. Communication skills are paramount, both for writing your reports and presenting your findings clearly and completely to professionals in the field.

EXPLORING

To explore your interest in archaeology, see if your local Boy Scout and Girl Scout group participate in camping or hiking expeditions. A trip to a museum also will introduce you to the world of archaeology. Better yet, see if your local museum offers part-time work or volunteer opportunities. You should also visit the Earthwatch Institute's website (http://www.earthwatch.org) to learn more about its many exploration trips to locations as close as North America and as far as Africa or Asia.

EMPLOYERS

Archaeologists work for universities and community colleges. They also work for museums that may be independent or affiliated with universities. Government agencies, such as the National Park Service and state historic preservation offices, employ archaeologists. More and more archaeologists are finding jobs in the private sector, for consulting firms, environmental companies, and other businesses.

STARTING OUT

You may have an opportunity to work as a research assistant or a teaching fellow while in graduate school, and frequently this experience is of tremendous help in qualifying for your first job. Your graduate school professors should be able to help you establish contacts in the field.

While in school, you should also be involved in internships to gain experience. Internship opportunities may be available through your graduate program, or you may have to seek them out yourself. You can check with your state's archaeological society or the National Forest Service to find out about volunteer opportunities.

ADVANCEMENT

Because of the relatively small size of this field, advancement opportunities can be scarce. Most archaeology teachers start as assistant professors and move into associate professor and possibly full professor positions. Archaeology researchers at the college level have the opportunity to head research areas and to gain recognition among colleagues as an expert in many areas of study.

Those working in museums also have an opportunity to advance within the institution in terms of higher pay or increased responsibility. Archaeologists working outside academia and museums will be promoted according to the standards of the individual companies and organizations for which they work.

EARNINGS

A large percentage of archaeologists work in academia. A 2001–02 survey by the American Association of University Professors reported that the average salary for professors at the bachelor's level was $67,000. At the doctorate level, professors earned an average of $94,788 a year.

For those working in the field, salaries ranged widely. The Bureau of Labor Statistics reports that the median annual salaries for archaeologists and anthropologists were $38,890 in 2001. The lowest paid 10 percent earned less than $23,260; the highest paid 10 percent earned more than $66,670.

WORK ENVIRONMENT

Archaeologists working in educational facilities have normally clean, well lit, and ventilated environments. Fieldwork presents a tougher environment, working in all types of weather and, depending on the area to which they are assigned, having to deal with potentially difficult living conditions.

Archaeologists work about 40 hours a week, and the hours may be irregular. Physical strength and stamina are necessary for fieldwork of all types. Those working on excavations, for instance, may work during most of the daylight hours and spend the evening planning the next day's activities. Excavation work may be tough, but most find the work interesting and well worth the irregular hours or primitive living conditions.

"You can convince yourself that you're doing something good for the world, trying to get important stuff preserved," King says, citing the pros and cons of the work, "but it's possible to get pretty cynical about the whole business, since preserving stuff is, on balance, often a losing game."

OUTLOOK

"Recognize that the number of Indiana Jones jobs available are strictly limited," King advises. "On the other hand, there are lots more jobs than there used to be in 'applied' archaeology, in the context of cultural resource management. Think about being more than an archaeologist. If you can also do cultural anthropology, history, geomorphology, law, or politics, your career opportunities will expand exponentially."

The U.S. Department of Labor predicts that employment for archaeologists will grow about as fast as the average for all other occupations over the next several years. Most new jobs in the near future will probably be nonteaching positions in consulting firms, research institutes, corporations, and federal, state, and local government agencies. Among the factors contributing to this growth is increased environmental, historic, and cultural preservation legislation. There is a particular demand for people with the ability to write environmental impact statements.

Overall, the number of job applicants for university faculty positions will be greater than the number of openings available.

Competition will be great even for those with doctorates who are seeking faculty positions, and many will find only temporary or nontenured jobs.

FOR MORE INFORMATION

The following organization offers valuable information about anthropological careers and student associations.

American Anthropological Association
2200 Wilson Boulevard, Suite 600
Arlington, VA 22201
Tel: 703-528-1902
http://www.aaanet.org

To learn more about the Student Challenge Awards, and the other programs available, contact

Earthwatch Institute
3 Clock Tower Place, Suite 100
Box 75
Maynard, MA 01754
Tel: 800-776-0188
Email: info@earthwatch.org
http://www.earthwatch.org

To learn about field excavations and specific programs, contact

Archaeological Research Institute
PO Box 853
Bountiful, UT 84011-0853
Tel: 801-292-7061
http://www.ari-aerc.org

Society for American Archaeology
900 Second Street, NE, Suite 12
Washington, DC 20002-3557
Tel: 202-789-8200
Email: headquarters@saa.org
http://www.saa.org

ARCHIVISTS

QUICK FACTS

School Subjects English Foreign language History	**Certification or Licensing** Voluntary
	Outlook About as fast as the average
Personal Skills Communication/ideas Leadership/management	**DOT** 101
Work Environment Primarily indoors Primarily one location	**GOE** 11.03.03
	NOC 5113
Minimum Education Level Master's degree	
	O*NET-SOC 25-4011.00
Salary Range $18,910 to $34,190 to $63,299+	

OVERVIEW

Archivists contribute to the study of the arts and sciences by analyzing, acquiring, and preserving for research historical documents, organizational and personal records, and information systems that are significant enough to be preserved for future generations. Archivists keep track of artifacts such as letters, contracts, photographs, filmstrips, blueprints, electronic information, and other items of potential historical significance.

HISTORY

For centuries, archives have served as repositories for the official records of governments, educational institutions, businesses, religious organizations, families, and countless other groups. From the first time information was recorded, there has been a need to preserve those accounts. The evolution of archiving information in a manner similar to what we know today can be traced back to the Middle Ages.

As the feudal system in Europe gave way to nations and a more systematic order of law, precise record-keeping became increasingly important to keep track of land ownership and official policy. These records helped governments serve the needs of their nations and protected the rights of the common people in civil matters.

In America, early settlers maintained records using skills they brought from their European homelands. Families kept records of the journey to their new country and saved correspondence with family members still in Europe. Religious institutions kept records of the births, deaths, and marriages of their members. Settlers kept track of their business transactions, such as a land purchases, crop trades, and building constructions.

In the early 18th century, similar to what occurred in Europe in the Middle Ages, civic records in America became more prevalent as towns became incorporated. Leaders needed to maintain accurate records of property ownership and laws made by—and for—citizens.

Although archives have been incorporated in one form or another for centuries, archivists have established themselves as professionals only in the last hundred years or so. In the past, museums and societies accumulated records and objects rapidly and sometimes indiscriminately, accepting items regardless of their actual merit. Each archive had its own system of documenting, organizing, and storing materials. In 1884, the American Historical Association was formed to develop archival standards and help boost interaction among archivists.

Each year, as new scientific discoveries are made and new works are published, the need for sifting through and classifying items increases. More advanced computer systems will help archivists catalog archival materials as well as make archives more readily available to users. Advances in conservation techniques will help extend the life of fragile items, making them available to future generations.

THE JOB

Archivists analyze documents and materials such as government records, minutes of corporate board meetings, letters from famous people, charters of nonprofit foundations, historical photographs, maps, coins, works of art, and nearly anything else that may have historical significance. To determine which documents should be saved, they consider such factors as when each was written, who wrote it, and for whom it was written. In deciding on other items to archive, the archivist needs to consider the provenance, or history of creation and ownership, of the materials. They also take into account the capacity of their organization's archives. For instance, a repository with very little space for new materials may need to decline the gift of a large or bulky item, despite its potential value.

Archives are kept by various organizations, including government agencies, corporations, universities, and museums, and the value of documents is generally dictated by whichever group owns them. For example, the U.S. Army may not be interested in General Motors' corporate charter, and General Motors may not be interested in a Civil War battle plan. Archivists understand and serve the needs of their employers and collect items that are most relevant to their organizations.

Archivists may also be in charge of collecting items of historical significance to the institution for which they work. An archivist at a university, for instance, may collect new copies of the student newspaper to keep historical documentation of student activities and issues up to date. An archivist at a public library may prepare, present, and store annual reports of the branch libraries in order to keep an accurate record of library statistics.

After selecting appropriate materials, archivists help make them accessible to others by preparing reference aids such as indexes, guides, bibliographies, descriptions, and microfilmed copies of documents. These finding aids may be printed up and kept in the organization's stack area, put online so off-site researchers have access to the information, or put on floppy disk or CD-ROM for distribution to other individuals or organizations. Archivists also file and cross-index archived items for easy retrieval when a user wishes to consult a collection.

Archivists may preserve and repair historical documents or send damaged items to a professional conservator. They may also appraise the items based on their knowledge of political, economic, military, and social history, as well as by the materials' physical condition, research potential, and rarity.

Archivists play an integral role in the exhibition programs of their organizations. A university library, for instance, may present an exhibit that honors former Nobel Prize-winning faculty members. Most accomplished faculty leave their papers—notes, research, experiments, articles—to their institution. An exhibition might display first drafts of articles, early versions of experiments, or letters between two distinguished scientists debating some aspect of a project's design. Exhibits allow members of the university and the community to learn about the history of an organization and how research has advanced the field. The archivist helps to sort through archival materials and decide what items would make for an interesting exhibition at the institution.

Many archivists conduct research using the archival materials at their disposal, and they may publish articles detailing their findings. They may advise government agencies, scholars, journalists, and others conducting research by supplying available materials and information. Archivists also act as reference contacts and teachers. An employee doing research at the company archives may have little knowledge of how and where to begin. The archivist may suggest the worker consult specific reference guides or browse through an online catalog. After the employee decides which materials will be of most use, the archivist may retrieve the archives from storage, circulate the collection to the user, and perhaps even instruct the user as to the proper handling of fragile or oversize materials.

Archivists may have assistants who help them with the sorting and indexing of archival collections. At a university library, undergraduate or graduate students usually act as archival assistants. Small community historical societies may rely on trained volunteers to assist the archivist.

Depending on the size of their employing organization, archivists may perform many or few administrative duties. Such duties may include preparing budgets, representing their institutions at scientific or association conferences, soliciting support for institutions, and interviewing and hiring personnel. Some help formulate and interpret institutional policy. In addition, archivists may plan or participate in special research projects and write articles for scientific journals.

REQUIREMENTS
High School

If you are interested in doing archival work, you should start your training in high school. Since it is usually necessary to earn a master's degree to become an archivist, you should select a college preparatory curriculum and pay special attention to learning library and research skills. Classes in English, history, science, and mathematics will provide you with basic skills and knowledge for university study. Journalism courses will hone your research skills, and political science courses will help you identify events of societal importance. You should also plan on learning at least one foreign language; if you are interested in doing archival work at a religious organization, Latin or Hebrew may be good language options. If you would like to work in a specialized archive, such as a medical school archive, you should also focus on classes in the sciences, such as anatomy, biology, and chemistry.

Postsecondary Training

To prepare for archival work in college, you should get a degree in the liberal arts. You will probably want to study history, library science, or a related field, since there are currently no undergraduate or graduate programs that deal solely with the archival sciences. You should take any specific courses in archival methods that are available to you as an undergraduate. Since many employers prefer to hire archivists with a graduate degree, consider any course load that may help you gain entrance into a program to earn a master's degree in library science, library and information science, or history.

Graduate school will give you the opportunity to learn more specific details about archival work. Over 65 colleges and universities offer classes in the archival sciences as part of other degree programs. These courses will teach you how to do many aspects of archival work, from selecting items and organizing collections to preparing documentation and conserving materials. While in graduate school, you may be able to secure a part-time job or assistantship at your school's archives. Many university archives rely on their own students to provide valuable help maintaining collections, and students who work there gain firsthand knowledge and experience in the archival field.

For many positions, a second master's degree in a specific field or a doctorate is prerequisite. An archivist at a historical society may need a master's degree in history and another master's in library and information science. Candidates with bachelor's degrees may serve as assistants while they complete their formal training.

Certification or Licensing

Although not currently required by most employers, voluntary certification for archivists is available from the Academy of Certified Archivists. Certification is earned by gaining practical experience in archival work, taking requisite courses, and passing an examination on the history, theory, and practice of archival science. Tests are offered each year, usually in conjunction with the annual meeting of the Society of American Archivists. Groups of six or more archivists can petition the organization for an alternate exam location. Archivists need to renew their certification status every five years, usually by examination. Certification can be especially useful to archivists wishing to work in the corporate world.

Other Requirements

Archivists need to have excellent research and organizational skills. They should be comfortable working with rare and fragile materials. They need to maintain archives with absolute discretion, especially in the case of closed archives or archives available only for specific users. Archivists also need to be able to communicate effectively with all types of people that may use the archives, since they will be explaining the research methods and the policies and procedures of their organization. Finally, archivists may be responsible for moving heavy boxes and other awkward materials. An archivist should have the physical capabilities of bending, lifting, and carrying, although requirements may be different for various organizations and archival specialties, and arrangements can often be made for professionals with different abilities.

EXPLORING

If you are interested in archival work, a good way to learn about the field is by using archives for your own research. If you have a report due on Abraham Lincoln, for instance, you could visit an archive near your home that houses some of Lincoln's personal papers and letters. A visit to the archives of a candy manufacturer could help you with an assignment on the history of a specific type of production method. Since institutions may limit access to their collections, be sure to contact the organization about your project before you make the trip.

Getting to know an archivist can give you a good perspective of the field and the specific duties of the professional archivist. You could also see if a professional archival or historical association offers special student memberships or mentoring opportunities.

A personal project might be to construct a "family archive," consisting of letters, birth and marriage certificates, special awards, and any other documents that would help someone understand your family's history.

Another way to gain practical experience is to obtain part-time or volunteer positions in archives, historical societies, or libraries. Many museums and cultural centers train volunteer guides called docents to give tours of their institutions. If you already volunteer for an organization in another capacity, ask to have a personal tour of the archives.

EMPLOYERS

Archivists can find employment in various fields. In 2000, nearly one-third of the nation's archivists were employed in government positions, working for the Department of Defense, the National Archives and Records Administration, and other local, state, and federal repositories. Approximately 18 percent of archivists worked in academia, working in college and university libraries. Other archivists worked in positions for museums, historical societies, and zoos.

Archivists are also on staff at corporations, religious institutions, and professional associations. Many of these organizations need archivists to manage massive amounts of records that will be kept for posterity, or to comply with state or federal regulations. Some private collectors may also employ an archivist to process, organize, and catalog their personal holdings.

STARTING OUT

There is no best way to become an archivist. Since there is no formal archivist degree, many people working in the field today have had to pave their own way. Daniel Meyer, associate curator of special collections and university archivist at the University of Chicago Library, began by earning a master's degree in history and then a Ph.D. In graduate school, he worked processing collections in his university's archives. By enhancing his educational credentials with practical experience in the field, he gradually moved on to positions with greater degrees of responsibility.

Another archivist approached her career from the other direction: she had a master's degree in French and then went on to earn a library degree, with a concentration in archival management. With her language background and the M.L.S., she was able to begin working in archival positions in several colleges and universities.

Candidates for positions as archivists should apply to institutions for entry-level positions only after completing their undergraduate degrees, usually a degree in history. An archivist going into a particular area of archival work, however, may wish to earn a degree in that field; if you are interested in working in a museum's archives, for instance, you may wish to pursue a degree in art or art history.

Many potential archivists choose to work part-time as research assistants, interns, or volunteers, in order to gain archival experience. School placement offices are good starting points in looking for research assistantships and internships, and professional librarian and archivist associations often have job listings for those new to the field.

ADVANCEMENT

Archivists usually work in small sections, units, or departments, so internal promotion opportunities are often limited. Promising archivists advance by gaining more responsibility for the administration of the collections. They will spend more time supervising the work of others. Archivists can also advance by transferring to larger repositories and taking more administration-based positions.

Because the best jobs as archivists are contingent upon education, the surest path to the top is to pursue more education. Ambitious archivists should also attend conferences and workshops to stay current with developments in their fields. Archivists can enhance their status by conducting independent research and publishing their findings. In a public or private library, an archivist may move on to a position such as curator, chief librarian, or library director.

Archivists may also move outside of the standard archival field entirely. With their background and skills, archivists may become teachers, university professors, or instructors at a library school. They may also set up shop for themselves as archival consultants to corporations or private collectors.

EARNINGS

Salaries for archivists vary considerably by institution and may depend on education and experience. People employed by the federal government or by prestigious museums generally earn far more than those working for small organizations. The U.S. Department of Labor reported that the average annual salary for an experienced archivist working for the federal government was $63,299 in 2001. The median annual salary for all archivists was $34,190 in 2001. A beginning archivist at a small, nonprofit organization, however, could earn as little as $18,910 per year.

Archivists who work for large corporations, institutions, or government agencies generally receive a full range of benefits, including health care coverage, vacation days, paid holidays, paid sick time, and retirement savings plans. Self-employed archival consultants usually have to provide their own benefits. All archivists have the added benefit of working with rare and unique materials. They have the opportunity to work with history and create documentation of the past.

WORK ENVIRONMENT
Because dirt, sunlight, and moisture can damage the materials they handle, archivists generally work in clean, climate-controlled surroundings with artificial lighting rather than windows. Many archives are small offices, often employing the archivist alone, or with one or two part-time volunteers. Other archives are part of a larger department within an organization; the archives for DePaul University in Chicago, for instance, are part of the special collections department and are managed by the curator. With this type of arrangement, the archivist generally has a number of graduate assistants to help with the processing of materials and departmental support staff to assist with clerical tasks.

Archivists often have little opportunity for physical activity, save for the bending, lifting, and reaching they may need to do in order to arrange collections and make room for new materials. Also, some archival collections include not only paper records but some oversized items as well. The archives of an elite fraternal organization, for example, may house a collection of hats or uniforms that members wore throughout the years, each of which must be processed, cataloged, preserved, and stored.

Most archivists work 40 hours a week, usually during regular, weekday working hours. Depending on the needs of their department and the community they serve, an archive may be open some weekend hours, thus requiring the archivist to be on hand for users. Also, archivists spend some of their time traveling to the homes of donors to view materials that may complement an archival collection.

OUTLOOK
Job opportunities for archivists are expected to increase about as fast as the average over the next several years, according to the U.S. Department of Labor. But since qualified job applicants outnumber the positions available, competition for jobs as archivists is keen. Candidates with specialized training, such as a master's degree in history and in library science, will have better opportunities. A doctorate in history or a related field can also be a boon to job-seeking archivists. Graduates who have studied archival work or records management will be in higher demand than those without that background. Also, by gaining related work or volunteer experience,

many potential archivists will be in a better position to find full-time employment. As archival work begins to reflect an increasingly digital society, an archivist with extensive knowledge of computers is likely to advance more quickly than an archivist with little experience with or interest in computers.

Jobs are expected to increase as more corporations and private organizations establish an archival history. Archivists will also be needed to fill positions left vacant by retirees and archivists who leave the occupation. On the other hand, budget cuts in educational institutions, museums, and cultural institutions often reduce demand for archivists. Overall, there will always be positions available for archivists, but the aspiring archivist may need to be creative, flexible, and determined in forging a career path.

FOR MORE INFORMATION

To find out about archival certification procedures, contact
Academy of Certified Archivists
48 Howard Street
Albany, NY 12207
Tel: 518-463-8644
Email: aca@caphill.com
http://www.certifiedarchivists.org

To request information about archival programs, activities, and publications in North America, contact
American Institute for Conservation
of Historic and Artistic Works
1717 K Street, NW, Suite 200
Washington, DC 20006
Tel: 202-452-9545
Email: info@aic-faic.org
http://aic.stanford.edu

If you are interested in working with the archives of film and television, contact
Association of Moving Image Archivists
1313 North Vine Street
Hollywood, CA 90028
Tel: 323-463-1500
Email: amia@amianet.org
http://amianet.org

For educational information as well as information about professional activities and publications, contact
Society of American Archivists
527 South Wells, Fifth Floor
Chicago, IL 60607-3922
Tel: 312-922-0140
http://www.archivists.org

For archival programs and activities in Canada, contact
Association of Canadian Archivists
PO Box 2596, Station D
Ottawa, ON K1P 5W6 Canada
Tel: 613-445-4564
http://archivists.ca

For information on archival work and publications in the United Kingdom, contact
Society of Archivists
40 Northampton Road
London, EC1R 0HB England
Email: societyofarchivists@archives.org.uk
http://www.archives.org.uk

BOOK CONSERVATORS

QUICK FACTS

School Subjects
Art
History

Personal Skills
Artistic
Mechanical/manipulative

Work Environment
Primarily indoors
Primarily one location

Minimum Education Level
Some postsecondary
training

Salary Range
$19,200 to $33,080 to
$61,490+

Certification or Licensing
Voluntary

Outlook
About as fast as the average

DOT
102

GOE
01.06.02

NOC
5112

O*NET-SOC
25-4013.00

OVERVIEW

Book conservators treat the bindings and pages of books and nonbook items to help preserve original materials for future use. Their work often includes removing a book block from its binding, sewing, measuring, gluing, rebinding, and using special chemical treatments to maintain the integrity of the item. Most conservators work in libraries, in museums, or for special conservation centers.

HISTORY

Before the invention of the printing press, religious orders were often charged with copying texts by hand. These same monastic groups also assumed the roles of bookbinder and conservator. One of the main goals in creating books is the conservation and dissemination of knowledge.

In order to pass that knowledge on to future generations, many early bookbinders began the legacy of conservation by using high quality materials and excellent craftsmanship; a book that is well-crafted in the first place will need less invasive conservation as the material ages. Historically, then, the people who created the books had the specialized knowledge to conserve them.

Conservators today share many of the same traits of early bookbinders: They have the specialized knowledge of how books have traditionally been crafted, but they use technologically advanced adhesives, papers, and binding techniques to ensure that materials created centuries ago will be around for years to come.

The establishment of book conservation as a career field apart from bookbinding probably began when the first courses in conservation and preservation were taught at a library school, or when a professional library association first addressed the topic. Thus, although early bookbinders dealt with issues of material longevity, conservation as a field has only been around for 100 years or so.

THE JOB
Book conservators work to slow down or stabilize the deterioration of books and other print-based materials. They repair books that have been damaged by misuse, accident, pests, or normal wear and tear; treat items that may have been produced or repaired with inferior materials or methods; and work to ensure that the books will be around for the future.

Before beginning any conservation efforts, book conservators must examine the item to be restored, determine the extent and cause of the deterioration, evaluate their own conservation skills, and decide on a proper course of action. In deciding how to treat an item, the book conservator must first consider the history of the item. Book conservators must have a good knowledge of the history of bookmaking in order to serve the needs of the item. A book bound by hand in Italy in 1600 will have different needs than a volume bound by machine in 1980.

The book conservator also needs to consider what other repairs have been made to the book over the years. Sometimes a shoddy repair job in the past can create more work for today's conservator. For example, someone thirty years ago may have taped a torn page to keep it from ripping out entirely. Unfortunately, this hasty action, coupled with tape that will not stand the test of time, could lead to cracked, yellowing tape and stained book pages. When repairing a ripped sheet, book conservators use a pH-neutral (acid-free) adhesive, such as wheat paste, and Japanese paper, or a special acid-free book tape. Since high levels of acidity in papers and materials increase the rate of deterioration, all materials that conservators use must be acid-free and of archival quality.

Book conservators also think about the current and future use of the book. For a common, high-use volume that will be checked out of the library frequently, they may repair the book with cheaper, lower quality materials that will survive being jostled in backpacks and undergoing repeated trips through the return chute. For a textbook that is reprinted each year, for example, a thick piece of tape may be an adequate conservation method. If such a book is falling out of its cover, the conservator may need to remove the bookblock entirely, repair or replace the end sheets and headbands, and reglue the bookblock back into the cover. If the cover of the book is broken, the conservator may need to fit the text block into a new cover. This involves measuring out the binder's board and book cloth, cutting the materials to size, gluing the cloth onto the board, sizing in the bookblock, gluing, and setting. After the glue is dry, the conservator will inspect the item to ensure that all materials were fitted in properly, and that all problems were corrected.

Rare books that are handled less frequently or only by specially trained and careful users can have less invasive repairs in order to maintain the integrity of the original item. For instance, a conservator may choose to make a box to house a book rather than repair a broken spine. If the conservation work would lessen the value of the book, sometimes it's better to simply stop the deterioration rather than repair the damage.

The historical and monetary value of a book is a key factor in deciding upon treatment. As with any antique, often less restoration is more. On a recent antiques television program, an owner refinished an antique table and thereby reduced its resale value by thousands of dollars. The same can be said for books. Many old and rare books have great value because of the historical materials and methods in evidence.

Sometimes pests are encountered in conservation work. Beetle larvae and other insects may feast upon crumbs left in books, the pulp of the paper, or the adhesive, and make holes in the text. The conservator will assess the extent of the damage and prescribe a treatment. For critter damage to books, the most important thing is to ensure that any infestation is under control. The conservator needs to make sure that all bugs in a book are dead; if not, the items may need to be taken to a professional for fumigation. Once that is complete, the conservator can look at possible repair options. If the damage is under control, the conservator will probably opt for further damage prevention in lieu of repair.

Often conservators treat books for only part of their day. They might also spend much time working on ways to minimize the need for conservation and repair work in the first place. Book conservators who work as part of a large department have other duties, such as dealing with patrons, reference work, security, training assistants, fielding calls from the public, giving seminars, and teaching. Conservators may also serve on groups and committees devoted to preservation, conservation, and the administration of a conservation lab or department.

REQUIREMENTS
High School

You should plan on taking a college preparatory course load while in high school. Classes, such as history, literature, art, foreign languages, chemistry, and mathematics will all help you build a strong background for book conservation. By studying history, you can learn the social and historical contexts of books and knowledge. Understanding the history of an item can give you a better perspective on approaching the material as a conservator. Strong knowledge of literature can help you appraise the potential value of a book. A comprehension of foreign languages allows you to deal with a wider variety of books from around the globe. Chemistry and math will begin to teach you about the composition and measurement of the materials you will be using. Art will teach you how to use your hands to create beautiful works that last.

Postsecondary Training

After high school, you should strongly consider getting a bachelor's degree. Although most employers don't currently require a college degree for book conservator jobs, earning a bachelor's can only help your chances of advancing to positions with more responsibility. A degree in art, art history, or one of the fine arts may help you gain entry into a book conservation apprenticeship or internship program. Your school may offer courses in the book or paper arts, which often include classes in preservation and conservation. You will also need to take courses that help you learn how to select items for conservation, purchase and best utilize your conservation materials, and prepare documentation on the conservation methods and treatments you provide to an item.

Upon earning a bachelor's degree, you may wish to attend library school to earn a master's degree in library science with a concentration in book and document conservation. Again, advanced degrees may not be necessary for some positions, but they can always help you gain more prominent positions—particularly in administration—and perhaps command a higher salary. Additionally, any special skills you gain through advanced education will make you more attractive to potential employers and private clients.

Certification or Licensing

Some book conservators gain certification from their library school or from a special certifying organization. The certification process generally requires a mix of formal study of theory and practice, as well as a certain amount of actual experience in the field. Certification is not officially required by any federal, state, or local agencies, but some employers may request, or require, a certified book conservationist for particular positions or projects. Also, the certifying organization compiles a list of all certified conservators; if someone contacts the organization looking for a conservator, the agency will refer the client to member book conservators in the area.

Other Requirements

Book conservators need be able to think creatively. Conservation projects require the conservator to visualize the end product before beginning work. Conservators should enjoy problem solving and be able to decide the best way to conserve the materials. Having a hands-on nature is key as well, since book conservators spend a majority of their time inspecting materials and making repairs by hand.

Since book conservators routinely work with musty, moldy, and mildewed books, they should not be overly sensitive to odors. They also deal with sharp instruments, such as awls, knives, and paper cutters, so for safety reasons they should have a certain amount of facility with their hands. Book conservators also work with adhesives and chemicals, so they must take care not to spill materials.

Although much of their day is spent working with the materials, many conservators deal with the public as well. Book conservators, therefore, should be able to communicate well, and with a certain measure of tact, with many types of people. They should be able to explain conservation options to clients and to best determine what procedures will meet the needs of the material and the owner.

EXPLORING

If you are interested in becoming a book conservator, you should start out by learning all you can about how books are made. Study the history of books and of binding. Purchase an inexpensive, hardcover book at a used bookstore and take it apart to see how the bookblock is sewn together and how it is connected to the cover. Then try to put the book back together. There are many "how to" bookbinding guides to help you. Check out *Hand Bookbinding: A Manual of Instruction* by Aldren A. Watson (Dover Publications, 1996) or *ABC of Bookbinding* by Jane Greenfield (Oak Knoll Books, 1998) for the history of different styles of bookbinding and definitions of terms used in the field.

Contact the conservation or preservation department at your local library. The department may offer tours of its facilities or workshops on the proper care of books. Contact professional librarian associations; they may have divisions devoted to conservation. Community colleges and art museums often have weekend or evening classes in the conservation and book arts.

Finally, you might try contacting your local park district or community center to suggest sessions about book conservation. Many such groups offer summer day camps or after-school programs and look for input from participants about what types of activities are of interest. Plus, if you have had some conservation experience of your own, you could offer to teach younger students about how they can begin conserving books by taking good care of their own materials and the books they check out of the library.

EMPLOYERS

College and university libraries, public libraries, institutional libraries, and special libraries all employ book conservators. These organizations may have an entire department devoted to the conservation and preservation of materials, or the tasks of conservation may be bestowed upon another division, such as an archival or rare book collection. Museums sometimes have a specific book conservator post, or they may offer such duties to an interested art conservationist. Book conservators also work for companies devoted to material conservation. Binderies may hire a conservationist as a quality control consultant.

A number of book conservators are self-employed, working on a freelance or part-time basis for organizations and private citizens. They may be part of a nationwide network of certified book conservators. Often, potential clients contact book conservators through membership in professional organizations.

STARTING OUT
Book conservation is a field that relies heavily on skill, reputation, and word-of-mouth communication. While earning your bachelor's or master's degree, you should try to get an internship, apprenticeship, or assistantship in conservation or a related field. Take all the courses you can that will help you gain conservation skills.

You may also be able to get a part-time or summer job in your school library's preservation or conservation department. Many part time positions or internships can turn into full-time jobs after the incumbent has proven his or her skills or completed specific educational requirements.

Once you complete a training period, you might consider becoming certified. Certification can be a deciding factor in gaining employment, since certain companies and organizations may require book conservators to have official affirmation of their qualifications from an outside agency.

You should also join a conservator's organization in order to get to know professionals in the field. Since many conservator positions are in libraries, you may wish to join a professional library association as well. Professional organizations often have job listings available to members. They also publish journals and newsletters to keep members up-to-date on new developments in the field.

If you are looking to be a self-employed conservator, you may wish to volunteer your services until you have established yourself. Volunteering to assist nonprofit organizations with their conservation needs will give you good exposure to the book conservator world and the skills that potential clients are seeking.

ADVANCEMENT
Book conservators who demonstrate a high level of skill in their craft can move on to positions with more responsibility. They may be called upon to train assistants in book conservation or to teach conservation techniques at a library school, certification program, or conservation lab.

They may also transfer their skill in dealing with rare and fine materials and work more in the art community as art conservators, appraisers, or artists. With more experience and education, a book conservator can become an archivist, curator, or librarian. Many book conservators prefer to move away from full-time conservation and work on freelance projects instead.

With advanced computer knowledge, book conservators can help bring rare and fragile materials into the digital age. They may learn how to make materials available on the Internet and become virtual curators. They may also move on to actual exhibition work. Knowing how to preserve materials gives them the advantage in knowing how to exhibit them safely.

As book conservators gain more prominent positions, the trend is away from materials and toward administration. Beginning conservators will often spend most of their day dealing directly with the materials to be conserved. Conservators who move on to more advanced positions generally spend more time training others; evaluating materials and methods; dealing with outside suppliers, customers, and associations; attending meetings; and planning for the future of the department and the field.

EARNINGS

It is difficult to say how much the average book conservator makes, since many conservators work part time, are self-employed, or have positions that encompass other duties as well. In general, the salary range for book conservators may fall within the range the U.S. Department of Labor reports for all conservators, archivists, and other museum workers. In 2000 this group of professionals had a median annual income of $33,080. The lowest paid 10 percent earned less than $19,200 yearly, and the highest paid 10 percent made more than $61,490 per year. Often the size of the employer affects how much a conservator earns, with larger employers able to pay more. In addition, book conservators in major metropolitan areas generally earn more than those in small cities, and those with greater skills also command higher salaries.

Conservators who work for libraries, conservation organizations, large corporations, institutions, or government agencies generally receive a full range of benefits, including health care coverage, vacation days, paid holidays, paid sick time, and retirement savings plans. Self-employed book conservators usually have to provide their own benefits. All conservators have the added benefit of working with rare and unique materials. They have the opportunity to work with history and preserve an artifact for the future.

WORK ENVIRONMENT

Because of the damage that dirt, humidity, and the sun can cause to books, most conservators work in clean, climate-controlled areas away from direct sunlight. Many conservation labs are small offices, which often employ the conservator alone or perhaps with one or two part-time assistants. Other labs are part of a larger department within an organization; the University of Chicago's Regenstein Library, for instance, has a conservation lab within the Special Collections department. With this type of arrangement, the book conservator generally has a few student and nonstudent assistants who work part-time to help with some of the conservation duties.

Book conservators are always on the move. They use their hands constantly to measure, cut, and paste materials. They also bend, lift, and twist in order to reach items they work on and make room for new materials. Also, books are not always an easy size or weight to handle. Some oversized items need to be transported on a book truck from the stack area to the conservation area for treatment.

Most book conservators work 40 hours a week, usually during regular, weekday working hours. Depending on the needs of their department and the clientele they serve, book conservators may need to be available some weekend hours. Also, some book conservators may agree to travel to the homes of clients to view materials that may require conservation.

OUTLOOK

The future of book conservation as a profession will most likely grow about as fast as the average through 2010. The U.S. Department of Labor notes that while the outlook for conservators in general is favorable, there is strong competition for jobs. Book conservators who are graduates of conservation programs and are willing to relocate should have the best opportunities for employment. Those who can use their conservation skills in tandem with other abilities may also find more job openings. Book conservators with an artistic bent, for instance, could bring their conservation skills to an exhibition program at an art museum. Conservators who enjoy public contact could use their practical experience to teach classes in conservation techniques.

Some people are concerned that our increasingly digital society will create fewer opportunities for book conservators. They claim that technologies, such as television, computers, telephones, and the Internet have changed communication styles so drastically that printed books will eventually become obsolete. New technologies will bring new challenges to conservation. These trends will probably increase opportunities for conservators who can mesh traditional conservation efforts with new technologies. For example, a book conservator with excellent computer skills and Web authoring knowledge can work on a project to digitize rare book collections and make them available to people all over the world.

FOR MORE INFORMATION

For information about how to become a conservator, contact
**American Institute for Conservation
of Historic and Artistic Works**
1717 K Street, NW, Suite 200
Washington, DC 20006
Tel: 202-452-9545
Email: info@aic-faic.org
http://aic.stanford.edu

For information about preservation methods, services, and opportunities, contact
Library of Congress Preservation Directorate
101 Independence Avenue, SE
Washington, DC 20540-4500
Tel: 202-707-5213
Email: preserve@loc.gov
http://lcweb.loc.gov/preserv

For information on internship programs in Canada, contact
Canadian Conservation Institute
1030 Innes Road
Ottawa, ON K1A 0M5 Canada
Tel: 613-741-4390
http://www.pch.gc.ca/cci-icc

For a wealth of information about conservation topics, check out the following project of the Preservation Department of Stanford University Libraries.
Conservation OnLine
http://palimpsest.stanford.edu

BOOK EDITORS

QUICK FACTS

School Subjects Computer science English Journalism	**Certification or Licensing** None available **Outlook** Faster than the average
Personal Skills Artistic Communication/ideas	**DOT** 132
Work Environment Primarily indoors Primarily one location	**GOE** 01.01.01
Minimum Education Level Bachelor's degree	**NOC** 5122
Salary Range $23,090 to $37,550 to $73,460+	**O*NET-SOC** 27-3041.00

OVERVIEW

Book editors acquire and prepare written material for publication in book form. Such formats include trade books (fiction and nonfiction), textbooks, and technical and professional books (which include reference books). A book editor's duties include evaluating a manuscript, accepting or rejecting it, rewriting, correcting spelling and grammar, researching, and fact checking. Book editors may work directly with printers in arranging for proofs and with artists and designers in arranging for illustration matter and determining the physical specifications of the book.

Approximately 122,000 editors work for newspapers, magazines, and book publishers in the United States. Book editors are employed at small and large publishing houses, book packagers (companies that specialize in book production), associations, and government agencies.

HISTORY

Though the origins of publishing remain unknown, experts have proposed that publishing came into existence soon after people developed written language, perhaps in Sumer in approximately 4000 B.C. After it became possible to record information in writing, somebody had to decide which information was worth recording. Technically speaking, the first record-keepers were the first publishers and editors. Some of the first things deemed suitable for publication were accounting records, genealogies, laws, and religious rituals and beliefs.

In the early years of European publishing, the published works were intended for the small, elite group of educated people who could read and afford to buy books. For the most part, these people were clergymen and members of the upper class who had intellectual interests. Publishing was the business of printers, who also often performed what we would now call editorial tasks. Books of that era generally were written and edited in Latin, which was the language of intellectuals. Over time, however, literacy spread and books began to be written in the languages of the countries in which they were published.

Beginning in the 19th century, the various tasks performed by publishing concerns became more specialized. Whereas in early publishing a single person would often perform various functions, in later publishing employees performed a narrow range of tasks. Instead of having a single editor, a publication would have an editorial staff. One person would be responsible for acquisitions, another would copyedit, another would be responsible for editorial tasks that related to production, and so forth.

Editing has also been powerfully affected by technology. Publishing came into existence only after Gutenberg had invented the necessary technology, and it has changed in various ways as technology has developed. The most important recent developments have been those that have made it possible to transfer and edit information rapidly and efficiently. The development of the computer has revolutionized editing, making it possible to write and rewrite texts electronically and transmit corrected stories almost instantaneously from one part of the world to another.

THE JOB

The editorial department is generally the main core of any publishing house. Procedures and terminology may vary from one type of publishing house to another, but there is some general agreement among the essentials. Publishers of trade books, textbooks, and reference books all have somewhat different needs for which they have developed different editorial practices.

The editor has the principal responsibility in evaluating the manuscript. The editor responsible for seeing a book through to publication may hold any of several titles. The highest level editorial executive in a publishing house is usually the *editor in chief* or *editorial director*. The person holding either of these titles directs the overall operation of the editorial department. Sometimes an *executive editor* occupies the highest position in an editorial department. The next level of editor is often the *managing editor*, who keeps track of schedules and deadlines and must know where all manuscripts are at any given time. Other editors who handle copy include the *senior editors, associate editors, assistant editors, editorial assistants,* and *copy editors.*

In a trade-book house, the editor, usually at the senior or associate position, works with manuscripts that he or she has solicited from authors or that have been submitted by known authors or their agents. Editors who seek out authors to write manuscripts are also known as *acquisitions editors.*

In technical/professional book houses, editors commonly do more researching, revising, and rewriting than trade-book editors do. These editors are often required to be skilled in certain subjects. Editors must be sure that the subject is comprehensively covered and organized according to an agreed-upon outline. Editors contract for virtually all of the material that comes into technical/professional book houses. The authors they solicit are often scholars.

Editors who edit heavily or ask an author to revise extensively must learn to be highly diplomatic; the art of author-editor relations is a critical aspect of the editor's job.

When the editor is satisfied with the manuscript, it goes to the copy editor. The copy editor usually does the final editing of the manuscript before it goes to the typesetter. On almost any type of manuscript, the copy editor is responsible for correcting errors of spelling, punctuation, grammar, and usage.

The copy editor marks up the manuscript to indicate where different kinds of typefaces are used and where charts, illustrations, and photos may be inserted. It is important for the copy editor to discover any inconsistencies in the text and to query the author about them. The copy editor then usually acts as a liaison between the typesetter, the editor, and the author as the manuscript is typeset into galley proofs and then page proofs.

Notable History Graduates

Name	Job Title
Theodore Roosevelt	26th President of the United States
Martha Stewart	Business executive
Henry Cabot Lodge	U.S. statesman
George McGovern	U.S. statesman
Lee Iacocca	Business executive
Woodrow Wilson	28th President of the United States
Michael Palin	Actor
Chris Berman	Sportscaster
Carly Fiorina	CEO, Hewlett-Packard
Steve Forbes	CEO, Forbes, Inc.
Newt Gingrich	U.S. statesman
Penelope Lively	Author
Neil Tennant	Musician (Pet Shop Boys)
Salman Rushdie	Author
Richard Nixon	37th President of the United States
George W. Bush	43rd President of the United States

In a small house, one editor might do the work of all of the editors described here. There can also be separate fact checkers, proofreaders, style editors (also called line editors), and indexers. An assistant editor could be assigned to do many of the kinds of jobs handled by the senior or associate editors. Editorial assistants provide support for the other editors and may be required to proofread and handle some administrative duties.

REQUIREMENTS
High School
If you have an interest in a career as an editor, the most obvious classes that English, literature, and composition classes will offer

good preparation. You should also become comfortable working with word processing programs, either through taking a computer science class or through your own schoolwork. Taking journalism classes will give you the opportunity to practice different writing styles, including short feature pieces and long investigative stories. Take advantage of any clubs or extracurricular activities that will give you a chance to write or edit. Joining the school newspaper staff is a great way to explore different tasks in publishing, such as writing, editing, layout, and printing.

Postsecondary Training

A college degree is a requirement for entry into the field of book editing. For general editing, a degree in English or journalism is particularly valuable, although most degrees in the liberal arts are acceptable. Degrees in other fields, such as the sciences, psychology, mathematics, or applied arts, can be useful in publishing houses that produce books related to those fields. Textbook and technical/professional book houses in particular seek out editors with strengths in certain subject areas.

Other Requirements

Book editors should have a sharp eye for detail and a compulsion for accuracy (of both grammar and content). Intellectual curiosity, self-motivation, and a respect for deadlines are important characteristics for book editors to have. Knowledge of word processing and desktop publishing programs is necessary as well.

It goes without saying that if you are seeking a career in book editing, you should not only love to read, but love books for their own sake, as well. If you are not an avid reader, you are not likely to go far as a book editor. The craft and history of bookmaking itself is also something in which a young book editor should be interested. A keen interest in any subject, be it a sport, a hobby, or an avocation, can lead you into special areas of book publishing.

EXPLORING

As previously mentioned, joining your school's newspaper staff is a great way to explore editing and writing while in high school. Even if your duties are not strictly editorial, gaining experience by writing, doing layout work, or even securing advertisements will help you to understand how the editing stage relates to the entire field of publishing. Joining your school's yearbook staff or starting your own literary magazine are other ways to gain valuable experience.

You might be able to find a part-time job with a local book publisher or newspaper. You could also try to publish your own magazine or newsletter. Combine one of your other interests with your desire to edit. For example, if you are interested in sports, you could try writing and editing your own sports report to distribute to family and friends.

Since editing and writing are inextricably linked, be sure to keep your writing skills sharp. Outside of any class assignments, try keeping a journal. Try to write something every day and gain practice at reworking your writing until it is as good as you can make it. Explore different kinds of writing, such as short stories, poetry, fiction, essays, comedic prose, and plays.

If you are interested in becoming a book editor, you might consider joining a book club. Check Web Magic's list of book clubs at http://www.literature.com. Other interesting book websites, such as http://www.literarymarketplace.com, may be of interest if you'd like to learn more about publishing companies.

EMPLOYERS

Book editors may find employment with small publishing houses, large publishing houses, the federal government, or book packagers, or they may be self-employed as freelancers. The major book publishers are located in larger cities, such as New York, Chicago, Los Angeles, Boston, Philadelphia, San Francisco, and Washington, D.C. Publishers of professional, religious, business, and technical books are dispersed throughout the country. There are approximately 122,000 editors employed in the United States (including book editors and all other editors).

STARTING OUT

New graduates can find editing positions through their local newspaper or through contacts made in college. College career counselors may be able to assist in finding book publishers to apply for jobs. Another option is to simply look them up in the Yellow Pages or Internet and apply for positions directly. Many publishers will advertise job openings on their corporate websites or on job sites such as monster.com. Starting positions are generally at the assistant level and can include administrative duties in addition to basic editing tasks.

ADVANCEMENT

An editor's career path is dependent on the size and structure of the book publisher. Those who start as editorial assistants or proofreaders generally become copy editors. The next step may be a position as a senior copy editor, which involves overseeing the work of junior copy editors, or as a *project editor*. The project editor performs a wide variety of tasks, including copyediting, coordinating the work of in-house and freelance copy editors, and managing the schedule of a particular project. From this position, an editor may move up to become first assistant editor, then managing editor, then editor-in-chief. As editors advance, they are usually involved in more management work and decision-making. The editor-in-chief works with the publisher to ensure that a suitable editorial policy is being followed, while the managing editor is responsible for all aspects of the editorial department. Head editors employed by a publisher may choose to start their own editing business, freelancing full time.

WORK ENVIRONMENT

Book editors do most of their work on a computer, either in an office setting or at home. When working alone, the environment is generally quiet to allow the editor to concentrate on the work at hand. Editors also work in teams, allowing for an exchange of ideas and collaboration. They typically work a normal workweek schedule of 40 hours per week, though if a book is near a deadline, they may work longer hours to get assignments done on schedule.

EARNINGS

Earnings for book editors vary based on the size of the employer and the types of books it publishes, geographic location, and experience of the editor. The U.S. Department of Labor reports the median yearly salary for book editors was $37,550 in 2000. For all editors in 2001, the salaries ranged from a low of less than $23,090 to a high of more than $73,460 annually. The median salary for all editors in 2001 was $39,960. In general, editors are paid higher salaries at large companies, in major cities, and on the east and west coasts.

Publishers usually offer employee benefits that are about average for U.S. industry. There are other benefits, however. Most editors enjoy working with people who like books, and the atmosphere of an editorial department is generally intellectual and stimulating. Some book editors have the opportunity to travel in order to attend meetings, to meet with authors, or to do research.

OUTLOOK

According to the U.S. Department of Labor, job growth for writers and editors should be faster than the average, although competition for positions will be strong. The growth of online publishing will increase the need for editors who are Web experts. Other areas where editors may find work include advertising, public relations, and businesses with their own publications, such as company newsletters. Turnover is relatively high in publishing—editors often advance by moving to another firm or by establishing a freelance business. There are many publishers and organizations that operate with a minimal salaried staff and hire freelance editors for everything from project management to proofreading and production.

FOR MORE INFORMATION

Literary Market Place, published annually by R. R. Bowker, lists the names of publishing companies in the United States and Canada as well as their specialties and the names of their key personnel. For additional information about careers in publishing, contact the following:

Association of American Publishers
71 Fifth Avenue
New York, NY 10003-3004
Tel: 212-255-0200
http://www.publishers.org

Publishers Marketing Association
627 Aviation Way
Manhattan Beach, CA 90266
Tel: 310-372-2732
Email: info@pma-online.org
http://www.pma-online.org

Small Publishers Association of North America
PO Box 1306
425 Cedar Street
Buena Vista, CO 81211
Tel: 719-395-4790
Email: span@spannet.org
http://www.spannet.org

COLLEGE PROFESSORS

QUICK FACTS

School Subjects
English
History
Speech

Personal Skills
Communication/ideas
Helping/teaching

Work Environment
Primarily indoors
Primarily one location

Minimum Education Level
Master's degree

Salary Range
$35,790 to $60,000 to
$108,000+

Certification or Licensing
None available

Outlook
Faster than the average

DOT
090

GOE
11.02.01

NOC
4121

O*NET-SOC
25.1031.00, 25-1061.00,
25-1062.00, 25-1063.00,
25-1064.00, 25-1065.00,
25-1066.00, 25-1067.00,
25-1081.00, 25-1082.00,
25-1112.00, 25-1113.00,
25-1121.00, 25-1122.00,
25-1123.00, 25-1124.00,
25-1125.00, 25-1126.00,
25-1191.00

OVERVIEW

College professors instruct undergraduate and graduate students in specific subjects at colleges and universities. They are responsible for lecturing classes, leading small seminar groups, and creating and grading examinations. They also may conduct research, write for publication, and aid in administration. Approximately 1.3 million postsecondary teachers are employed in the United States.

HISTORY

The concept of colleges and universities goes back many centuries. Two of the most notable early European universities were the

University of Bologna in Italy, thought to have been established in the 12th century, and the University of Paris, which was chartered in 1201. These universities were considered to be the models after which other European universities were patterned. Oxford University in England was probably established during the 12th century. Oxford served as a model for early American colleges and universities and today is still considered one of the world's leading institutions.

Harvard, the first U.S. college, was established in 1636. Its stated purpose was to train men for the ministry; the early colleges were all established for religious training. With the growth of state-supported institutions in the early 18th century, the process of freeing the curriculum from ties with the church began. The University of Virginia established the first liberal arts curriculum in 1825, and these innovations were later adopted by many other colleges and universities.

Although the original colleges in the United States were patterned after Oxford University, they later came under the influence of German universities. During the 19th century, more than 9,000 Americans went to Germany to study. The emphasis in German universities was on the scientific method. Most of the people who had studied in Germany returned to the United States to teach in universities, bringing this objective, factual approach to education and to other fields of learning.

In 1833, Oberlin College in Oberlin, Ohio became the first college founded as a coeducational institution. In 1836, the first women-only college, Wesleyan Female College, was founded in Macon, Georgia.

The junior college movement in the United States has been one of the most rapidly growing educational developments. Junior colleges first came into being just after the turn of the 20th century.

THE JOB

College and university faculty members teach at junior colleges or at four-year colleges and universities. At four-year institutions, most faculty members are *assistant professors, associate professors,* or *full professors.* These three types of professorships differ in status, job responsibilities, and salary. Assistant professors are new faculty members who are working to get tenure (status as a permanent professor); they seek to advance to associate and then to full professorships.

College professors perform three main functions: teaching, advising, and research. Their most important responsibility is to teach students. Their role within a college department will determine the level of courses they teach and the number of courses per semester.

Most professors work with students at all levels, from college freshmen to graduate students. They may head several classes a semester or only a few a year. Some of their classes will have large enrollment, while graduate seminars may consist of only 12 or fewer students. Though college professors may spend fewer than 10 hours a week in the actual classroom, they spend many hours preparing lectures and lesson plans, grading papers and exams, and preparing grade reports. They also schedule office hours during the week to be available to students outside of the lecture hall, and they meet with students individually throughout the semester. In the classroom, professors lecture, lead discussions, administer exams, and assign textbook reading and other research. In some courses, they rely heavily on laboratories to transmit course material.

Another important professorial responsibility is advising students. Not all faculty members serve as advisers, but those who do must set aside large blocks of time to guide students through the program. College professors who serve as advisers may have any number of students assigned to them, from fewer than 10 to more than 100, depending on the administrative policies of the college. Their responsibility may involve looking over a planned program of study to make sure the students meet requirements for graduation, or it may involve working intensively with each student on many aspects of college life.

The third responsibility of college and university faculty members is research and publication. Faculty members who are heavily involved in research programs sometimes are assigned a smaller teaching load. College professors publish their research findings in various scholarly journals. They also write books based on their research or on their own knowledge and experience in the field. Most textbooks are written by college and university teachers. In arts-based programs, such as master's of fine arts programs in painting, writing, and theater, professors practice their craft and exhibit their art work in various ways. For example, a painter or photographer will have gallery showings, while a poet will publish in literary journals.

Publishing a significant amount of work has been the traditional standard by which assistant professors prove themselves worthy of becoming permanent, tenured faculty. Typically, pressure to publish is greatest for assistant professors. Pressure to publish increases again if an associate professor wishes to be considered for a promotion to full professorship.

In recent years, some liberal arts colleges have recognized that the pressure to publish is taking faculty away from their primary duties to the students, and these institutions have begun to place a decreasing emphasis on publishing and more on performance in the classroom. Professors in junior colleges face less pressure to publish than those in four-year institutions.

Some faculty members eventually rise to the position of *department chair*, where they govern the affairs of an entire department, such as English, mathematics, or biological sciences. Department chairs, faculty, and other professional staff members are aided in their myriad duties by *graduate assistants*, who may help develop teaching materials, conduct research, give examinations, teach lower level courses, and carry out other activities.

Some college professors may also conduct classes in an extension program. In such a program, they teach evening and weekend courses for the benefit of people who otherwise would not be able to take advantage of the institution's resources. They may travel away from the campus and meet with a group of students at another location. They may work full time for the extension division or may divide their time between on-campus and off-campus teaching.

Distance learning programs give professors the opportunity to use today's technologies to remain in one place while teaching students who are at a variety of locations simultaneously. The professor's duties, like those when teaching correspondence courses conducted by mail, include grading work that students send in at periodic intervals and advising students of their progress. Computers, the Internet, email, and video conferencing, however, are some of the technology tools that allow professors and students to communicate in "real time" in a virtual classroom setting. Meetings may be scheduled during the same time as traditional classes or during evenings and weekends. Professors who do this work are sometimes known as *extension work, correspondence,* or *distance learning instructors.* They may teach online courses in addition to other classes or may have distance learning as their major teaching responsibility.

The *junior college instructor* has many of the same kinds of responsibilities as the teacher in a four-year college or university. Because junior colleges offer only a two-year program, they teach only undergraduates.

REQUIREMENTS
High School

Your high school's college preparatory program likely includes courses in English, science, foreign language, history, math, and government. In addition, you should take courses in speech to get a sense of what it will be like to lecture to a group of students. Your school's debate team can also help you develop public speaking skills, along with research skills.

Postsecondary Training

At least one advanced degree in your field of study is required to be a professor in a college or university. The master's degree is considered the minimum standard, and graduate work beyond the master's is usually desirable. If you hope to advance in academic rank above instructor, most institutions require a doctorate.

In the last year of your undergraduate program, you'll apply to graduate programs in your area of study. Standards for admission to a graduate program can be high and the competition heavy, depending on the school. Once accepted into a program, your responsibilities will be similar to those of your professors—in addition to attending seminars, you'll research, prepare articles for publication, and teach some undergraduate courses.

You may find employment in a junior college with only a master's degree. Advancement in responsibility and in salary, however, is more likely to come if you have earned a doctorate.

Other Requirements

You should enjoy reading, writing, and researching. Not only will you spend many years studying in school, but your whole career will be based on communicating your thoughts and ideas. People skills are important because you'll be dealing directly with students, administrators, and other faculty members on a daily basis. You should feel comfortable in a role of authority and possess self-confidence.

EXPLORING

Your high school teachers use many of the same skills as college professors, so talk to your teachers about their careers and their college experiences. You can develop your own teaching experience by volunteering at a community center, working at a day care center, or working at a summer camp. Also, spend some time on a college campus to get a sense of the environment. Write to colleges for their admissions brochures and course catalogs (or check them out online); read about the faculty members and the courses they teach. Before visiting college campuses, make arrangements to speak to professors who teach courses that interest you. These professors may allow you to sit in on their classes and observe. Also, make appointments with college advisers and with people in the admissions and recruitment offices. If your grades are good enough, you might be able to serve as a teaching assistant during your undergraduate years, which can give you experience leading discussions and grading papers.

EMPLOYERS

Employment opportunities vary based on area of study and education. Most universities have many different departments that hire faculty. With a doctorate, a number of publications, and a record of good teaching, professors should find opportunities in universities all across the country. There are more than 3,800 colleges and universities in the United States. Professors teach in undergraduate and graduate programs. The teaching jobs at doctorate institutions are usually better paying and more prestigious. The most sought-after positions are those that offer tenure. Teachers that have only a master's degree will be limited to opportunities with junior colleges, community colleges, and some small private institutions. There are approximately 1.3 million postsecondary teachers employed in the United States.

STARTING OUT

You should start the process of finding a teaching position while you are in graduate school. The process includes developing a curriculum vitae (a detailed, academic resume), writing for publication, assisting with research, attending conferences, and gaining teaching experience and recommendations. Many students begin applying for teaching positions while finishing their graduate program. For most positions at four-year institutions, you must travel to large conferences where interviews can be arranged with representatives from the universities to which you have applied.

Because of the competition for tenure-track positions, you may have to work for a few years in temporary positions, visiting various schools as an *adjunct professor*. Some professional associations maintain lists of teaching opportunities in their areas. They may also make lists of applicants available to college administrators looking to fill an available position.

ADVANCEMENT

The normal pattern of advancement is from instructor to assistant professor, to associate professor, to full professor. All four academic ranks are concerned primarily with teaching and research. College faculty members who have an interest in and a talent for administration may be advanced to chair of a department or to dean of their college. A few become college or university presidents or other types of administrators.

The instructor is usually an inexperienced college teacher. He or she may hold a doctorate or may have completed all the Ph.D. requirements except for the dissertation. Most colleges look upon the rank of instructor as the period during which the college is trying out the teacher. Instructors usually are advanced to the position of assistant professors within three to four years. Assistant professors are given up to about six years to prove themselves worthy of tenure, and if they do so, they become associate professors. Some professors choose to remain at the associate level. Others strive to become full professors and receive greater status, salary, and responsibilities.

Most colleges have clearly defined promotion policies from rank to rank for faculty members, and many have written statements about the number of years in which instructors and assistant professors may remain in grade. Administrators in many colleges hope to encourage younger faculty members to increase their skills and competencies and thus to qualify for the more responsible positions of associate professor and full professor.

EARNINGS

Earnings vary depending on the departments professors work in, the size of the school, the type of school (for example, public, private, or women's only), and by the level of position the professor holds. In its 2000–2001 salary survey, the American Association of University Professors (AAUP) reported the average yearly income for all full-time faculty was $60,000. It also reports that professors averaged the following salaries by rank: full professors, $78,912; associate professors, $57,380; assistant professors, $47,358; and instructors, $35,790. Full professors working in disciplines such as law, business, health professions, computer and information sciences, and engineering have the highest salaries. Lower paying disciplines include visual and performing arts, agricultural studies, education, and communications. The American Association for the Advancement of Science reports that, according to findings from its member salary survey, the median earnings for full professors in the life science fields were approximately $108,000 in 2001. Associate professors in life sciences earned a median of $72,000 that same year.

According to a study by the College and University Professional Association for Human Resources, the average salary in all fields at public institutions was $60,893 for 2001–2002. At private colleges, the average was $60,289. Law professors earned top salaries of $107,696 at private colleges, and library science faculty members were near the bottom of the salary scale, earning $44,206 per year.

Many professors try to increase their earnings by completing research, publishing in their field, or teaching additional courses. Professors working on the west coast and the east coast of the United States and those working at doctorate-granting institutions tend to have the highest salaries.

Benefits for full-time faculty typically include health insurance and retirement funds and, in some cases, stipends for travel related to research, housing allowances, and tuition waivers for dependents.

WORK ENVIRONMENT

A college or university is usually a pleasant place in which to work. Campuses bustle with all types of activities and events, stimulating ideas, and a young, energetic population. Much prestige comes with success as a professor and scholar; professors have the respect of students, colleagues, and others in their community.

Depending on the size of the department, college professors may have their own office, or they may have to share an office with one or more colleagues. Their department may provide them with a computer, Internet access, and research assistants. College professors are also able to do much of their office work at home. They can arrange their schedule around class hours, academic meetings, and the established office hours when they meet with students. Most college teachers work more than 40 hours each week. Although college professors may teach only two or three classes a semester, they spend many hours preparing for lectures, examining student work, and conducting research.

OUTLOOK

The U.S. Department of Labor predicts faster than average employment growth for college and university professors over the next several years. College enrollment is projected to grow due to an increased number of 18- to 24-year-olds, an increased number of adults returning to college, and an increased number of foreign-born students. Additionally, opportunities for college teachers will be good in areas such as engineering, business, computer science, and health science, which offer strong career prospects in the world of work. Retirement of current faculty members will also provide job openings. However, competition for full-time, tenure-track positions at four-year schools will be very strong.

A number of factors threaten to change the way colleges and universities hire faculty. Some university leaders are developing more business-based methods of running their schools, focusing on profits and budgets. This can affect college professors in a number of ways. One of the biggest effects is in the replacement of tenure-track faculty positions with part-time instructors. These part-time instructors include adjunct faculty, visiting professors, and graduate students. Organizations such as the AAUP and the American Federation of Teachers are working to prevent the loss of these full-time jobs, as well as to help part-time instructors receive better pay and benefits. Other issues involve the development of long-distance education departments in many schools. Though these correspondence courses have become very popular in recent years, many professionals believe that students in long-distance education programs receive only a second-rate education. A related concern is about the proliferation of computers in the classroom. Some courses consist only of instruction by computer software and the Internet. The effects of these alternative methods on the teaching profession will be offset somewhat by the expected increases in college enrollment in coming years.

FOR MORE INFORMATION

To read about the issues affecting college professors, contact the following organizations:

American Association of University Professors
1012 14th Street, NW, Suite 500
Washington, DC 20005
Tel: 202-737-5900
Email: aaup@aaup.org
http://www.aaup.org

American Federation of Teachers
555 New Jersey Avenue, NW
Washington, DC 20001
Tel: 202-879-4400
Email: online@aft.org
http://www.aft.org

CONGRESSIONAL AIDES

QUICK FACTS

School Subjects Government History	**Certification or Licensing** None available
Personal Skills Communication/ideas Leadership/management	**Outlook** Little change or more slowly than the average
Work Environment Primarily indoors One location with some travel	**DOT** 209
	GOE 07.04.04
Minimum Education Level Bachelor's degree	**NOC** N/A
Salary Range $22,504 to $42,314 to $116,573+	**O*NET-SOC** N/A

OVERVIEW

Congressional aides are the men and women who staff the offices of the members of the United States Congress. Working for senators and representatives, congressional aides assist with a variety of duties, from administrative details to extensive research on legislation. Members of Congress typically have staff consisting of an administrative assistant, legislative assistants, a press secretary, an office manager, a personal secretary, and a legislative correspondent. Aides are generally divided into two groups: personal staff and committee staff. An aide may work in an office in Washington, D.C., or in a local district or state office.

HISTORY

Ever since members of Congress first began to hire stenographers and receptionists to assist with office duties, the role of congressional aides has stirred controversy. In the early 1800s, Congressmen worried they would look incapable of handling the responsibilities of their own jobs if they relied too much on assistants. This concern still exists today. Some members of Congress complain that having too many aides distances the senators and representatives from constituents, legislation, and the general requirements of their work.

Even these critics, however, admit that aides are very important to the lawmaking process. Since the end of World War II, with improvements in communications and transportation, voters have been making greater demands on their elected officials. Also, issues and casework have become increasingly complex. The Legislative Reorganization Act of 1946 was passed to allow each House and Senate standing committee to employ a campaign staff of four professional and six clerical workers. Another Reorganization Act passed years later, in 1970, which increased the number of professional staff to six members. The number of staff members has continued to grow, causing Congress to allocate more funds to construct new housing and office space.

THE JOB

Congressional aides see the lawmaking process at work—sometimes right on the Senate floor where laws are made. They work at the sides of important lawmakers, briefing them on legislation. The members of Congress (senators and representatives) rely on aides to assist them with a number of their responsibilities. Many constituents (the voters who elected members to Congress) rely on aides to help them make their voices and opinions heard. Aides answer letters, emails, and phone calls and distribute information to keep Congress members and the people they represent updated on the issues of national and local concern.

John Newsome worked on the staff of Congresswoman Barbara Lee as both a press secretary and legislative aide. Congresswoman Lee serves as the representative of California's 9th district and has been behind many important actions since taking office in April of 1998. Lee was involved in declaring an HIV crisis in the local African-American community, making Alameda County the first jurisdiction in the nation to issue such a declaration. She helped get a grant from the U.S. Department of Commerce for BAYTRADE, an organization that promotes the development of trade relations between Northern California and the African continent. She has also played a part in modifying and passing a bill authorizing a study of the barriers that women face in science, math, and technical fields. The congressional aide's job is to inform the public and the media of these actions and also to prepare the Congress member for press conferences and interviews. During his time at the office, Newsome did just that and also researched legislation. "I've been interested in politics all my life," Newsome says. "I wanted to work for someone with a real eye to grass roots advocacy." When Congress is in session, his days started at around 9:30 A.M. and lasted until 9:00 P.M. or even as late as 11:30 P.M.

In the office of a senator or representative, aides either serve on a personal or committee staff. A basic difference between the two types of staff is that the committee staffs are more strictly concerned with work that involves the construction and passage of legislation, while the personal staffs also deal with matters concerning the home state. Personal aides are generally loyal supporters of their members of Congress and their political philosophies. But this doesn't mean that aides don't sometimes have differing views. In some cases, aides may be more familiar with an issue and the general opinions of the constituents concerning an issue than the member of Congress. An aide's opinion can have an impact on a Congress member's decision.

The most important aide to a Congress member is the *chief of staff*, or *administrative assistant*. Those who achieve this position have worked closely with a Congress member for some time and have gained his or her trust and respect. The Congress member relies on the chief of staff's or administrative assistant's opinion and understanding of politics, legislation, and individual bills when making decisions. These aides also oversee the work of the other congressional aides.

Office managers handle the actual administration of the office. They attend to the management of office clerical staff, which includes hiring, staff scheduling, and other personnel matters. In addition to *administrative assistant secretaries* who provide clerical support to the chief of staff, a congressional staff also includes *personal secretaries*. They attend to the Congress member's administrative and clerical needs, which includes daily scheduling, expense accounts, and personal correspondence. This correspondence is delivered by *mailroom managers*, who are responsible for devising plans for handling the enormous crush of mail that arrives in congressional offices each day. They maintain mass mailing records and prepare reports on mail volume and contents.

The legislative staff in a congressional office assists the Congress member with research of bills and other legislative duties. The *leg-*

islative director directs the legislative staff and helps the Congress member keep up to date on important bills. They make sure the Congress member can make informed decisions on issues. Assisting the director are *legislative assistants* and *legislative correspondents.* Legislative assistants are each responsible for the coverage of issues in which they have developed some expertise. They brief the member of Congress on the status of legislation for which they are responsible and prepare floor statements and amendments for them; they may also write speeches for the member. Legislative correspondents are responsible for researching and drafting responses to letters received in the Congress member's offices.

Press secretaries are the primary spokespersons for members of Congress in their dealings with the media and the public. They respond to daily inquiries from the press, plan media coverage, coordinate press conferences, prepare press releases, and review daily newspapers.

State and district directors are responsible for state or district office operations, helping the Congress member to maintain close interaction with constituents. They represent their Congress member in all areas of the state or district and keep the office in Washington, D.C. informed on issues important to the local voters. Directors also plan the Congress member's visits to the state, sometimes accompanying him or her on a state tour.

A congressional staff also includes *schedulers,* who handle all the Congress member's scheduling of appointments; *computer operators,* who are responsible for computerized correspondence systems; and *caseworkers,* who work directly with people having difficulties with the federal government in such areas as veterans' claims, social security, and tax returns.

REQUIREMENTS
High School

Having a careful understanding of the government and how it works is important to anyone working for a member of Congress. You should take courses in U.S. government, political science, civics, social studies, and history, and get involved in school government and school committees. Attend formal meetings of various school clubs to learn about parliamentary procedure. Writing press releases and letters, and researching current issues are important aspects of congressional work. Journalism classes and reporting for your school newspaper will develop these communication skills.

Postsecondary Training

A well-rounded college education is very important for this career. Many congressional aides, such as chiefs of staff and legislative directors, have graduate degrees or law degrees. Consider undergraduate programs in political science, journalism, or economics. Political science programs offer courses in government, political theory, international relations, sociology, and public speaking. Look for internship opportunities in local, state, and federal government, and in political campaigns. Journalism programs offer courses in news reporting, communications law, and editing. Contact the offices of your state's members of Congress about applying for internships.

Other Requirements

Congressional aides need good problem-solving skills. They must have leadership abilities as well as the ability to follow instructions. Communication skills are very important, including writing, speaking, and listening. Before working as press secretary, John Newsome held other writing-related jobs, which involved writing grants and writing for the media. "I'm a very detail-oriented writer," he says. "I love writing. But to get a story sold also requires networking and advocacy. You have to maintain good relationships with people."

Aides must have a good temperament to deal with the stress of preparing a congressperson for voting sessions, and patience when dealing with constituents who have serious concerns about political issues. As with any job in politics, diplomacy is important in helping a Congress member effectively serve a large constituency with widely varying views.

EXPLORING

An extremely valuable—but highly competitive—learning opportunity is to work as a *page*. Pages serve members of Congress, running messages across Capitol Hill. The length of a page's service varies from one summer to one year. Students at least 16 years old are eligible to apply. Contact your state's senator or representative for an application.

You can also gain some insight into the work of a congressional aide through local efforts: volunteer for various school committees, take an active part in clubs, and become involved in school government. Campaigns for local elections rely heavily on volunteers, so find out about ways you can support your favorite candidate. Keep a close watch over current events by reading newspapers and news magazines. With an understanding of current issues, you can take a stand and express your opinions to your local, state, and federal representatives. An annual publication called the *Congressional Staff Directory* (http://www.csd.cq.com) contains the addresses, phone numbers, and biographical information for members of Congress and their aides. You can use this directory to express your views on an issue to your representatives. By contacting your Congress members' offices, you'll be talking to congressional aides and learning something about their responsibilities. (Print or online versions of this directory are available for purchase.)

EMPLOYERS

Congressional aides are federal employees. There are 100 senators and 435 representatives who hire congressional aides. This number won't change without an amendment to the constitution or the addition of another state. For fair representation in the U.S. Congress, each state is allowed two senators; the number of representatives for each state is determined by the state's population. California has the most representatives (53). Most congressional aides work in Washington, D.C., on Capitol Hill. Some find work in the home-state offices of their members of Congress.

STARTING OUT

Assistants are needed at every level of government. While in college, make personal contacts by volunteering on political campaigns. But be prepared to volunteer your services for some time in order to advance into positions of responsibility for candidates and elected officials. John Newsome has been involved since high school in grass roots advocacy. Over the years, he's been involved in HIV activism and community service with mentally disabled youth. Experience with these issues helped him to get his job with Congresswoman Lee. You can also gain valuable experience working in the offices of your state capitol building. State legislators require aides to answer phones, send letters, and research new bills.

Become familiar with the *Congressional Staff Directory*, available at your library or online. Getting a job as a congressional aide can be a difficult task—you may need to regularly submit resumes to placement offices of the House and the Senate. An internship can be a great way to get a foot in the door. The Congressional Management Foundation publishes information on internships.

ADVANCEMENT

Advancement in any of the congressional aide jobs is directly related to a congressional aide's ability, experience on Capitol Hill, and willingness to make personal sacrifices to complete work efficiently and on time. The highest office on congressional staffs is that of administrative assistant. It is possible for anyone on staff to rise up through the ranks to fill this position. Obviously, everyone cannot reach the top position, but advancement to higher staff positions is available to those who show they have the ability to take on greater responsibility. Legislative directors and state and district directors are probably the most likely candidates for the job of chief of staff. Legislative assistants, state office managers, and district office managers are in the best position to move into their respective directors' jobs. The top secretarial position is that of personal secretary, and any of the other secretaries can aspire to that position or that of scheduler. Any of the administrative staff, such as the receptionist or the mail room manager, can work toward the office manager's position.

EARNINGS

Congressional aides' salaries vary a great deal from office to office. Aides working in Senate positions generally have higher salaries than those working in House positions. Earnings also vary by position. A chief of staff, for example, has a much higher salary than a staff assistant working in the same office. Experience also plays a role in aides' earnings, with the highest salaries going to staffers with the most experience. Additionally, aides' earnings vary by the location of the office, that is, Washington, D.C., or the Congress person's home district, in which they work.

The Congressional Management Foundation (CMF), a nonprofit organization in Washington, D.C., publishes periodic reports on congressional employment practices that include salary information. In 2001, the average Senate salary for all positions (including aides) was $45,847. In 2000 (the most recent data available), the average House salary for all positions was $42,314.

According to CMF's *1999 Senate Staff Employment Study* (the latest available for this publication), the average annual salary earned by a Senate chief of staff was $116,573. Senate office managers averaged $57,330; systems administrators averaged $39,612; and staff assistants averaged $22,504. These averages are for positions in Washington, D.C. CMF's *2000 House Staff Employment Study* found that the average annual salary for a House chief of staff was $97,615.

House office managers averaged $44,009; systems administrators averaged $30,205; and staff assistants averaged $23,849. Again, these averages are for positions in Washington, D.C. More information on these reports is available from the CMF at http://www.cmfweb.org.

WORK ENVIRONMENT

Oddly enough, while Congress makes laws to protect workers and to ensure civil rights among the general populace, it has, in many cases, exempted itself from those same laws. Members of Congress contend that they should not be regulated like firms in the private sector because of the political nature of their institution and the necessity of choosing staff on the basis of loyalty. They also feel that it would breach the principle of the separation of powers if the executive branch had the power to enforce labor regulations in Congress.

Congressional aides are often faced with long hours, cramped quarters, and constant pressure. But many people thrive on the fast pace and appreciate the opportunity to get to know federal legislation from the inside. "The opportunities to meet people are endless," John Newsome says. "And it's incredibly challenging work." Despite the high pressure and deadlines, Newsome liked being a member of a staff involved in making positive changes.

OUTLOOK

Members of Congress will continue to hire aides regularly, but this is not a large employment field. The need for new workers will be steady but limited. Additionally, aides' positions are linked to the success of the Congressman or Congresswoman for whom they work. If their employer is voted out of office, aides also lose their jobs. Despite the long hours and (often) low pay, these jobs are prestigious, making competition for them strong.

Few people make working as a congressional aide a lifelong career. Those with excellent educational backgrounds and comfortable using technologies should have the best chances for jobs. The Internet is making it easier for constituents to express their views quickly and to access press releases, information about current legislation, and the positions of their representatives. Advocacy groups will expand their use of the Internet, gaining more support and encouraging voters to express their views via email. In the future, aides will work with a constituency much more knowledgeable about current legislation. The Internet will also serve aides in their research of bills, their interaction with the media, and their gauging of public views.

FOR MORE INFORMATION

For more information about House and Senate employment studies and other publications, such as The Congressional Intern Handbook, *contact*
Congressional Management Foundation
513 Capitol Court, NE, Suite 300
Washington, DC 20002
Tel: 202-546-0100
Email: cmf@cmfweb.org
http://www.cmfweb.org

Visit the websites of the House and the Senate for extensive information about individual Congress members and legislation. To write to your Congress members, contact
Office of Senator (Name)
U.S. Senate
Washington, DC 20510
http://www.senate.gov

Office of Congressperson (Name)
U.S. House of Representatives
Washington, DC 20510
http://www.house.gov

For employment opportunities, mail resume and cover letters to
Senate Placement Office
Room SH-142B
Washington, DC 20510

U.S. House of Representatives
Office of Human Resources
175 Ford House Office Building
Washington, DC 20515-6610

CULTURAL ADVISERS

QUICK FACTS

School Subjects	**Certification or Licensing**
Business	None available
Foreign language	
Speech	**Outlook**
	Faster than the average
Personal Skills	
Communication/ideas	**DOT**
Helping/teaching	N/A
Work Environment	**GOE**
Primarily indoors	N/A
Primarily multiple locations	**NOC**
	N/A
Minimum Education Level	
Bachelor's degree	**O*NET-SOC**
	N/A
Salary Range	
$65 to $100 to	
$265 per hour	

OVERVIEW

Cultural advisers, also known as *bilingual consultants,* work with businesses and organizations to help them communicate effectively with others who are from different cultural and language backgrounds. Cultural advisers usually have a specialty such as business management, banking, education, or computer technology. They help bridge both language and cultural barriers in our increasingly global business world.

HISTORY

Communication has always been a challenge when cultures come into contact with each other. In the early days of the United States, settlers and explorers relied on interpreters to assist them. One of those famous interpreters, Sacajawea, a member of the Shoshone Indian tribe, was a precursor of the cultural advisers of today. As she helped guide Meriwether Lewis and William Clark across the West to the Pacific Ocean, she acted as interpreter when they encountered Native American tribes. She also helped the explorers adapt to the different cultures and customs.

Today's cultural advisers work with companies or organizations that need to communicate effectively and do business with other cultures. Cultural advisers are becoming even more valuable because it is now relatively quick and easy to travel throughout the world. Each year, more trade barriers are broken down by legislation, such as the North American Free Trade Agreement, implemented in 1994.

THE JOB

Cultural advisers work to bridge gaps in communication and culture. They usually have a second specialty that is complimented by their bilingual skills. For example, a banking and finance expert who has traveled extensively in Japan and is familiar with Japanese language and customs would have the marketable skills to become a cultural adviser for American companies interested in doing business in Japan.

Cultural advisers work in a wide variety of settings. They may hold full-time staff positions with organizations or they may work as independent consultants providing services to a number of clients. Cultural advisers work in education. They provide translation services and help foreign or immigrant students adjust to a new culture. They also educate teachers and administrators to make them aware of cultural differences, so that programs and classes can be adapted to include everyone. Colleges and universities that have large international student populations often have cultural advisers on staff.

In industry, cultural advisers train workers in safety procedures and worker rights. The health care industry benefits from the use of advisers to communicate with non-English-speaking patients. Cultural advisers also hold training sessions for health care professionals to teach them how to better understand and instruct their patients.

Large business enterprises that have overseas interests hire cultural advisers to research new markets and help with negotiations. Some advisers work primarily in employment, finding foreign experts to work for American businesses or finding overseas jobs for American workers. In addition to advising American business leaders, cultural advisers sometimes work with foreign entities who want to do business in the United States. They provide English language instruction and training in American business practices.

Cultural advisers also work in the legal system, the media, advertising, the travel industry, social services, and government agencies. Whatever the setting, cultural advisers help their clients—foreign and American—understand and respect other cultures and communicate effectively with each other.

REQUIREMENTS
High School
Classes in business, speech, and foreign language will give you an excellent head start to becoming a cultural adviser. Also take other classes in your high school's college prep curriculum, such as history, mathematics, sciences, and English. Accounting classes and computer science classes will also help prepare you for working in business.

Postsecondary Training
If you are planning a career as a cultural adviser, fluency in two or more languages is a requirement, so college courses in those languages are necessary. Courses in business, world history, world geography, and sociology would be useful as well. You will need at least a bachelor's degree to find work as a cultural adviser, and you may want to consider pursuing a master's degree to have more job opportunities. Many universities offer programs in cultural studies, and there are master's programs that offer a concentration in international business.

Take advantage of every opportunity to learn about the people and area you want to work with, whether Latin America, Europe, Japan, or another region or country. Studying abroad for a semester or year is also recommended.

Other Requirements
Cultural sensitivity is the number one requirement for an adviser. Knowing the history, culture, and social conventions of a people as well as the language is a very important part of the job. Also, expertise in another area, such as business, education, law, or computers, is necessary to be a cultural adviser.

EXPLORING
A good way to explore this field is to join one of your high school's foreign language clubs. In addition to using the foreign language,

these clubs often have activities related to the culture where the language is spoken. You may also find it helpful to join your school's business club, which will give you an opportunity to learn about business tactics and finances, as well as give you an idea of how to run your own business.

Learn as much as you can about people and life in other parts of the world. You can do this by joining groups such as American Field Service International (AFS) and getting to know a student from another country who is attending your school. There are also study and living aboard programs you can apply to even while in high school. Rotary International and AFS offer such opportunities; see the end of the article for contact information.

EMPLOYERS

Cultural advisers are employed on a contract or project basis by businesses, associations, and educational institutions. Large global companies are the most significant source of employment for cultural advisers as they seek to serve the global population. Small- to medium-sized companies that conduct business in a particular region also employ cultural advisers. Companies in large cities offer the most opportunities for cultural advisers, especially those cities that border other countries and their economies.

Miguel Orta is a cultural adviser in North Miami Beach, Florida. He works with Latin American companies and American companies doing business in Central America and South America. He also has a background in law and business management. Orta is fluent in English, Spanish, and Portuguese. He uses his location in Florida to help businesses in the United States interact with a growing Hispanic population. His Florida location also allows him to be only a short plane flight from his Latin American clients.

STARTING OUT

Most cultural advisers do not begin this career right after college. Some real life experience is necessary to be qualified to fill the cultural adviser's role. "Education is very important," says Miguel Orta. "But first you need some work in the trenches." Once that experience is obtained, you will be ready to try advising.

After graduating with a law degree, Orta spent several years as a private attorney representing many Latin American clients. He practiced corporate, international, and labor law. When the opportunity came to serve one of his Venezuelan clients as a cultural adviser,

Orta enjoyed the work and decided to become an adviser to others in need of those services.

ADVANCEMENT

Working with larger companies on more extensive projects is one way for a cultural adviser to advance. If an adviser decides to trade in the flexibility and freedom of the job, opportunities to become a salaried employee would most likely be available.

EARNINGS

Cultural advisers are well compensated for the time they spend on projects. Rates can range from approximately $65 to as high as $265 per hour. The median rate is close to $100 per hour. Advisers may incur business expenses, but their clients generally pay many of the expenses associated with the work, such as travel, meals, and lodging.

WORK ENVIRONMENT

The work environment of cultural advisers largely depends on their specialties. A smaller company may offer a more informal setting than a multinational corporation. A cultural adviser who is employed by a large, international bank may travel much more than an adviser who works for an educational institution or association.

While cultural advisers generally work independently on projects, they must also communicate with a large number of people to complete their tasks. In the middle of a project, a cultural adviser may work 50–60 hours per week and travel may be necessary. Between projects, cultural advisers manage their businesses and solicit new clients.

OUTLOOK

The field of cultural advising is predicted to grow faster than average in the next decade. Demand will grow as trade barriers are continually loosened and U.S. companies conduct more business on a global scale. Latin America and Asia are two promising areas for American businesses.

Cultural advisers will also be needed to address the interests of the increasingly diverse population of the United States. However, competition is keen, and those with graduate degrees and specific expertise will be the most successful.

FOR MORE INFORMATION

Management consulting firms employ a large number of cultural advisers. For more information on the consulting business, contact

Association of Career Management Consulting Firms International
204 E Street, NE
Washington, DC 20002
Tel: 202-547-6344
Email: aocfi@aocfi.org
http://www.aocfi.org

For information about cultural exchanges, contact
American Field Service International
71 West 23rd Street, 17th Floor
New York, NY 10010
Tel: 212-807-8686
Email: info@afs.org
http://www.afs.org

Rotary International
One Rotary Center
1560 Sherman Avenue
Evanston, IL 60201
Tel: 847-866-3000
http://www.rotary.org

For information on etiquette and cross-cultural training, contact
Multi-Language Consultants, Inc.
Tel: 212-726-2164
Email: contact@mlc.com
http://www.mlc.com

Protocol Advisors, Inc.
241 Beacon Street
Boston, MA 02116
Tel: 617-267-6950
http://www.protocoladvisors.com

DEMOGRAPHERS

QUICK FACTS

School Subjects Computer science Mathematics Sociology	**Certification or Licensing** None available **Outlook** About as fast as the average
Personal Skills Communication/ideas Technical/scientific	**DOT** 054
Work Environment Primarily indoors One location with some travel	**GOE** 11.03.02 **NOC** 2161
Minimum Education Level Bachelor's degree	**O*NET-SOC** 15-2041.00, 19-3093.00
Salary Range $21,900 to $48,330 to $76,530	

OVERVIEW

Demographers are population specialists who collect and analyze vital statistics related to human population changes, such as births, marriages, and deaths. They plan and conduct research surveys to study population trends and assess the effects of population movements. Demographers work for government organizations as well as at private companies across the country.

HISTORY

Throughout history, people have conducted population studies of one kind or another for various reasons. As early as the mid-1600s, for example, the English were the first to systematically record and register all births and deaths. Over the years, recording techniques were refined and expanded to conduct more sophisticated population surveys so that governments could collect information, such as number of people and extent of property holdings, to measure wealth and levy taxes.

In recent years, census taking has become much more comprehensive, and the scientific methods of collecting and interpreting demographic information have also improved extensively. Demographers now have a leading role in developing detailed population studies that are designed to reveal the essential characteristics of a society, such as the availability of health care or average income levels.

THE JOB

Demography is the statistical study of human populations. A demographer works to establish ways in which numbers may be organized to produce new and useful information. For example, demographers may study data collected on the frequency of disease in a certain area, develop graphs and charts to plot the spread of that disease, and then forecast the probability that the medical problem may spread.

Many demographers work on the basis of a "sampling" technique in which the characteristics of the whole population are judged by taking a sample of a part of it. For example, demographers may collect data on the educational level of residents living in various locations throughout a community. They can use this information to make a projection of the average educational level of the community as a whole. In this way, demographers conduct research and forecast trends on various social and economic patterns throughout an area.

Demographers not only conduct their own surveys but often work with statistics gathered from government sources, private surveys, and public opinion polls. They may compare different statistical information, such as an area's average income level and its population, and use it to forecast the community's future educational and medical needs. They may tabulate the average age, income, educational levels, crime rate, and poverty rate of a farming community and compare the results with the same statistics of an urban environment.

Computers have radically changed the role of the demographer. Now, much greater amounts of data can be collected and analyzed. In the U.S. Census Bureau, for example, demographers work with material that has been compiled from the nationwide census conducted every 10 years. Millions of pieces of demographic information, such as age, gender, occupation, educational level, and country of origin, are collected from people around the country. A demographer may take this statistical information, analyze it, and then use it to forecast population growth or economic trends.

Demographers investigate and analyze a variety of social science questions for the government, such as rates of illness, availability of police services, and other issues that define a community. Private companies, such as retail chains, may use the information to make marketing decisions, such as where to open a new store and how to best reach possible customers.

Demographers may work on long-range planning. Population trends are especially important in such areas as educational and economic planning, and a demographer's analysis is often used to help set policy on health care issues and a host of other social science concerns. Local, state, and national government agencies all use the demographer's statistical forecasts in an attempt to accurately provide transportation, education, and other services.

Demographers may teach demographic research techniques to students. They also work as consultants to private businesses. Much of their time is spent doing library research, analyzing demographic information of various population groups.

An *applied statistician*, a specialized type of demographer, uses accepted theories and known statistical formulas to collect and analyze data in a specific area, such as the availability of health care in a specified location.

REQUIREMENTS
High School
Since you will need at least a bachelor's degree to find work as a demographer, you should take college preparatory courses, such as social studies, English, and mathematics (algebra and geometry) while in high school. In addition, take any statistics classes that your school offers. Training in computer science is also advantageous because computers are used extensively for research and statistical analysis.

Postsecondary Training
College course work should include classes in social research methods, economics, public policy, public health, statistics, and computer applications. Keep in mind that while you can get some starting jobs in the field with a bachelor's degree, most social scientists go on to attain advanced degrees. Many demographers get a doctorate in statistics, sociology, or demography. Approximately 110 universities offer master's programs in statistics, and about 60 have statistics departments offering doctorate programs.

Other Requirements

To work as a demographer, you should enjoy using logic to solve problems and have an aptitude for mathematics. You should also enjoy detailed work and must like to study and learn. Research experience is helpful. Other qualities that are helpful include intellectual curiosity and creativity, good written and oral communication skills, objectivity, and systematic work habits.

EXPLORING

A part-time or summer job at a company with a statistical research department is a good way of gaining insight into the career of demographer. Discussions with professional demographers are another way of learning about the rewards and responsibilities in this field. While in high school, ask your mathematics teachers to give you some simple statistical problems related to population changes to practice the kinds of statistical techniques that demographers use. Exploring statistical surveys and information from the Gallup Organization on the Internet (http://www.gallup.com) is another way to learn about this career. Additionally, undertaking your own demographic survey of an organization or group, such as your school or after-school club, is a project worth considering.

EMPLOYERS

Federal agencies such as the U.S. Census Bureau and the Bureau of Labor Statistics employ a large number of demographers, as do local and state government agencies. Private industry uses the services of demographers, as do universities, colleges, and foundations. Some demographers work as independent consultants rather than full-time employees for any one organization.

STARTING OUT

The usual method of entering the profession is through completion of an undergraduate or graduate degree in sociology or public health with an emphasis in demographic methods. However, according to Cary Davis, former vice president of the Population Reference Bureau in Washington, D.C., most entry-level positions require a graduate degree. "In fact," says Davis, "no one on my staff knows of any demographer who has less than a master's degree. Focus on an area that interests you, such as births and deaths or public health."

Qualified applicants can apply directly to private research firms or other companies that do population studies. University placement offices can help identify such organizations. Government jobs are listed with the Civil Service Commission.

ADVANCEMENT

According to Cary Davis, demographers who narrow their focus and become specialized in an area of interest are most likely to advance. Those with the highest degree of education are also most likely to be promoted.

EARNINGS

Earnings vary widely according to education, training, and place of employment. Social scientists (including sociologists who specialize in demography) earned a median annual salary of approximately $48,330 in 2000, according to the U.S. Department of Labor. Those with a bachelor's degree who started to work for the federal government began in the $21,900–$27,200 range in 2001. Social scientists with a master's degree working for the federal government started at about $33,300, while those with a doctorate started at about $40,200.

In 2001, statisticians working for the federal government (often including demographers) averaged an annual salary of $68,900. Those working in mathematical positions averaged $76,530.

Vacation days and other benefits, such as sick leave, group insurance, and a retirement plan, are typically offered to demographers working full time for any large organization.

WORK ENVIRONMENT

Most demographers work in offices or classrooms during a regular 40-hour week. Depending on the project and deadlines, however, overtime may be required. Those engaged in research may work with other demographers assembling related information. Most of the work revolves around analyzing population data or interpreting computer information. A demographer is also usually responsible for writing a report detailing the findings. Some travel may be required, such as to attend a conference or complete limited field research.

OUTLOOK

According to the U.S. Department of Labor, the social science field is expected to grow about as fast as the average over the next several years. However, there will be keen competition in many areas. Those with the most training and greatest amount of education, preferably a Ph.D., should find the best job prospects. Employment opportunities should be greatest in and around large metropolitan areas, where many colleges, universities, research facilities, and federal agencies are located. Individuals with statistical training will have an advantage.

FOR MORE INFORMATION

For career publications, lists of accredited schools, and job information, contact

American Sociological Association
1307 New York Avenue, NW, Suite 700
Washington, DC 20005
Tel: 202-383-9005
Email: executive.office@asanet.org
http://www.asanet.org

This organization includes demographers, sociologists, economists, public health professionals, and other individuals interested in research and education in the population field. For information on job opportunities, publications, and annual conferences and workshops, contact

Population Association of America
8630 Fenton Street, Suite 722
Silver Spring, MD 20910-3812
Tel: 301-565-6710
Email: info@popassoc.org
http://www.popassoc.org

For publications, special reports, and global population information, contact

Population Reference Bureau
1875 Connecticut Avenue, NW, Suite 520
Washington, DC 20009-5728
Tel: 800-877-9881
Email: popref@prb.org
http://www.prb.org

For population statistics, as well as information on regional offices, jobs, and a calendar of events, contact

U.S. Census Bureau
Washington, DC 20233
Tel: 301-457-4608
Email: recruiter@census.gov
http://www.census.gov

Top History Graduate Programs by Specialty

U.S. News & World Report prepares annual ranking lists for graduate school programs. The following lists show the top-ranked schools for various history specialties.

Modern U.S. History

1. Yale University (Conn.)
   http://www.yale.edu/history
2. Columbia University (N.Y.)
   http://www.columbia.edu/cu/history
3. University of California—Berkeley
   http://history.berkeley.edu
4. Stanford University (Calif.)
   http://history.stanford.edu
5. Princeton University (N.J.)
   http://history.princeton.edu
6. Harvard University (Mass.)
   http://www.fas.harvard.edu/~history
7. University of Wisconsin-Madison
   http://history.wisc.edu
8. University of Chicago
   http://history.uchicago.edu
9. University of North Carolina—Chapel Hill
   http://www.unc.edu/depts/history
10. University of Michigan-—Ann Arbor
    http://www.lsa.umich.edu/history

U.S. Colonial History

1. Yale University (Conn.)
   http://www.yale.edu/history
2. College of William and Mary (Va.)
   http://www.wm.edu/history
3. Harvard University (Mass.)
   http://www.fas.harvard.edu/~history
4. Johns Hopkins University (Md.)
   http://www.jhu.edu/~history

(continues)

Top History Graduate Programs by Specialty
(continued)

5. Princeton University (N.J.)
   http://history.princeton.edu

6. University of Pennsylvania
   http://www.history.upenn.edu

7. University of California—Los Angeles
   http://www.sscnet.ucla.edu/history

8. Columbia University (N.Y.)
   http://www.columbia.edu/cu/history

9. University of Virginia
   http://www.virginia.edu/history

10. Brown University (R.I.)
    http://www.brown.edu/Departments/History

European History

1. Princeton University (N.J.)
   http://history.princeton.edu

2. University of California—Berkeley
   http://history.berkeley.edu

3. Yale University (Conn.)
   http://www.yale.edu/history

4. University of Chicago
   http://history.uchicago.edu

5. Harvard University (Mass.)
   http://www.fas.harvard.edu/~history

6. University of Michigan—Ann Arbor
   http://www.lsa.umich.edu/history

7. University of California—Los Angeles
   http://www.sscnet.ucla.edu/history

8. Stanford University (Calif.)
   http://history.stanford.edu

9. Columbia University (N.Y.)
   http://www.columbia.edu/cu/history

10. Johns Hopkins University (Md.)
    http://www.jhu.edu/~history

(continues)

Top History Graduate Programs by Specialty
(continued)

Latin American History

1. University of Texas-Austin
   http://www.utexas.edu/cola/depts/history

2. Yale University (Conn.)
   http://www.yale.edu/history

3. University of California—Berkeley
   http://history.berkeley.edu

4. University of California—Los Angeles
   http://www.sscnet.ucla.edu/history

5. University of Chicago
   http://history.uchicago.edu

6. University of Wisconsin-Madison
   http://history.wisc.edu

7. Harvard University (Mass.)
   http://www.fas.harvard.edu/~history

8. Indiana University—Bloomington
   http://www.indiana.edu/~histweb

9. University of California—San Diego
   http://historyweb.ucsd.edu

10. Duke University (N.C.)
    http://www-history.aas.duke.edu

11. University of Arizona
    http://datamonster.sbs.arizona.edu/history

African-American History

1. University of Michigan—Ann Arbor
   http://www.lsa.umich.edu/history

2. Harvard University (Mass.)
   http://www.fas.harvard.edu/~history

3. New York University
   http://www.nyu.edu/gsas/dept/history

4. Columbia University (N.Y.)
   http://www.columbia.edu/cu/history

(continues)

Top History Graduate Programs by Specialty
(continued)

5. Princeton University (N.J.)
   http://history.princeton.edu

6. Rutgers State University—New Brunswick (N.J.)
   http://history.rutgers.edu/undergrad/under_index.html

7. Yale University (Conn.)
   http://www.yale.edu/history

8. Duke University (N.C.)
   http://www-history.aas.duke.edu

9. University of Chicago
   http://history.uchicago.edu

10. Stanford University (Calif.)
    http://history.stanford.edu

11. University of California-Berkeley
    http://history.berkeley.edu

12. University of Wisconsin-Madison
    http://history.wisc.edu

Asian History

1. University of California-Berkeley
   http://history.berkeley.edu

2. Harvard University (Mass.)
   http://www.fas.harvard.edu/~history

3. University of California-Los Angeles
   http://www.sscnet.ucla.edu/history

4. Stanford University (Calif.)
   http://history.stanford.edu

5. Yale University (Conn.)
   http://www.yale.edu/history

6. University of Chicago
   http://history.uchicago.edu

7. Columbia University (N.Y.)
   http://www.columbia.edu/cu/history

8. Princeton University (N.J.)
   http://history.princeton.edu

(continues)

Top History Graduate Programs by Specialty
(continued)

9. University of Michigan-Ann Arbor
   http://www.lsa.umich.edu/history

10. Cornell University (N.Y.)
    http://falcon.arts.cornell.edu/History

11. University of Washington (Wash.)
    http://depts.washington.edu/clio

Women's History

1. Rutgers University—New Brunswick (N.J.)
   http://history.rutgers.edu/graduate/programwomgen.htm

2. University of Michigan-Ann Arbor
   http://www.lsa.umich.edu/history

3. University of Wisconsin-Madison
   http://history.wisc.edu

4. Yale University (CT)
   http://www.yale.edu/history

5. University of California—Los Angeles
   http://www.sscnet.ucla.edu/history

6. University of North Carolina—Chapel Hill
   http://www.unc.edu/depts/history

7. University of California-Berkeley
   http://history.berkeley.edu

8. University of Minnesota—Twin Cities
   http://www.hist.umn.edu

9. Stanford University (Calif.)
   http://history.stanford.edu

10. New York University
    http://www.nyu.edu/gsas/dept/history

Cultural History

1. University of California—Berkeley
   http://history.berkeley.edu

2. University of Chicago
   http://history.uchicago.edu

(continues)

Top History Graduate Programs by Specialty
(continued)

3. Princeton University (N.J.)
   http://history.princeton.edu

4. University of California—Los Angeles
   http://www.sscnet.ucla.edu/history

5. Yale University (Conn.)
   http://www.yale.edu/history

6. Columbia University (N.Y.)
   http://www.columbia.edu/cu/history

7. Harvard University (Mass.)
   http://www.fas.harvard.edu/~history

8. New York University
   http://www.nyu.edu/gsas/dept/history

9. University of Michigan—Ann Arbor
   http://www.lsa.umich.edu/history

10. Stanford University (Calif.)
    http://history.stanford.edu

Source: *U.S. News & World Report* (ranked in 2001)

EDUCATION DIRECTORS AND MUSEUM TEACHERS

QUICK FACTS

School Subjects
English
History
Speech

Personal Skills
Communication/ideas
Helping/teaching

Work Environment
Primarily indoors
One location with some travel

Minimum Education Level
Bachelor's degree

Salary Range
$18,000 to $32,000 to $60,000+

Certification or Licensing
None available

Outlook
Little change or more slowly than the average

DOT
099

GOE
11.07.03

NOC
5124

O*NET-SOC
N/A

OVERVIEW

People visit museums, zoos, and botanical gardens to learn and observe. *Education directors,* or *curators of education,* are responsible for helping these people enrich their visits. Education directors plan, develop, and administer educational programs at museums and other similar institutions. They plan tours, lectures, and classes for individuals, school groups, and special interest groups.

Museum teachers also provide information, share insight, and offer explanations of exhibits. Direct communication ranges from informal explanations at staff previews of a new exhibit, to addressing corporate donor groups, to aiding groups of school-children. Museum teachers may write exhibit labels, prepare cata-logs, or contribute to multimedia installations. Museum teachers also teach by demonstration, by conducting studio classes, or by leading field trips.

HISTORY

In early times, churches displayed art and furnishings for worshipers to view. The early equivalents of education directors were the priests or laypeople who developed expertise in the collections. As public museums grew, so did their need for education directors. When Europeans began to encourage the idea of universal education, museums began to draw in uneducated visitors who needed to be taught about their collections.

Similarly, zoos and arboretums, which were originally organized to exhibit their animals and plants to experts, began to teach others about their collections. Education directors were hired to plan programs and tours for visitors.

In the United States, early museums displayed objects relating to colonial history. Some were in former homes of wealthy colonists and others were established at the first U.S. universities and colleges. In these early museums *curators* or *archivists* maintained the collections and also explained the collections to visitors. As the collections grew and more visitors and groups of visitors came, education directors were hired by the curators to coordinate educational programs.

THE JOB

Education directors carry out the educational goals of a museum, zoo, botanical garden, or other similar institution. The educational goals of most of these institutions include nurturing curiosity and answering questions of visitors, regardless of age or background. Education directors work with administrators and museum or zoo boards to determine the scope of their educational programs. Large museums may offer full schedules of classes and tours, while smaller ones may only provide tours or lectures at the request of a school or other group.

Education directors plan schedules of courses to be offered through the zoo or museum. They may hire lecturers from local colleges or universities as well as regular educational staff members to lead tours or discussion groups. Education directors are usually responsible for training the staff members and may also work with professionals or university faculty to determine the content of a particular lecture, class, or series of lectures. They prepare course outlines and establish the credentials necessary for those who will teach the courses.

In smaller institutions the education director may do much of the teaching, lecturing, or tour leading. In zoos, the education director can arrange for small children to watch cows being milked or for the children to pet or feed smaller animals such as goats. In museums, the education director's job often depends on the museum's collection. In art museums, visitors are often older than in natural history museums, and the education director may plan programs that allow older children to explore parts of the collection at their own pace.

Education directors often promote their programs on local radio or television or in newspapers. They may speak to community or school groups about the museum's education department and encourage the groups to attend. Sometimes, education directors deliver lectures or offer classes away from the museum or zoo.

The education director is responsible for the budget for all educational programs. Directors prepare budgets and supervise the records of income and spending. Often, schools or other groups are charged lower rates for tours or classes at museums or zoos. Education directors work with resource coordinators to establish budgets for resource materials. These need to be updated regularly in most institutions. Even in natural history museums, where the collections may change less than in other museums, slide collections may need to be updated or presentations altered if new research has led to different interpretations of the objects. The education director may also prepare grant proposals or help with fundraising efforts for the museum's educational program. Once a grant has been received or a large gift has been offered to the education department, the education director plans for the best use of the funds within the department.

Education directors often work with exhibit designers to help create displays that are most effective for visitors. They may also work with illustrators to produce illustrations or signs that enhance exhibits. Zoos, for example, often display maps near the animals to show their countries of origin.

Education directors train their staff members as well as volunteers to work with individual visitors and groups. Some volunteers are trained to assist in presentations or to help large groups on tours. It is the responsibility of the education director to see that the educational program is helpful and interesting to all of the people who visit the museum or zoo.

Education directors plan special activities that vary widely depending on the institution. Film programs, field trips, lectures, and full-day school programs may be offered weekly, monthly, or annually.

In larger museums, education directors may have a staff of educators. Museum teachers may serve as *docents* or *interpreters* who interact directly with visitors. Docents also give prepared talks or provide information in a loosely structured format, asking and answering questions informally. Good content knowledge is required, as well as sensitivity to visitor group composition. Scholarly researchers, for example, have a different knowledge base and attention span than children.

Other museum teachers, such as *storytellers,* may be self-employed people who contract with a museum to provide special programs a few times a year. Many teachers are volunteers or part-time workers.

Education specialists are experts in a particular field, which may be education itself or an area in which the museum has large holdings, such as Asian textiles, North American fossils, or pre-Columbian pottery. Education specialists divide their time between planning programs and direct teaching. They may supervise other teachers, conduct field trips, or teach classes in local schools as part of joint programs of study between museums and schools.

Educational resource coordinators are responsible for the collection of education materials used in the educational programs. These may include slides, posters, videotapes, books, or materials for special projects. Educational resource coordinators prepare, buy, catalog, and maintain all of the materials used by the education department. They sometimes have a lending library of films, videos, books, or slides that people may borrow. Resource coordinators keep track of the circulation of materials. They may also lead tours or workshops for educators or school personnel to teach them about the collection of the museum or zoo and to keep them apprised of new materials the educators may use in their tours or in their own classrooms. Resource coordinators and directors attend conventions and teachers' meetings to promote their institution's educational program and to encourage participation in their classes or tours.

REQUIREMENTS
High School

As an education director or a museum professional, you will need a diverse educational background to perform well in your job. At the high school level, you should follow a well rounded college preparatory curriculum, including courses in creative writing, literature, history of world civilizations, American history, science, foreign language, art, and speech. These courses will give you general background knowledge you can use to interpret collections, write letters to school principals, design curriculum materials, develop multicultural education, and lecture to public audiences. You should also develop strong math and computer skills. You will use these skills when preparing budgets and calculating the number of visitors that can fit in an exhibit space, and when writing grants or asking corporations and federal agencies for program funding.

Postsecondary Training

In order to be an education director, you must have a bachelor's degree. Many museums, zoos, and botanical gardens also require a master's degree. The largest zoos and museums prefer to hire education directors who have doctorate degrees.

Some colleges in the United States offer programs of instruction leading to a degree in museology (the study of museums). Most education directors work in museums that specialize in art, history, or science. These directors often have degrees in fields related

A New Take on History

In years past, most history scholars worked solely in academia, researching and publishing for the scholarly community. However, history scholars gained new opportunities in the public sector in the last half of the 19th century as the general public took new interest in the history of their own country and its role in the world. Everyday people suddenly wanted to know about historical figures and events, and institutions were created to educate the public. As early as 1836, the Smithsonian Institution in Washington, D.C., was established—a museum campus which is now home to 16 different institutions.

This new nonacademic branch of history has been labeled public history, mainly because of its audience: the general public. Public historians not only work for museums, but they are also employed to work on television documentaries, write for widely read publications (such as *National Geographic*), and even contribute to popular historical websites (such as History Matters at http://historymatters.gmu.edu).

Source: Public History Resource Center (http://www.publichistory.org)

to the museum's specialty. Those who work in zoos usually have studied biology or zoology or have worked closely with animals. Education directors who work in more specialized museums often have studied such specialized fields as early American art, wood-carvings, or the history of circuses. As an education director, you must have a good working knowledge of the animals, plants, or artifacts in the collection.

Museum teachers and education specialists must also have a bachelor's degree in an academic discipline or in education.

Other Requirements

Excellent communication skills are essential in this field. Your primary responsibility will be to interpret and present collections to a broad public audience. The ability to motivate and teach many individuals from a wide range of cultural backgrounds, age groups, and educational levels is necessary. You should also be organized and flexible. You will be at a great advantage if you know a foreign language, sign language, and/or CPR.

EXPLORING

If you are interested in becoming an education director or museum teacher, you can easily obtain volunteer experience: Most zoos and museums need and have student volunteers. You can request a position or apply for an internship in the education department, where you may help with elementary school tours, organize files or audio-visual materials, or assist a lecturer in a class.

The American Association of Museums publishes an annual museum directory, a monthly newsletter, and a bimonthly magazine. It also publishes *Museum Careers: A Variety of Vocations*. This report is helpful for anyone considering a career in the museum field. *Introduction to Museum Work*, published by the American Association for State and Local History, discusses the educational programs at various museums. In addition, the American Association of Botanical Gardens and Arboreta publishes a directory of over 500 internships offered through public gardens each year.

EMPLOYERS

Institutions with a primary goal to educate the public about their collections hire education directors. Depending on each institution's monetary resources, most museums (large and small), zoos, botanical gardens, and occasionally historical societies employ education directors to ensure public access to their collections. Institutions with small operating budgets or limited visitor access sometimes hire part-time educators or rely on volunteer support.

STARTING OUT

Your first job in a museum or zoo will likely be as a teacher or resource coordinator working in the education department. With a few years of experience and improved understanding of the institution's collection, you may enter competition for promotion to education director. Many people in the field transfer from one museum to another or from one zoo to another, in order to be promoted to the position of education director.

ADVANCEMENT

Once in the education department, most people learn much of their work on the job. Experience in working with different people and groups becomes very important. Education directors must continually improve their understanding of their own institution's collection so that they can present it to school and other groups in the best way possible. Some education directors work for the federal government in specific subject areas such as aeronautics, philately (stamp collecting), or branches of science and technology. They must be proficient in these fields as well as in education.

Museum teachers with experience and appropriate academic or teaching credentials may become content specialists in one area of the museum's collection or may become a director of education, assuming responsibility for the departmental budget, educational policies and community outreach programs, and training and supervision of numerous staff and volunteer workers. Advancement may depend on acquisition of an advanced degree in education or in an academic field. Because professional supervisory positions are few in comparison to the large corps of teachers, museum teachers desiring advancement may need to look beyond their home institution, perhaps accepting a smaller salary at a smaller museum in return for a supervisory title.

Teachers who leave museum work are well positioned to seek employment elsewhere in the nonprofit sector, especially with grant-funding agencies involved in community-based programs. In the for-profit sector, excellent communication skills and the ability to express an institution's philosophy both in writing and in interviews are skills valued by the public relations departments of corporations.

EARNINGS

Salaries for education directors vary widely depending on the size, type, and location of the institution, as well as the education and experience of the director. The average beginning salary for education directors with bachelor's degrees plus one year of related experience or equivalent advanced education is $30,000. Those with master's degrees may earn starting salaries of $35,000 to $45,000. Salaries can range from as little as $6,000 for a part-time position at a small museum to $60,000 at a large institution. Salary.com reports that a typical education manager working in the United States is expected to earn a median base salary of $52,996. According to the *Wall Street Journal's Career Journal,* the 2001 median annual salary for an education director at a nonprofit institution was $59,817.

Educational assistants and museum teachers can expect to earn from $18,000 to $22,000 to start. Those with experience earn from $25,000 to $32,000.

Fringe benefits, including medical and dental insurance, paid vacations and sick leave, and retirement plans, vary according to each employer's policies.

WORK ENVIRONMENT

Most people who choose to be education directors like to be in museums, botanical gardens, or zoos. They also enjoy teaching, planning activities, organizing projects, and carrying a great deal of responsibility. Those in zoos usually enjoy animals and like being outdoors. Those in museums like the quiet of a natural history museum or the energy and life of a science museum aimed at children. Education directors should enjoy being in an academic environment where they work closely with scholars, researchers, and scientists.

Education directors in larger institutions usually have their own offices where they do planning and other administrative work, but they spend the majority of their time in other parts of the museum and at other locations where they lead education programs.

Most museum teachers have a base of operation in the museum but may not have a private office, since the bulk of their work is carried out in exhibit areas, in resource centers or study rooms within the museum, in classrooms outside of the museum, or in the field. Permanent staff work a normal workweek, with occasional weekend or evening assignments.

Museum teaching varies from day to day and offers innovative teachers a chance to devise different programs. However, museum teaching is different from conventional classroom teaching where educators have the benefit of more time to convey ideas and facts.

OUTLOOK

The employment outlook for education directors and museum teachers is expected to increase more slowly than average through the next decade, according to the U.S. Department of Labor. Budget cutbacks have affected many museums and other cultural institutions, which have in turn reduced the size of their education departments. Museums in the United States have seen significant reduction in the number of visitors, which is directly related to the slowdown in the travel industry.

Many educators with specialties in sciences, the arts, or zoology are interested in becoming education directors at museums and zoos. Competition is especially intense for positions in large cities and those with more prestigious reputations. Some smaller museums and botanical gardens may cut out their education director position altogether until the economic climate improves, or they may get by with part-time education directors.

FOR MORE INFORMATION

For information about publications, meetings, seminars, and workshops, contact

American Association for State and Local History
1717 Church Street
Nashville, TN 37203-2991
Tel: 615-320-3203
Email: history@aaslh.org
http://www.aaslh.org

For a directory of museums and other information, contact

American Association of Museums
1575 Eye Street, NW, Suite 400
Washington, DC 20005
Tel: 202-289-1818
http://www.aam-us.org

ELEMENTARY
SCHOOL TEACHERS

QUICK FACTS

School Subjects English Speech	**Certification or Licensing** Required by all states
Personal Skills Communication/ideas Helping/teaching	**Outlook** About as fast as the average **DOT** 092
Work Environment Primarily indoors Primarily one location	**GOE** 11.02.01
Minimum Education Level Bachelor's degree	**NOC** 4142
Salary Range $27,000 to $41,080 to $64,280+	**O*NET-SOC** 25-2021.00

OVERVIEW

Elementary school teachers instruct students from the first through sixth or eighth grades. They develop teaching outlines and lesson plans, give lectures, facilitate discussions and activities, keep class attendance records, assign homework, and evaluate student progress. Most teachers work with one group of children throughout the day, teaching several subjects and supervising such activities as lunch and recess. More than 1.4 million elementary school teachers are employed in the United States.

HISTORY

The history of elementary education can be traced back to about 100 B.C., when the people of Judah established schools for young children as part of their religious training.

In the early days of Western elementary education, the teacher only had to have completed elementary school to be considered qualified to teach. There was little incentive for an elementary school teacher to seek further education. School terms were generally short (about six months) and buildings were often cramped and poorly heated. Many elementary schools combined the entire eight grades into one room, teaching the same course of study for all ages. In these earliest schools, teachers were not well paid and had little status or recognition in the community.

When people began to realize that teachers should be better educated, schools designed to train teachers, called normal schools, were established. The first normal school was private and opened in Concord, Vermont, in 1823. The first state-supported normal school was established in Lexington, Massachusetts, in 1839. By 1900, nearly every state had at least one state-supported normal school.

The forerunner of the present-day college or school of education in large universities was the normal department established at Indiana University in 1852. Normal schools have since then given way to teachers' colleges and today almost every university in the country has a school or college of education.

THE JOB

Depending on the school, elementary school teachers teach grades one through six or eight. In smaller schools, grades may be combined. There are still a few one-room, one-teacher elementary schools in remote rural areas. However, in most cases, teachers instruct approximately 20–30 children of the same grade. They teach a variety of subjects in the prescribed course of study, including language, science, mathematics, and social studies. In the classroom, teachers use various methods to educate their students, such as reading to them, assigning group projects, and showing films for discussion. Teachers also use educational games to help their pupils come up with creative ways to remember lessons.

In the first and second grades, elementary school teachers cover the basic skills: reading, writing, counting, and telling time. With older students, teachers instruct history, geography, math, English, and handwriting. To capture attention and teach new concepts, they use arts and crafts projects, workbooks, music, and other interactive activities. In the upper grades, teachers assign written and oral reports and involve students in projects and competitions such as spelling bees, science fairs, and math contests. Although they are usually required to follow a curriculum designed by state or local administrators, teachers study new learning methods to incorporate into the classroom, such as using computers to surf the Internet.

"I utilize many different, some unorthodox, teaching tools," says Andrea LoCastro, a sixth-grade teacher in Clayton, New Jersey. "I have a lunchtime chess club. Students give up their recess to listen to classical music and play, or learn to play, chess." She has also found that role-playing activities keep her students interested in the various subjects. "We are studying ancient Greece," she says, "and I currently have my students writing persuasive essays as either part of Odysseus' legal team or the Cyclops' legal team. I intend to culminate the activity with a mock trial, Athenian style."

To create unique exercises and activities such as those LoCastro uses, teachers need to devote a fair amount of time to preparation outside of the classroom. They prepare daily lesson plans and assignments, grade papers and tests, and keep a record of each student's progress. Other responsibilities include communicating with parents through written reports and scheduled meetings, keeping their classroom orderly, and decorating desks and bulletin boards to keep the learning environment visually stimulating.

Elementary school teachers may also teach music, art, and physical education, but these areas are often covered by specialized teachers. *Art teachers* are responsible for developing art projects, procuring supplies, and helping students develop drawing, painting, sculpture, mural design, ceramics, and other artistic abilities. Some art teachers also teach students about the history of art and lead field trips to local museums. *Music teachers* teach music appreciation and history. They direct organized student groups such as choruses, bands, or orchestras, or guide music classes by accompanying them in singing songs or playing instruments. Often, music teachers are responsible for organizing school pageants, musicals, and plays. *Physical education teachers* help students develop physical skills such as coordination, strength, and stamina and social skills such as self-confidence and good sportsmanship. Physical education teachers often serve as sports coaches and may be responsible for organizing field days and intramural activities.

When working with elementary-aged children, teachers need to instruct social skills along with general school subjects. They serve as disciplinarians, establishing and enforcing rules of conduct to help students learn right from wrong. To keep the classroom manageable, teachers maintain a system of rewards and punishments to encourage students to behave, stay interested, and participate. In cases of classroom disputes, teachers must also be mediators, teaching their pupils to peacefully work through arguments.

Recent developments in school curricula have led to new teaching arrangements and methods. In some schools, one or more teachers work with students within a small age range instead of with particular grades. Other schools are adopting bilingual education, where students are instructed throughout the day in two languages by either a *bilingual teacher* or two separate teachers.

Many teachers find it rewarding to witness students develop and hone new skills and adopt an appreciation for learning. In fact, many teachers inspire their own students to later join the teaching profession themselves. "Teaching is not just a career," says LoCastro, "It is a commitment—a commitment to the 20-plus children that walk into your classroom door each September eager for enlightenment and fun."

REQUIREMENTS
High School
Follow your school's college preparatory program and take advanced courses in English, mathematics, science, history, and government to prepare for an education degree. Art, music, physical education, and extracurricular activities will contribute to the broad base of knowledge necessary to teach a variety of subjects. Composition, journalism, and communications classes are also important for developing your writing and speaking skills.

Postsecondary Training
All 50 states and the District of Columbia require public elementary education teachers to have a bachelor's degree in either education or in the subject they plan to teach. Prospective teachers must also complete an approved training program. In the United States, there are over 500 accredited teacher education programs, which combine subject and educational classes with work experience in the classroom.

Though programs vary by state, courses cover how to instruct language arts, mathematics, physical science, social science, art, and music. Additionally, prospective teachers must take educational training courses, such as philosophy of education, child psychology, and learning methods. To gain experience in the classroom, student teachers are placed in a school to work with a full-time teacher. During this training period, student teachers observe the ways in which lessons are presented and the classroom is managed, learn how to keep records of attendance and grades, and gain experience in handling the class, both under supervision and alone.

Some states require prospective teachers to have master's degrees in education and specialized technology training to keep them familiar with more modern teaching methods using computers and the Internet.

Certification or Licensing

Public school teachers must be licensed under regulations established by the state in which they are teaching. If they relocate, teachers have to comply with any other regulations in their new state to be able to teach, though many states have reciprocity agreements that make it easier for teachers to change locations.

Licensure examinations test prospective teachers for competency in basic subjects such as mathematics, reading, writing, teaching, and other subject matter proficiency. In addition, many states are moving towards a performance-based evaluation for licensing. In this case, after passing the teaching examination, prospective teachers are given provisional licenses. Only after proving themselves capable in the classroom are they eligible for a full license.

Another growing trend spurred by recent teacher shortages is alternative licensure arrangements. For those who have a bachelor's degree but lack formal education courses and training in the classroom, states can issue a provisional license. These workers immediately begin teaching under the supervision of a licensed educator for one to two years and take education classes outside of their working hours. Once they have completed the required coursework and gained experience in the classroom, they are granted a full license. This flexible licensing arrangement has helped to bring additional teachers into school systems needing instructors.

Other Requirements

Many consider the desire to teach a calling. This calling is based on a love of children and a dedication to their welfare. If you want to become a teacher, you must respect children as individuals, with personalities, strengths, and weaknesses of their own. You must also be patient and self-disciplined to manage a large group independently. Teachers make a powerful impression on children, so they need to serve as good role models. "Treat students with kindness and understanding, rules and consequences," LoCastro suggests. "Be nice, yet strict. They'll love you for it."

EXPLORING

To explore the teaching career, look for leadership opportunities that involve working with children. You might find summer work as a counselor in a summer camp, as a leader of a scout troop, or as an assistant in a public park or community center. Look for opportunities to tutor younger students or coach children's athletic teams. Local community theaters may need directors and assistants for summer children's productions. Day care centers often hire high school students for late afternoon and weekend work.

EMPLOYERS

There are more than 1.4 million elementary school teachers employed in the United States. Teachers are needed at public and private institutions, including parochial schools and Montessori schools, which focus more on the child's own initiatives. Teachers are also needed in day care centers that offer full-day elementary programs and charter schools, which are smaller, deregulated schools that receive public funding. Although rural areas maintain schools, more teaching positions are available in urban or suburban areas.

STARTING OUT

After obtaining a college degree, finishing the student teaching program, and becoming certified, prospective teachers have many avenues for finding a job. College placement offices and state departments of education maintain listings of job openings. Many local schools advertise teaching positions in newspapers. Another option is directly contacting the administration in the schools in which you'd like to work. While looking for a full-time position, you can work as a substitute teacher. In more urban areas with many schools, you may be able to find full-time substitute work.

ADVANCEMENT

As teachers acquire experience or additional education, they can expect higher wages and more responsibilities. Teachers with leadership skills and an interest in administrative work may advance to serve as principals or supervisors, though the number of these positions is limited and competition is fierce. Others may advance to work as *senior* or *mentor teachers* who assist less experienced staff. Another move may be into higher education, teaching education classes at a college or university. For most of these positions, additional education is required.

Other common career transitions are into related fields. With additional preparation, teachers can become librarians, reading specialists, or counselors.

"I intend to continue teaching as my career," says Andrea LoCastro. "I am not at all interested in moving up to administration. I will, however, pursue a master's in teaching after receiving tenure."

EARNINGS

According to the Bureau of Labor Statistics, the median annual salary for elementary school teachers was $41,080 in 2001. The lowest 10 percent earned $27,000 or less; the highest 10 percent earned $64,280 or more.

The American Federation of Teachers reports that the average salary for beginning teachers with a bachelor's degree was $28,986 in 2001. The estimated average salary of all public elementary and secondary school teachers was $43,250.

Teachers often supplement their earnings through teaching summer classes, coaching sports, sponsoring a club, or other extracurricular work. More than half of all teachers belong to unions such as the American Federation of Teachers or the National Education Association. These unions bargain with schools over contract conditions such as wages, hours, and benefits. Depending on the state, teachers usually receive a retirement plan, sick leave, and health and life insurance. Some systems grant teachers sabbatical leave.

WORK ENVIRONMENT

Most teachers are contracted to work 10 months out of the year, with a two-month vacation during the summer. During their summer break, many continue their education to renew or upgrade their teaching licenses and earn higher salaries. Teachers in schools that operate year-round work eight-week sessions with one-week breaks in between and a five-week vacation in the winter.

Teachers work in generally pleasant conditions, although some older schools may have poor heating or electrical systems. The work can seem confining, requiring them to remain in the classroom throughout most of the day. Although the job is not overly strenuous, dealing with busy children all day can be tiring and trying. Teachers must stand for many hours each day, do a lot of talking, show energy and enthusiasm, and may have to handle discipline problems. But, according to Andrea LoCastro, problems with students are usually overshadowed by their successes. "Just knowing a child is learning something because of you is the most rewarding feeling, especially when you and the child have struggled together to understand it."

OUTLOOK

According to the *Occupational Outlook Handbook,* employment opportunities for teachers (grades K–12) are expected to grow as fast as the average for all occupations over the next several years. The need to replace retiring teachers will provide many opportunities nationwide.

The demand for teachers varies widely depending on geographic area. Inner-city schools characterized by poor working conditions and low salaries often suffer a shortage of teachers. In addition, more opportunities exist for those who specialize in a subject in which it is harder to attract qualified teachers, such as mathematics, science, or foreign languages.

The National Education Association believes it will be a difficult challenge to hire enough new teachers to meet rising enrollments and replace the large number of retiring teachers, primarily because of low teacher salaries. Approximately 2.4 million teachers will be needed to fill classrooms in the next decade. Higher salaries along with other necessary changes, such as smaller classroom sizes and safer schools, will be necessary to attract new teachers and retain experienced ones. Other challenges for the profession involve attracting more men into teaching. The percentage of male teachers continues to decline.

In order to improve education, drastic changes are being considered by some districts. Some private companies are managing public schools in the hope of providing better facilities, faculty, and equipment. Teacher organizations are concerned about taking school management away from communities and turning it over to remote corporate headquarters.

Charter schools and voucher programs are two other controversial alternatives to traditional public education. Publicly funded charter schools are not guided by the rules and regulations of traditional public schools. Some view these schools as places of innovation and improved educational methods; others see them as ill-equipped and unfairly funded with money that could better benefit local school districts. Vouchers, which exist only in a few cities, use public tax dollars to allow students to attend private schools. In theory, the vouchers allow for more choices in education for poor and minority students. Teacher organizations see some danger in giving public funds to unregulated private schools.

FOR MORE INFORMATION

For information about careers, education, and union membership, contact the following organizations:

American Federation of Teachers
555 New Jersey Avenue, NW
Washington, DC 20001
Tel: 202-879-4400
Email: online@aft.org
http://www.aft.org

National Council for Accreditation of Teacher Education
2010 Massachusetts Avenue, NW, Suite 500
Washington, DC 20036
Tel: 202-466-7496
Email: ncate@ncate.org
http://www.ncate.org

National Education Association
1201 16th Street, NW
Washington, DC 20036
Tel: 202-833-4000
http://www.nea.org

ETHNOSCIENTISTS

QUICK FACTS

School Subjects Foreign language History Sociology	**Certification or Licensing** None available **Outlook** About as fast as the average
Personal Skills Communication/ideas Technical/scientific	**DOT** N/A
Work Environment Indoors and outdoors Primarily multiple locations	**GOE** N/A **NOC** N/A
Minimum Education Level Doctorate degree	**O*NET-SOC** N/A
Salary Range $21,700 to $46,330 to $87,850+	

OVERVIEW

Ethnoscientist is a broad term that covers various specialties, such as ethnoarchaeology, ethnobiology, ethnomusicology, ethnoveterinary medicine, and ethnozoology. Ethnoscientists study a particular subject, usually a social or life science, (e.g., archaeology, biology, veterinary medicine, or zoology) from the perspective of one or more cultural groups.

Ethnoscientists are usually Western practitioners who are interested in exploring the knowledge, beliefs, traditions, and practices of cultures in nonindustrialized areas of the world, such as the Maoris of New Zealand, the Shona of south-central Africa, or the Inuit of Alaska. These cultures have unique, often undocumented, ways of perceiving, interacting with, and understanding each other and their environment. Ethnoscientists study these cultures to record and learn from their perspectives.

HISTORY

Although the term is relatively new, ethnoscientific study has been around since people first began exploring the relationship between people and their environment, by studying music, language, biology, history, and all the elements that form societies and cultures.

According to an ethnobotany lecture from the Khon Kaen University (Thailand) department of pharmacognosy and pharmaceutical botany (see http://www.rbgkew.org.uk/peopleplants/regions/thailand/lecture1.htm), ethnoscience evolved as a subfield of ethnography, the study of cultural groups. "Towards the end of the 19th century, academics began to use the prefix *ethno-* to refer to the way that indigenous people see the natural world, in contrast to the perspective of natural scientists trained in the Western tradition." The prefix became more widespread as the disciplines of ethnobotany, ethnobiology, and ethnoecology developed in about 1895, 1935, and 1954, respectively. Ethnohistory gained popularity in the 1930s and 1940s. Eugene Hunn, an anthropology professor with a specialization in ethnobiology at the University of Washington, says, "The term 'ethnobotany' was first used to refer to museum studies of native peoples' uses of plants.

"Ethnoscience was a common label in the 1960s and 1970s for a particular focus in anthropology," Hunn continues. "This has evolved into cognitive anthropology, an emphasis within sociocultural anthropology and linguistic anthropology that focuses on cultural knowledge systems, particularly their linguistic expression."

Evelyn Mathias, an independent consultant focusing on integrated livestock development, says that interest in indigenous knowledge and ethnoveterinary medicine arose with the failure of many development projects that had regarded Western technology and approaches as superior and tried to use them in southern countries with little adaptation and modification. "Over the last two or three decades, it became increasingly obvious that this type of development is inappropriate and not sustainable. Scientists and development professionals have come to realize that local people's knowledge is a valuable resource for development and they have started to study and use it in projects."

Sound-recording devices, beginning with the phonograph, have enabled ethnoscientists to record and keep sounds, such as language (ethnolinguists) and music (ethnomusicologists). More recent innovations include CD-ROM multimedia technology, which, according to Hunn, "is being used more frequently to present the complex data of ethnobiology, which often must include images of plants and animals, recordings of sounds of animals, recordings of the pronunciation of native names, video footage of processing activities, etc."

THE JOB

Ethnoscientists generally perform the same or similar duties as their counterparts in the traditional sciences, but from the perspective of the knowledge and belief systems of a particular indigenous group or culture. Not only do ethnoscientists conduct research in their particular area of study but they immerse themselves in the culture and talk to the inhabitants to find out about, for example, the local knowledge and use (medicinally or otherwise) of plants (*ethnobotanist* or *ethnopharmacologist*), the local use of language (*ethnolinguist*), or the local use of implements, utensils, tools, or other items (*ethnoarchaeologists*). Ethnoscientists classify information based on traditional methods and concepts while at the same time drawing on linguistic and cognitive theories.

Because ethnoscientists study other cultural groups, they often have to travel to conduct their research and talk to the local people. Eugene Hunn says, "Summers or perhaps at other times when I can arrange to travel to do ethnobiological field research, I will go to Oaxaca, Mexico, Australia, or Alaska to visit villages where indigenous peoples still hunt, fish, gather, or farm their ancestral lands. With their permission and with their help, I collect plants, insects, and fungi, and observe birds, reptiles, and mammals—always with local guides who can explain to me what they call each organism and what importance each plant or bug might have for their lives. I spend a lot of time studying foreign languages and learning Latin names of plants and animals." It is important that ethnoscientists are not intrusive when conducting research. They must always remember that they are acting as observers rather than agents of change.

Hunn defines an *ethnobiologist* as "a scholar who studies what people in cultures around the world know about biology. Most often this means what they know about the plants and animals of their local environment. Ethnobiology includes ethnobotany (study of knowledge of local plants), ethnozoology (local animals), ethnoentomology (local insects), etc. Ethnobotany may focus on naming and classifying or on how plants are used, for example, for food, medicine, or construction materials. Ethnozoology could emphasize how animals are imagined in folklore or how domestic animals are cared for and utilized. Some ethnobiologists are archaeologists who analyze plant or animal remains for evidence of past use."

Hunn notes, "There are few, if any, jobs specifically for ethnobiologists, as it is a specialty that crosses the boundaries of typical academic disciplines." This also holds true for the other ethnosciences.

An ethnobiologist's primary duties are "to develop research proposals for funding that allow the researcher to travel to the field site for extended periods," explains Hunn. "An ethnobiologist collects voucher specimens (especially of plants, insects, fungi) in conjunction with recording the ethnographic information in the native language of the people of the community where the research takes place. There are ethical expectations that the ethnobiologist will publish his or her finding not only in academic journals and books but also in the local languages in a form readily accessible to the people of the study community and to the scholars of the host country (if outside the United States). Ethnobiologists in universities are expected to teach ethnobiology courses and to train students in ethnobiology."

In describing his typical day, Hunn reports, "Most of the time I work in my office preparing for classes, talking with students, reading other people's work, writing articles or books, sorting and analyzing my own data, and preparing grant proposals so that I can get out of the office and into the field, which is where I most like to be."

Evelyn Mathias explains ethnoveterinary medicine as the study of how people manage animal health care and production. "It covers everything herders and small farmers do and know to keep their animals healthy and productive." According to Mathias, there are two types of ethnoveterinarians. First there are the "local practitioners, such as herders, farmers, or healers, who use indigenous techniques to treat animals." And second are the "Western academics or development professionals who study and promote the use of indigenous techniques in agricultural development. Most of these are either veterinarians who are interested in traditional health care practices or anthropologists who study veterinary medicine."

Mathias's primary duties include doing laboratory research or a participatory research study in the field, collecting and summarizing literature, running a network on raising the awareness of the value of local knowledge, and doing project evaluations. Research entails documentation, laboratory and fieldwork, studying how to integrate local practices, and incorporating ethnoveterinary medicine into education programs.

Ethnobiologists and ethnoveterinarians account for only two of the many ethnoscience specialties. Given the multidisciplinary approach of the ethnosciences, there is great variance in definition, focus, and process among its many areas. But at the core of the ethnosciences is an immersion in other cultures and a desire to learn what is known, believed, and practiced by local inhabitants.

Ethnoarchaeologists study contemporary cultural groups with the goal of understanding cultures of the past. They examine current customs and rituals, gather ancient and current artifacts, and talk to local inhabitants about their lifestyle. Based on their findings, ethnoarchaeologists hypothesize about a group's social organization and history.

Ethnobotanists study the use and classification of indigenous plants by a particular cultural group. Plants may be used as drugs, food, cosmetics, clothing, building material, or as part of religious ceremonies. Ethnobotanists also evaluate whether these plants have more widespread value outside the region, especially in the case of medicinal plants.

Many wild plants can only be grown in their native environment—the Amazon rainforest, for example. Ethnobotanists must be especially aware that taking plants from their environment affects the entire ecosystem, including its human inhabitants.

Economic botany, the study of plants that are commercially important, is closely related to ethnobotany. *Ethnopharmacologists* conduct research that is similar to that of ethnobotanists. The difference is that ethnopharmacologists study indigenous plants focusing on their medicinal value and use only. Ethnopharmacologists examine current indigenous remedies derived from either plant or animal substances and look for ways to develop new and better drugs. Both ethnobotanists and ethnopharmacologists must be sure that the intellectual property rights of the local people are observed, that they receive a share in whatever financial returns may result from knowledge or use elsewhere of indigenous plants.

Ethnoecologists focus on the knowledge and understanding that indigenous peoples have of their local ecology—that is, how they interact with their environment and other organisms.

Ethnohistorians research the history of various cultures, such as Native Americans and other non-European peoples. They study maps, music, paintings, photography, folklore, oral tradition, ecology, archaeological sites and materials, museum collections, enduring customs, language, and place names.

Ethnolinguists examine the relationship between the language and the culture of a specific people. They study the structure of speech and modification of language. They look at how language is used to convey understanding and knowledge.

Enthnomusicologists study the music made by certain (usually non-European) cultural groups as well as studying the musicians themselves. The process of making music, the sound of the music being made, musical instruments, what the music means to the creators and listeners, and dances or ceremonies associated with certain music all are components of ethnomusicology. In order to preserve a culture's music, ethnomusicologists usually make audio and video recordings in addition to written notation.

Ethnopsychiatrists are concerned with how indigenous peoples perceive and treat mental, emotional, or behavioral disorders of others within their own societies. *Ethnopsychologists* explore cultural influences on human behavior and mental characteristics of indigenous peoples, as well as their own theories of psychology.

No matter what the specialty, membership in professional organizations and reading scholarly journals are important aspects of an ethnoscientist's job. Mathias is a member of the German Veterinary Association, the League for Pastoral Peoples, and AGRECOL (Agricultural and Ecological Association). She comments that the latter two associations are particularly important to her "because they are interested in alternative approaches to development. This gives me the opportunity of exchanging information and getting some peer support." She continues, "It is important to stay up to date with the latest developments. I read books and scientific journals mainly on veterinary medicine in the tropics, development, indigenous knowledge, and related fields."

REQUIREMENTS
High School

Sociology courses will teach you the basics of research methods and observation techniques. If your school offers any anthropology classes, be sure to take them. Learning another foreign language can be helpful if you conduct field research. The foreign language you take in high school may not be the one you will need later, but learning a second language should make it easier for you to learn others. History and art classes will expose you to the cultures of different peoples of the world.

Biology and chemistry will be useful if you're considering ethnobiology, ethnobotany, or ethnopharmacology. Evelyn Mathias recommends an assortment of classes if you're interested in ethnoveterinary medicine: geography, cultural studies, biology, zoology, botany, and agriculture. She stresses the importance of classes that highlight the value of cultural diversity. Math and computer classes are also helpful.

Postsecondary Training

To teach at the university level, you will need a Ph.D. The particular field of study will depend on the line of work you want to enter. Anthropology classes, especially cultural anthropology, will be useful for study in just about any discipline. Classes in archaeology, linguistics, history, sociology, religion, and mythology can help prepare you to work with indigenous peoples. Some schools offer concentrations or courses in specific ethnosciences (e.g., ethnomusicology or ethnobiology).

If you want to pursue ethnoveterinary medicine, Mathias recommends getting a degree in a technical field, such as veterinary medicine, animal husbandry, biology, pharmacology, or botany, in addition to social science courses. To prepare for a career in ethnobotany, it is recommended that you get your degree in anthropology, botany, or pharmacology. Other important areas of study include chemistry, ecology, and medicine. According to Eugene Hunn, "Most professional ethnobiologists have doctorate degrees in anthropology or biology."

Consult relevant professional organizations such as the Centre for International Ethnomedicinal Education and Research, the American Society for Ethnohistory, and the Society for Ethnomusicology for lists of postsecondary programs in your area of interest. (See the end of this article for contact information.)

Other Requirements

It is important that ethnoscientists possess an "openness and understanding for other cultures and the ability and willingness to learn from others and work with other peoples," notes Mathias. "Someone who has prejudices against other peoples and who believes that high-tech is the only solution possible" will not be suitable for this line of work. Many cultural groups of the world live lives that are far less technologically oriented than in the Western world. Ethnoscientists embrace those differences.

Ethnoscientists need a healthy curiosity and should enjoy research. They should be able to work independently and as part of a team.

Many ethnoscientists are away from home for extended periods and must be able to tolerate different climates, rustic accommodations, unusual foods, and other physical conditions. Adaptability is a key personality trait for ethnoscientists doing fieldwork.

EXPLORING

A fascination with birds, bugs, snakes, fish, or plants is what got many of Eugene Hunn's ethnobiological colleagues started early. "Later they realized that they weren't just interested in the plants and animals but in how those plants and animals fit into people's lives. So they studied anthropology or linguistics to better understand the human side of the equation."

Explore extracurricular, volunteer, or part-time opportunities that will give you some background experience in your field of interest. If it's ethnobotany, look for a summer job working in a city park or with a local florist or nursery. If it's ethnoveterinary medicine, look for part-time or volunteer work at a veterinarian's office or animal shelter. To explore your interest in ethnozoology, work at a zoo. If enthnolinguistics interests you, try learning a language that is not offered at your school; for example, learn Swahili, Hawaiian, or Tagalog. To explore ethnomusicology, listen to recorded and live world music and visit museums and music stores that carry indigenous instruments. Museums offer a wealth of information on different cultures, including exhibits, reading materials, lectures, and workshops.

Take any opportunity offered you to travel, particularly to non-industrialized countries and more remote areas of the world that have been less influenced by Western culture. Explore study-abroad programs or consider volunteering with the Peace Corps to get an intense, long-term experience living in another culture.

Visit the websites of professional organizations, such as the Society of Ethnobiology, the Botanical Society of America, the American Society for Ethnohistory, and the Society for Ethnomusicology.

EMPLOYERS

Ethnoscientists work in the same places as other social and life scientists—universities, research institutes, government and non-government organizations, museums, and alternative medical firms.

Sometimes ethnoscientists become independent consultants, as is the case with Evelyn Mathias.

Eugene Hunn says, "Most ethnobiologists work at universities as faculty members or researchers. Some may be employed by government agencies, for example, to advise National Park Service or Forest Service staff on issues relating to how local communities, such as Native American groups, interact with local plants and animals. They study how traditional and modern subsistence activities, such as hunting, fishing, gathering, herding, or farming, might affect protected areas. Some ethnoscientists work at museums and herbaria. A few jobs may be available in the private sector, with companies developing new products modeled on how indigenous peoples use plants or animals—for example, drugs, cosmetics, or teas."

STARTING OUT

While working on your degree, be sure to communicate your interests to your professors. They may be aware of opportunities at the university or elsewhere. You might be able to participate in a university research project or become a research assistant or teaching fellow. Professional organizations are another important resource when it comes to finding a job. If you network with others in your field, you have a good chance of hearing about job opportunities. Also, organizations might post information on jobs or apprenticeships in their journals or on their websites.

There is strong competition for academic positions. Most students begin their job search while finishing their graduate degrees. Your first position is likely to be an instructor in general courses in anthropology, sociology, history, biology, or botany, depending on your specialty. In order to advance to higher ranks of professor, you will be required to do research, during which you can focus on your ethnoscience specialty. Evelyn Mathias suggests that, because research opportunities are difficult to come by, you might have to create your own opportunities, perhaps by proposing research projects.

ADVANCEMENT

Ethnoscientists advance by producing high-quality research and publishing articles or books. They might come to be known as experts in their field. They might become the head of a research project. The advancement path of ethnoscientists who teach in universities is instructor to assistant professor to associate professor to full professor. A full professor might eventually become a department head.

EARNINGS

The U.S. Department of Labor reports that the median salary of biological scientists, which includes biologists, botanists, ecologists, and zoologists, was $49,239 in 2000. Anthropologists and archaeologists had median annual earnings of $38,890 in 2001, while historians earned $42,930. The median salary of veterinarians was $62,010 in 2001. Postsecondary teachers received median annual earnings of $46,330 in 2000. Salaries for teachers ranged from less than $21,700 to more than $87,850 during that same year.

Eugene Hunn cautions, "If you want to get rich, you don't want to become an ethnobiologist. Most ethnobiologists—if they are lucky enough to get a good job at a university or museum—may earn $40,000–$70,000 with a Ph.D. and some years of experience. Mostly we do it because it's fascinating and we get to travel a lot." Evelyn Mathias notes that the same thing is true in her field. "Unless you have the very rare dream job as a fully paid ethnoveterinarian (e.g., as a project researcher), ethnoveterinary work is chronically underpaid. Ethnoveterinary medicine is not for persons hoping to earn lots of money quickly. It is rather for solid scientists and idealists."

WORK ENVIRONMENT

Ethnoscientists in academia mainly work indoors. Their time is spent teaching, meeting with students, writing texts or grant proposals, or compiling and analyzing data. For Evelyn Mathias, the hardest parts of her job include networking and getting financial support so she can conduct fieldwork. Ethnoscientists who travel to do research on different cultural groups conduct fieldwork outdoors. When in the field, ethnoscientists encounter climates that are different from their own, such as the tropical rainforest or the Arctic tundra. Ethnoscientists must be ready to work outdoors, sometimes for long periods of time, no matter what the weather, and they must be prepared to stay in primitive living conditions.

OUTLOOK

The *Occupational Outlook Handbook* reports that employment for postsecondary teachers in general will grow faster than the average over the next several years. This is largely because enrollment is expected to increase, creating a greater need for professors. Employment for social scientists is expected to grow about as fast as the average over the next several years. Faster-than-average job growth is expected for medical and biological scientists, but scientists holding Ph.D.'s may face strong competition when trying to get basic research positions.

Eugene Hunn thinks that ethnobiology is a growing field "primarily because humanity is facing environmental and political crises that often have their roots in conflicts over how to use the earth's biological resources. Ethnobiologists document many alternative ways that people can live in harmony with the land, and so our research may help educate people about better ways to use the earth's resources." Evelyn Mathias believes that interest in ethnoveterinary medicine will grow as the limitations of modern medicine and development are becoming more obvious.

While interest may increase, it is difficult to say whether funding will increase as well. If there are federal budget cuts, there might be a decrease in the amount of money devoted to new government research projects, or existing projects might not get renewed.

FOR MORE INFORMATION

For information on careers in anthropology, contact
American Anthropological Association
2200 Wilson Boulevard, Suite 600
Arlington, VA 22201
Tel: 703-528-1902
http://www.aaanet.org

The AVMA website provides information on student chapters and educational resources.
American Veterinary Medical Association (AVMA)
1931 North Meacham Road, Suite 100
Schaumburg, IL 60173
Tel: 847-925-8070
Email: avmainfo@avma.org
http://www.avma.org

For information on careers in zoos and aquariums, contact
American Zoo and Aquarium Association
8403 Colesville Road, Suite 710
Silver Spring, MD 20910-3314
Tel: 301-562-0777
http://www.aza.org

For information on botany careers, contact
Botanical Society of America
PO Box 299
St. Louis, MO 63166-0299
Tel: 314-577-9566
Email: bsa-manager@botany.org
http://www.botany.org

For information on ethnomedicine, contact
Centre for International Ethnomedicinal Education and
  Research
http://www.cieer.org

The LSA website provides descriptions of the various areas of linguistics and a directory of linguistics programs.
Linguistic Society of America (LSA)
1325 18th Street, NW, Suite 211
Washington, DC 20036-6501
Email: lsa@lsadc.org
http://www.lsadc.org

The SAA website lists archaeology programs and features career resources.
Society for American Archaeology (SAA)
900 Second Street, NE, #12
Washington, DC 20002-3557
Tel: 202-789-8200
Web: http://www.saa.org

This society offers student membership and presents its newsletter online.
Society for Economic Botany
PO Box 1897
Lawrence, KS 66044
Tel: 800-627-0629
http://www.econbot.org

This website features descriptions of and links to ethnomusicology degree programs.
Society for Ethnomusicology
1165 East 3rd Street
Morrison Hall 005
Indiana University
Bloomington, IN 47405-3700

Email: sem@indiana.edu
http://www.ethnomusicology.org

This society offers student memberships.
Society of Ethnobiology
Department of Anthropology
CB 3115, Alumni Building
University of North Carolina-Chapel Hill
Chapel Hill, NC 27599-3155
http://ethnobiology.org

For background information on the field of ethnohistory along with links to schools offering ethnohistory courses, see
American Society for Ethnohistory
http://ethnohistory.org

For materials specifically dealing with ethnoveterinary medicine, including an introduction to the field by Evelyn Mathias, see
Ethnovetweb
http://www.ethnovetweb.com

ISE offers a useful list of links to other websites of interest.
International Society for Ethnopharmacology (ISE)
http://www.etnobotanica.de

FBI AGENTS

QUICK FACTS

School Subjects English Foreign language Government	**Certification or Licensing** None available
Personal Skills Communication/ideas Leadership/management	**Outlook** About as fast as the average **DOT** 375
Work Environment Indoors and outdoors Primarily multiple locations	**GOE** 04.01.02 **NOC** N/A
Minimum Education Level Bachelor's degree	**O*NET-SOC** N/A
Salary Range $39,115 to $61,251 to $100,000+	

OVERVIEW

FBI agents, special agents of the Federal Bureau of Investigation, are employees of the federal government. The FBI, a part of the U.S. Department of Justice, investigates violations of more than 350 federal laws in the areas of criminal and civil law and government intelligence. To carry out its mission, the FBI needs men and women who can fill a variety of demanding positions. There are approximately 11,000 FBI agents employed in the United States.

HISTORY

The Federal Bureau of Investigation was founded in 1908 as the investigative branch of the U.S. Department of Justice. In its earliest years, the FBI's responsibilities were limited. However, the creation of new federal laws gave the FBI jurisdiction over criminal matters that had previously been regulated by the individual states, such as those involving the interstate transportation of stolen vehicles. By the 1920s, the FBI was also used for political purposes, such as tracking down alleged subversive elements and spying on political enemies.

Early in its history, the FBI developed a reputation for corruption. In 1924, J. Edgar Hoover was appointed as director of the Bureau and charged with the twin goals of cleaning up the agency and making the agency's work independent from politics. Hoover established stricter professional standards, eliminating corruption, and, partly because of Hoover's own ambitions, the FBI's responsibilities increased. Soon the FBI was the most powerful law enforcement agency in the country.

The FBI established its Identification Division in 1924 and the Bureau's scientific laboratory in 1932. Then, in 1934, the FBI was given the general authority to handle federal crime investigation. Within three years, more than 11,000 federal criminals were convicted through the FBI's efforts. As its prestige grew, the FBI was further designated, in 1939, as the central clearinghouse for all matters pertaining to the internal security of the United States. During World War II, FBI agents rendered many security services for plants involved in war production and worked to gather evidence on espionage activities within the plants.

Since its inception in 1932, the FBI Laboratory has become one of the largest and most comprehensive crime laboratories in the world, providing leadership and service in the scientific solution and prosecution of crimes. It is the only full-service federal forensic laboratory in the United States. As a result, today the FBI is involved in a wide variety of law-enforcement activities using the latest scientific methods and forms of analysis available.

The FBI's Identification Division serves as the nation's repository and clearinghouse for fingerprint records. The fingerprint section of the FBI Laboratory is the largest in the world, containing millions of sets of fingerprints. In this capacity, the division provides the following services: identifying and maintaining fingerprint records for arrested criminal suspects and for applicants to sensitive jobs; posting notices for people wanted for crimes and for parole or probation violations; examining physical evidence for fingerprints and providing occasional court testimony on the results of examinations; training in fingerprint science; maintaining fingerprint records of people currently reported missing; and identifying amnesia victims and unknown deceased people.

In addition to its own activities, the FBI provides support and cooperation for many other criminal justice agencies in the United States and around the world.

THE JOB

The headquarters of the FBI is located in Washington, D.C., and from this location the work of 56 field offices is supervised. FBI agents can be assigned to investigate any case, irrespective of its nature, unless they have skills in some particular field. In such situations they are most likely assigned to work on those cases that demand their specialized talents.

For any case, the responsibility of the FBI agent is to investigate violations of federal laws. Violations may include such crimes as bank robbery, extortion, kidnapping, fraud and theft against the federal government, espionage, interstate transportation of stolen property, mail fraud, sabotage, and infractions of the Atomic Energy Act. FBI special agents are responsible for protecting the security of the United States and for investigating any subversive acts that might threaten that security. In performing investigative work, agents have at their disposal a vast network of communication systems and the crime detection laboratory in Washington, D.C. When cases are completed, agents submit full reports to the bureau's headquarters.

FBI agents usually carry special badges to identify themselves as employees of the bureau. They wear ordinary business suits almost all the time, not special uniforms such as police wear. Agents are required to carry firearms while on duty.

FBI agents usually work on their own unless there is potential danger or the nature of the case demands two or more people. An agent's work is always confidential and may not be discussed except among other authorized bureau members. This prevents any discussion of work assignments even with immediate family or friends. The Bureau and its agents work in close cooperation with law enforcement agencies from all over the country and around the world, although the FBI does not function as a law enforcement agency. FBI agents function strictly as investigators.

Agents perform their work in various ways, depending upon the nature of the case. They may need to travel for extended periods or live in various cities. Agents may interview people to gather information, spend time searching various types of records, and observe people, especially those who are suspected of criminal intentions or acts. FBI agents take part in arrests and may participate in or lead raids of various kinds. On occasion, they are summoned to testify in court cases regarding their investigative work and findings. It is not the agent's role, however, to express judgments or opinions regarding the innocence or guilt of those people being tried in court. The agent's work is to gather facts and report them.

REQUIREMENTS
High School
A high school diploma, or its equivalent, is required. The FBI does not recommend specific courses for high school students. Rather, the bureau encourages students to do the best work they can. Since FBI agents perform a variety of work, agents can be skilled in numerous academic disciplines.

Postsecondary Training
All special agent candidates must hold a four-year degree from a college or university that is accredited by one of the six regional accrediting bodies of the Commission on Institutions of Higher Education. Candidates must fulfill additional requirements of one of four entry programs: Law, Accounting, Language, and Diversified. Entry through the law program requires a law degree from an accredited resident law school. The accounting program requires a bachelor's degree in accounting or related discipline, such as economics, business, or finance. Applicants for the accounting program must have passed the Uniform Certified Accountant Examination or at least show eligibility to take this exam. Language program applicants may hold a bachelor's degree in any discipline, but must demonstrate fluency in one or more foreign languages meeting the current needs of the FBI. In recent years, these languages have included Spanish, Arabic, Farsi, Pashtu, Urdu, Chinese, Japanese, Korean, Vietnamese, and Russian. The diversified program accepts applicants with a bachelor's degree in any discipline plus three years of full-time work experience or an advanced degree accompanied by two years of full-time work experience.

All candidates must complete a rigorous application process. For those who successfully complete the written tests and interview, the FBI conducts a thorough background investigation that includes credit and criminal record checks; interviews with associates; contact with personal and business references; interviews with past employers and neighbors; and verification of educational achievements. Drug testing, a physical examination, and a polygraph examination are required. The completed background investigation is then considered when the final hiring decision is made.

All newly appointed special agents must complete 16 weeks of intensive training at the FBI Academy in Quantico, Virginia. Classroom hours are spent studying a variety of academic and investigative subjects, accompanied by training in physical fitness, defensive tactics, and the proper use of firearms. Trainees must pass several exams with a minimum passing grade of 85 percent. Trainees may be disqualified and dismissed for failing two exams; for failing to demonstrate proficiency in defensive tactics, firearms use and handling, or simulated arrest exercises; or for violating the agency's rules and regulations for conduct.

After graduation from the FBI Academy, new agents are assigned to an FBI field office for a probationary period lasting one year, after which they become permanent special agents. During the first months of employment, the novice agent is guided by a veteran special agent who will help show how the lessons learned at the academy can be applied on the job. Assignments are determined by the individual's special skills and the current needs of the FBI. As a part of their duties, special agents may be required to relocate during their careers.

The education and training of FBI agents continue throughout their career. FBI agents are always expected to learn new techniques and better methods in criminal investigation, either through experience on the job, advanced study courses, in-service training, or special conferences.

Other Requirements

To qualify for training as an FBI agent, candidates must be U.S. citizens between the ages of 23 and 36. They must possess a valid driver's license, be available for assignment anywhere in the areas of the Bureau's jurisdiction, which includes Puerto Rico, and be in excellent physical condition. Their vision must not be worse than 20/200 uncorrected and correctable to 20/20 in one eye and no worse than 20/40 in the other eye. Applicants must also pass a color-vision test and hearing test. Applicants may not have physical disabilities that would interfere with the performance of their duties, including use of firearms and defensive tactics and taking part in raids. All applicants must be able to withstand rigorous physical strain and exertion.

FBI agents assume grave responsibilities as a normal part of their jobs. Their reputation, integrity, and character must be above reproach, and they must be dependable and courageous. Agents must be able to accept continual challenges in their jobs, realizing that no two days of work assignments may be exactly alike. FBI agents need to be stable and personally secure and able to work daily with challenge, change, and danger. For most agents, the FBI is a lifelong career.

EXPLORING

The best method of exploring a career with the FBI is to participate in the FBI Honors Internship Program, which is held every summer in Washington, D.C. Participation is open to undergraduate and graduate students selected by the FBI. This program is designed to give interns experience and insight into the inner workings of, and career opportunities available at, the FBI. Students are assigned to various divisions of the agency according to their academic disciplines, and they work alongside special agents under the supervision of assistant directors. Interns may work at FBI headquarters or other agency locations in the Washington, D.C. area. Acceptance into the internship program is highly competitive. Applicants must be full-time students intending to return to school after the internship program. They must achieve a cumulative grade point average of 3.0 or higher. Undergraduate applicants must be in their junior year at the time of application. In addition, applicants must submit letters of recommendation and complete a 500-word essay. Undergraduate interns are paid at the GS-6 level, which was approximately $26,130 per year in 2003. Graduate interns are paid at the GS-7 level of about $29,037 in 2003. Transportation to and from Washington, D.C. is also provided as part of the internship program. For more information on this program, visit http://www.fbi.gov/employment/honors.htm.

If you are interested in a career with the FBI, you may apply for internships and other programs offered through your local police departments, which will give you experience and insight into aspects of law enforcement in general. Good grades throughout high school and college will give you the best chance of winning a place in the Honors Internship Program.

EMPLOYERS

Agents work for the Federal Bureau of Investigation, which is head-quartered in Washington, D.C. and is the investigative arm of the U.S. Department of Justice. Agents are placed in one of 56 field offices or one of 40 foreign liaison posts. There are approximately 11,000 agents and 16,000 support personnel employed by the FBI.

STARTING OUT

If you are interested in the occupation of FBI special agent, you should contact the Applicant Coordinator at your local FBI field office. The Bureau will send you information on existing vacancies, requirements for the positions, how to file applications, and locations where examinations will be given. Examinations are scored by computer at FBI headquarters. Interviews are arranged based on the applicant's score and overall qualifications and the agency's current needs.

ADVANCEMENT

Although FBI special agents are not appointed under the Federal Civil Service Regulations like other federal workers, they are eligible to receive salary raises periodically within the grade set for their positions. These within-grade increases depend, of course, upon satisfactory job performance. Grade advancements may be earned as the agent gains experience on the job. Promotions within the FBI are usually given on the basis of performance rather than seniority.

Higher grade administrative and supervisory positions in the FBI are filled by those advancing within the ranks. Positions open to

Hooray for the History Major!

History and other liberal arts majors are no longer viewed as dead-end career paths. Today's employers realize that history and other liberal arts graduates possess a skill set that allows them to be successful in almost any work environment. Surveys indicate that businesses are hiring and promoting more history and other liberal arts graduates than ever before. *Fortune* magazine reports that 38 percent of today's CEOs majored in liberal arts. According to collegenews.org, 19 percent of U.S. presidents were liberal arts majors.

advancement may include special agent in charge of a field office, inspector, field supervisor, and assistant director.

EARNINGS

Special agent trainees at the Quantico training facility are paid at the GS-10 level, which was $39,115 in 2003. Upon graduation, the salary ranges from approximately $50,000 to $60,000, depending upon their location. Agents based in locations such as New York, Los Angeles, Miami, Boston, and other areas where the cost of living is higher are paid more. Experienced special agents averaged $61,251 (GS-13 level) per year in 2003, and the most experienced agents earned $72,381 (GS-14 level) per year. Supervisory positions began at $85,140 (GS-15 level) in 2003. Some agents then move into a different employment category called the Senior Executive Service, where they make more than $100,000 annually working for the FBI. Special agents may also earn as much as $6,000 per year in overtime pay. They are also eligible for cash awards under the federal employee Incentive Awards Program for outstanding achievement or suggestions for improving function and service.

As federal employees, FBI special agents enjoy generous benefits, including health and life insurance, and 13 days of paid sick leave. Vacation pay begins at 13 days for each of the first three years of service and rises to 20 to 26 days for each year after that. All special agents are required to retire at the age of 57; they may choose to retire at 50 if they have put in 20 years of service.

WORK ENVIRONMENT

Depending on their case assignments, FBI agents may work a very strenuous and variable schedule, frequently working more hours than the customary 40-hour week. They are on call for possible assignment 24 hours a day. Assignments may be given for any location at any time. Every aspect of the agent's work is of a confidential nature. As a result, agents may work under potentially dangerous circumstances in carrying out their assignments, and they may be confronted with unpleasant and even horrifying aspects of life. Because of the confidential nature of their work, they must refrain from speaking about their case work even with relatives or spouses. In addition, agents may be required to travel and perform their duties under many conditions, including severe weather. Nevertheless, a career with the FBI offers a great deal of respect, responsibility, and the possibility of adventure. No two days are ever the same for a special agent.

OUTLOOK

Most job vacancies within the FBI are expected to come as agents retire, advance, or resign. Turnover, in general, has traditionally been low, as most agents remain with the FBI throughout their working lives.

The numbers of FBI special agents are linked to the scope of the FBI's responsibilities. Increases in organized crimes, white-collar crimes, and terrorist threats on American soil have led the FBI to increase the number of agents in recent years. According to one FBI recruitment representative in a live chat on washingtonpost.com, the terrorist attacks on September 11, 2001 lead to an increase in hiring. In 2002, the FBI aimed to recruit 966 additional agents. However, the Bureau reports that there were over 70,000 applicants for these positions.

As the Bureau's responsibilities expand, it will create new positions to meet them. Despite increased recruitment, growth in the numbers of new agency hires is expected to remain somewhat limited. Competition for openings will continue to be extremely high. According to the *Chicago Tribune*, the typical recruit is between the ages of 27 and 31, has a graduate-level education, and is physically fit. Since the terrorist attacks, the FBI is particularly interested in recruits who are able to speak Arabic and are familiar with Middle and Far Eastern culture. Potential agents with backgrounds in information technology are also in high demand.

FOR MORE INFORMATION

For information on FBI jobs, internship programs (paid and unpaid), current news, and contact information for a field office in your area, visit the FBI website. Contact information for your local field office is also available in your telephone directory.

Federal Bureau of Investigation (FBI)
J. Edgar Hoover Building
935 Pennsylvania Avenue, NW
Washington, DC 20535-0001
Tel: 202-324-3000
http://www.fbi.gov

FEDERAL AND STATE OFFICIALS

QUICK FACTS

School Subjects English Government History	**Certification or Licensing** None available
	Outlook About as fast as the average
Personal Skills Communication/ideas Leadership/management	**DOT** 188
Work Environment Primarily indoors One location with some travel	**GOE** 11.05.03
	NOC 0011
Minimum Education Level Bachelor's degree	**O*NET-SOC** 11-1031.00
Salary Range $10,000 to $40,000 to $400,000+	

OVERVIEW

Federal and state officials hold positions in the legislative, executive, and judicial branches of government at the state and national levels. They include governors, judges, senators, representatives, and the president and vice president of the country. Government officials are responsible for preserving the government against external and domestic threats, supervising and resolving conflicts between private and public interest, regulating the economy, protecting political and social rights of the citizens, and providing goods and services. Officials may, among other things, pass laws, set up social service programs, and allocate the taxpayers' money on goods and services.

HISTORY

In ancient states, the scope of government was almost without limitation. As Aristotle put it, "What was not commanded by the government was forbidden." Government functions were challenged by Christianity during the Roman Empire, when the enforcement of religious sanctions became the focus of political authority. It was not until the 18th century that the modern concept of government as separate from the church came into being.

The Roman Republic had a great deal of influence on those who framed the U.S. Constitution. The supreme council of state in ancient Rome was called the Senate. Even the name Capitol Hill is derived from Capitoline Hill of Rome. The Congress of the United States was modeled after British Parliament and assumed the powers that London had held before American independence. Limiting the powers of the individual states, the U.S. Congress was empowered to levy taxes, engage in foreign diplomacy, and regulate Native American affairs.

THE JOB

As voters, we choose carefully when electing a government official, taking many different things into consideration. The decisions of state and federal lawmakers affect your daily life and your future. State and federal officials pass laws concerning the arts, education, taxes, employment, health care, and other areas, in efforts to change and improve communities and standards of living.

Besides the *president* and *vice president* of the United States, the executive branch of the national government consists of the president's Cabinet, including, among others, the secretaries of state, treasury, defense, interior, agriculture, homeland security, and health and human services. These officials are appointed by the president and approved by the Senate. The members of the Office of Management and Budget, the Council of Economic Advisors, and the National Security Council are also executive officers of the national government.

Just as the U.S. Congress is composed of the Senate and the House of Representatives, so does each state (with one exception, Nebraska) have a senate and a house. The executive branch of the U.S. government is headed by the president and vice president, while the states elect governors and lieutenant governors. The *governor* is the chief executive officer of a state. In all states, a large government administration handles a variety of functions related to agriculture, highway and motor vehicle supervision, public safety and corrections, regulation of intrastate business and industry, and some aspects of education, public health, and welfare. The governor's job is to manage this administration. Some states also have a *lieutenant governor,* who serves as the presiding officer of the state's senate. Other elected officials commonly include a secretary of state, state treasurer, state auditor, attorney general, and superintendent of public instruction.

State senators and *state representatives* are the legislators elected to represent the districts and regions of cities and counties within the state. The number of members of a state's legislature varies from state to state. In the U.S. Congress, there are 100 senators (as established by the Constitution—two senators from each state) and 435 representatives. The number of representatives each state is allowed to send to the U.S. Congress varies based on the state's population as determined by the national census. The primary function of all legislators, on both the state and national levels, is to make laws. With a staff of aides, senators and representatives attempt to learn as much as they can about the bills being considered. They research legislation, prepare reports, meet with constituents and interest groups, speak to the press, and discuss and debate legislation on the floor of the House or Senate. Legislators also may be involved in selecting other members of the government, supervising the government administration, appropriating funds, impeaching executive and judicial officials, and determining election procedures, among other activities. A state legislator may be involved in examining such situations as the state's relationship to Native American tribes, the level of school violence, and welfare reform.

"Time in each day goes by so quickly," says Don Preister, who serves on the state legislature in Nebraska, "there's no time to read up on all legislation and all the information the constituents send in." The state of Nebraska is the only state with a single-house system. When the state senate is in session, Preister commits many hours to discussing and debating issues with other state senators and gathering information on proposed legislation. In addition to senate sessions, Preister attends committee hearings. His committees include Natural Resources and Urban Affairs. "A hearing lasts from 20 minutes to three or four hours," he says, "depending on the intensity of the issues." Despite having to devote about 60 hours a week to the job when the Senate is in session, Preister finds his work a wonderful opportunity to be of service to the community and to improve lives.

"I take a lot of personal satisfaction from being a voice for people whose voices aren't often heard in government."

REQUIREMENTS
High School

Courses in government, civics, and history will give you an understanding of the structure of state and federal governments. English courses are important because you need good writing skills for communicating with constituents and other government officials. Math and accounting help you to develop the analytical skills needed for examining statistics and demographics. You should take science courses because you'll be making decisions concerning health, medicine, and technological advances. Journalism classes will help you learn about the print and broadcast media and the role they play in politics.

Postsecondary Training

State and federal legislators come from all walks of life. Some hold master's degrees and doctorates, while others have only a high school education. Although a majority of government officials hold law degrees, others have undergraduate or graduate degrees in such areas as journalism, economics, political science, history, and English. Regardless of your major as an undergraduate, it is important to take classes in English literature, statistics, foreign language, Western civilization, and economics. Graduate studies can focus more on one area of study; some prospective government officials pursue master's degrees in public administration or international affairs. Consider participating in an internship program that will involve you with local and state officials. Contact the offices of your state legislators and of your state's members of Congress to apply for internships directly.

Other Requirements

"You should have concern for people," Don Preister says. "You should have an ability to listen and understand people and their concerns." This attention to the needs of communities should be of foremost importance to anyone pursuing a government office. Although historically some politicians have had questionable purposes in their campaigns for office, most successful politicians are devoted to making positive changes and improvements. Good people skills will help you make connections, get elected, and make things happen once in office. You should also enjoy argument, debate, and opposition—

you'll get a lot of it as you attempt to get laws passed. A good temperament in such situations will earn you the respect of your colleagues. Strong character and a good background will help you to avoid the personal attacks that occasionally accompany government office.

EXPLORING

If you are 16 or older, you can gain experience in a legislature. The U.S. Congress and possibly your state legislature offer opportunities for young adults who have demonstrated a commitment to government study to work as *pages*. For Congress, pages run messages across Capitol Hill, and have the opportunity to see senators and representatives debating and discussing bills. The length of a page's service can be for one summer or up to one year. Contact your state's senator or representative for an application.

You can also explore government careers by becoming involved with local elections. Many candidates for local and state offices welcome young people to assist with campaigns. You might be asked to make calls, post signs, or hand out information about the candidate. Not only will you get to see the politician at work, but you will also meet others with an interest in government.

Another great way to learn about government is to become involved in an issue of interest to you. Participate with a grass roots advocacy group or read about the bills up for vote in the state legislature and U.S. Congress. When you feel strongly about an issue and are well educated on the subject, contact the offices of state legislators and members of Congress to express your views. Visit the websites of the House and Senate and of your state legislature to read about bills, schedules, and the legislators. The National Conference of State Legislators (NCSL) also hosts a website (http://www.ncsl.org) featuring legislative news and links to state legislatures.

EMPLOYERS

State legislators work for the state government, and many hold other jobs as well. Because of the part-time nature of some legislative offices, state legislators may hold part-time jobs or own their own businesses. Federal officials work full-time for the Senate, the House, or the executive branch.

STARTING OUT

There is no direct career path for state and federal officials. Some enter into their positions after some success with political activism on the grass roots level. Others work their way up from local government positions to state legislature and into federal office. Those who serve as U.S. Congress members have worked in the military, journalism, academics, business, and many other fields.

Many politicians get their start assisting someone else's campaign or advocating for an issue. Don Preister's beginnings with the Nebraska state legislature are particularly inspiring. Because of his involvement in grass roots organizing to improve his neighborhood, he was encouraged by friends and neighbors to run for senator of the district. Others, however, believed he'd never get elected running against a man who'd had a lot of political success, as well as great finances to back his campaign. "I didn't have any money," Preister says, "or any experience in campaigning. So I went door to door to meet the people of the district. I went to every house and apartment in the district." He won that election in 1992 and won again in 1996 and 2000.

ADVANCEMENT

Initiative is one key to success in politics. Advancement can be rapid for someone who is a fast learner and is independently motivated, but a career in politics most often takes a long time to establish. Most state and federal officials start by pursuing training and work experience in their particular field, while getting involved in politics at the local level. Many people progress from local politics to state politics. It is not uncommon for a state legislator to eventually run for a seat in Congress. Appointees to the president's Cabinet and presidential and vice presidential candidates frequently have held positions in Congress.

EARNINGS

In general, salaries for government officials tend to be lower than what the official could make working in the private sector. In the case of state legislators, the pay can be very much lower.

The Bureau of Labor Statistics reports that the median annual earnings of government legislators was $14,650 in 2001. Salaries generally ranged from less than $11,830 to more than $64,890, although some officials earn nothing at all.

According to the NCSL, state legislators make from $10,000 to $47,000 a year. A few states, however, don't pay state legislators anything but an expense allowance. But a state's executive officials get paid better: *The Book of the States* lists salaries of state governors as ranging from $60,000 in Arkansas to a high of $130,000 in New York.

In 2001, U.S. senators and representatives earned $145,100; the Senate and House majority and minority leaders earned $161,200; the vice president was paid $186,300; and the president earned $400,000.

Congressional leaders such as the Speaker of the House and the Senate majority leader receive higher salaries than the other Congress members. The Speaker of the House makes $186,300 a year. U.S. Congress members receive excellent insurance, vacation, and other benefits.

WORK ENVIRONMENT

Most government officials work in a typical office setting. Some may work a regular 40-hour week, while others will typically work long hours and weekends. One potential drawback to political life, particularly for the candidate running for office, is that there is no real off-duty time. One is continually under observation by the press and public, and the personal lives of candidates and officeholders are discussed frequently in the media.

Because these officials must be appointed or elected in order to keep their jobs, the ability to determine long-range job objectives is slim. There may be extended periods of unemployment, when living off of savings or working at other jobs may be necessary.

Frequent travel is involved in campaigning and in holding office, so some people with children may find the lifestyle demanding on their families.

OUTLOOK

The U.S. Department of Labor predicts that employment of federal and state officials will grow about as fast as the average over the next several years. To attract more candidates to run for legislative offices, states may consider salary increases and better benefits for state senators and representatives. But changes in pay and benefits for federal officials are unlikely. An increase in the number of representatives is possible as the U.S. population grows, but would require additional office space and other costly expansions. For the most part, the structures of state and federal legislatures will remain unchanged, although the topic of limiting the number of terms that a representative is allowed to serve does often arise in election years.

The federal government has made efforts to shift costs to the states; if this continues, it could change the way state legislatures and executive officers operate with regard to public funding. Already, welfare reform has resulted in state governments looking for financial aid in handling welfare cases and job programs. Arts funding may also become the sole responsibility of the states as the National Endowment for the Arts loses support from Congress.

With the government's commitment to developing a place on the Internet, contacting your state and federal representatives, learning about legislation, and organizing grass roots advocacy have become much easier. This voter awareness of candidates, public policy issues, and legislation will increase and may affect how future representatives make decisions. Also look for government programming to be part of cable television's expansion into digital broadcasting. New modes of communication will allow constituents to become even more involved in the actions of their representatives.

FOR MORE INFORMATION

Visit the Senate and House websites for extensive information about Congress, government history, current legislation, and links to state legislature sites. To inquire about internship opportunities with your Congress member, contact

U.S. Senate
Office of Senator (Name)
United States Senate
Washington, DC 20510
Tel: 202-224-3121
http://www.senate.gov

U.S. House of Representatives
Office of the Honorable (Name)
Washington, DC 20515
Tel: 202-224-3121
http://www.house.gov

To read about state legislatures, policy issues, legislative news, and other related information, visit the NCSL's website.
National Conference of State Legislatures (NCSL)
444 North Capitol Street, NW, Suite 515
Washington, DC 20001
Tel: 202-624-5400
Email: info@ncsl.org
http://www.ncsl.org

FOREIGN CORRESPONDENTS

QUICK FACTS

School Subjects English Foreign language Journalism	**Certification or Licensing** None available
	Outlook Little change or more slowly than the average
Personal Skills Communication/ideas Helping/teaching	**DOT** N/A
Work Environment Indoors and outdoors Primarily multiple locations	**GOE** N/A
Minimum Education Level Bachelor's degree	**NOC** 5123
Salary Range $17,320 to $50,000 to $100,000	**O*NET-SOC** 27-3022.00

OVERVIEW

Foreign correspondents report on news from countries outside of where their newspapers, radio or television networks, or wire services are located. They sometimes work for a particular newspaper, but since today's media are more interested in local and national news, they usually rely on reports from news wire services to handle international news coverage rather than dispatching their own reporters to the scene. Only the biggest newspapers and television networks employ foreign correspondents. These reporters are usually stationed in a particular city and cover a wide territory.

HISTORY

James Gordon Bennett, Sr., a prominent United States journalist and publisher of the *New York Herald*, was responsible for many firsts in the newspaper industry. He was the first publisher to sell papers through newsboys, the first to use illustrations for news stories, the first to publish stock-market prices and daily financial articles, and he was the first to employ European correspondents. Bennett's son, James Gordon Bennett, Jr., carried on the family business and in 1871 sent Henry M. Stanley to central Africa to find Dr. David Livingstone, a famous British explorer who had disappeared.

In the early days, even magazines employed foreign correspondents. Famous American poet Ezra Pound, for example, reported from London for *Poetry* and *The Little Review*.

The inventions of the telegraph, telephone, typewriter, portable typewriter, the portable laptop computer, and the Internet all have contributed to the field of foreign correspondence.

THE JOB

The foreign correspondent is stationed in a foreign country where his or her job is to report on the news there. Foreign news can range from the violent (wars, coups, and refugee situations) to the calm (cultural events and financial issues). Although a domestic correspondent is responsible for covering specific areas of the news, like politics, health, sports, consumer affairs, business, or religion, foreign correspondents are responsible for all of these areas in the country where they are stationed. A China-based correspondent, for example, could spend a day covering the new trade policy between the United States and China, and the next day report on the religious persecution of Christians by the Chinese government.

A foreign correspondent often is responsible for more than one country. Depending on where he or she is stationed, the foreign correspondent might have to act as a one-person band in gathering and preparing stories.

"There are times when the phone rings at five in the morning and you're told to go to Pakistan," said Michael Lev, Beijing, China, correspondent for the *Chicago Tribune*. "You must keep your wits about you and figure out what to do next."

For the most part, Lev decides on his own story ideas, choosing which ones interest him the most out of a myriad of possibilities. But foreign correspondents alone are responsible for getting the story done, and unlike reporters back home, they have little or no support staff to help them. Broadcast foreign correspondents, for example, may have to do their own audio editing after filming scenes. And just like other news reporters, foreign correspondents work under the pressure of deadlines. In addition, they often are thrown into unfamiliar situations in strange places.

Part of the importance of a foreign correspondent's job is keeping readers or viewers aware of the various cultures and practices held by the rest of the world. Lev says he tries to focus on similarities and differences between the Asian countries he covers and the United States. "If you don't understand another culture, you are more likely to come into conflict with it," he says.

Foreign correspondents are drawn to conflicts of all kinds, especially war. They may choose to go to the front of a battle to get an accurate picture of what's happening. Or they may be able to get the story from a safer position. Sometimes they face weapons targeted directly at them.

Much of a foreign correspondent's time is spent doing research, investigating leads, setting up appointments, making travel arrangements, making on-site observations, and interviewing local people or those involved in the situation. The foreign correspondent often must be experienced in taking photographs or shooting video.

Living conditions can be rough or primitive, sometimes with no running water. The job can sometimes be isolating.

After correspondents have interviewed sources and noted observations about an event or filmed it, they put their stories together, writing on computers and using modern technology like the Internet, email, satellite telephones, and fax machines to finish the job and transmit the story to their newspaper, broadcast station, or wire service. Many times, correspondents work out of hotel rooms.

REQUIREMENTS
High School

In addition to English and creative writing needed for a career in journalism, you should study languages, social studies, political science, history, and geography. Initial experience may be gained by working on your school newspaper or yearbook, or taking advantage of study-abroad programs.

Postsecondary Training

In college, pursuing a journalism major is helpful but may not be crucial to obtaining a job as a foreign correspondent. Classes, or even a major, in political science or literature could be beneficial. Economics and foreign languages are also beneficial.

Other Requirements

In addition to a definite love of adventure, to be a foreign correspondent you need to be curious about how other people live, diplomatic
when conducting interviews, courageous when confronting people on
uncomfortable topics, very communicative, and disciplined enough to
act as your own boss. You also need to be strong enough to hold up
under pressure yet flexible enough to adapt to other cultures.

EXPLORING

To explore this field, you can begin by honing your skills in different journalism media. Join your high school newspaper staff to
become a regular columnist or write special feature articles. Check
out your high school's TV station and audition to be an anchor. If
your school has a radio station, volunteer to be on the staff. If your
school has an online newspaper, get involved with that project. Gain
as much experience as you can with different media; learn about the
strengths and weaknesses of each and decide which suits you best.
You can also ask your high school journalism teacher or guidance
counselor to help you set up an informational interview with a local
journalist. Most are happy to speak with you when they know you
are interested in their careers. It may be possible to get a part-time
or summer job working at a local TV or radio station or at the newspaper office. Competition for one of these jobs, however, is strong
because many college students take such positions as interns and do
the work for little or no pay.

EMPLOYERS

Foreign correspondents work for news wire services, such as the
Associated Press, Reuters, and Agence-France Press; major metropolitan newspapers; newsmagazines; and television and radio networks. These media are located in the largest cities in the United
States and, in the case of Reuters and Agence-France Press, in Europe.

STARTING OUT

College graduates can pursue a couple of paths to become a foreign
correspondent. They can decide to experience what being a foreign correspondent is like immediately by going to another country, perhaps
one whose language is familiar to them, and freelancing or working as
a *stringer*. That means writing stories and offering them to anyone
who will buy them. This method can be hard to accomplish financially
in the short run but can pay off substantially in the long run.

Another path is to take the traditional route of a journalist and try to get hired upon graduation at any newspaper, radio station, or television station you can. It helps in this regard to have worked at a summer internship during your college years. Recent college graduates generally get hired at small newspapers or media stations, although a few major metropolitan dailies will employ top graduates for a year with no guarantee of their being kept on afterward. After building experience at a small paper or station, a reporter can try to find work at progressively bigger ones. Reporters who find employment at a major metropolitan daily that uses foreign correspondents can work their way through the ranks to become one. This is the path Michael Lev took, and he became a foreign correspondent when he was in his early 30s. He suggests that working for a wire service may allow a reporter to get abroad faster, but he thinks more freedom can be found working for a newspaper.

ADVANCEMENT

Foreign correspondents can advance to other locations that are more appealing to them or that offer a bigger challenge. Or they can return home to become columnists, editorial writers, editors, or network news directors.

EARNINGS

Salaries vary greatly depending on the publication, network, or station, and the cost of living and tax structure in various places around the world where foreign correspondents work. Generally, salaries range from $50,000 to an average of about $75,000 to a peak of $100,000 or more. Some media will pay for living expenses, such as the costs of a home, school for the reporter's children, and a car.

According to the Bureau of Labor Statistics, correspondents and other news reporters earned a median salary of $30,060 in 2001. The lowest 10 percent earned $17,320 or less, and the highest 10 percent earned $68,020 or more.

WORK ENVIRONMENT

Correspondents and other reporters may face a hectic work environment if they have tight deadlines and have to produce their reports with little time for preparation. Correspondents who work in countries that face great political or social problems risk their health and even their lives to report breaking news. Covering wars, political uprisings, fires, floods, and similar events can be extremely dangerous.

Working hours vary depending on the correspondent's deadlines. Their work often demands irregular or long hours. Because foreign correspondents report from international locations, this job involves travel. The amount of travel depends on the size of the region the correspondent covers.

OUTLOOK

Although employment at newspapers, radio stations, and television stations in general is expected to continue to decline, the number of foreign correspondent jobs has leveled off. The employment outlook is expected to remain relatively stable, or even increase should more major conflicts or wars occur.

Factors that keep the number of foreign correspondents low are the high cost of maintaining a foreign news bureau and the relative lack of interest Americans show in world news. Despite these factors, the number of correspondents is not expected to decrease. There are simply too few as it is; decreasing the number could put the job in danger of disappearing, which most journalists believe is not an option. For now and the near future, most job openings will arise from the need to replace those correspondents who leave the job.

FOR MORE INFORMATION

The ASJA promotes the interests of freelance writers. It provides information on court rulings dealing with writing issues, has a writers' referral service, and offers a newsletter.

American Society of Journalists and Authors (ASJA)
1501 Broadway, Suite 302
New York, NY 10036
Tel: 212-997-0947
http://www.asja.org

This association publishes the annual publication Journalism and Mass Communication Directory, which has information on educational programs in all areas of journalism (newspapers, magazines, television, and radio).

**Association for Education in Journalism and Mass
  Communication**
234 Outlet Pointe Boulevard
Columbia, SC 29210-5667
Tel: 803-798-0271

Email: aejmc@aejmc.org
http://www.aejmc.org

The NAB website's Career Center has information on jobs, scholarships, internships, college programs, and other resources. You can also purchase career publications from the online NAB Store.
National Association of Broadcasters (NAB)
1771 N Street, NW
Washington, DC 20036
Tel: 202-429-5300
Email: nab@nab.org
http://www.nab.org

The SPJ has chapters all over the United States. The SPJ website offers career information and information on internships and fellowships.
Society of Professional Journalists (SPJ)
Eugene S. Pulliam National Journalism Center
3909 North Meridian Street
Indianapolis, IN 46208
Tel: 317-927-8000
Email: questions@spj.org
http://www.spj.org

FOREIGN SERVICE OFFICERS

QUICK FACTS

School Subjects Foreign language Government History	**Certification or Licensing** None available
	Outlook About as fast as the average
Personal Skills Communication/ideas Leadership/management	**DOT** 188
Work Environment Primarily indoors Primarily multiple locations	**GOE** 11.09.03
	NOC 4168
Minimum Education Level Bachelor's degree	**O*NET-SOC** N/A
Salary Range $35,819 to $49,123 to $118,400	

OVERVIEW

Foreign Service officers represent the government and the people of the United States by conducting relations with foreign countries and international organizations. They promote and protect the United States' political, economic, and commercial interests overseas. They observe and analyze conditions and developments in foreign countries and report to the State Department and other agencies. Foreign Service officers guard the welfare of Americans abroad and help foreign nationals traveling to the United States. There are about 4,000 Foreign Service officers in more than 250 U.S. embassies and consulates and in Washington, D.C.

HISTORY

The Foreign Service is a branch of the U.S. Department of State, which plans and carries out U.S. foreign policy under the authority of the president. Established in 1789, the State Department was placed under the direction of Thomas Jefferson, the first U.S. secretary of state and the senior officer in President George Washington's cabinet. It was his responsibility to initiate foreign policy on behalf of the U.S. government, advise the president on matters related to foreign policy, and administer the foreign affairs of the United States with the help of employees both at home and abroad.

The Foreign Service wasn't actually established until 1924, when the Diplomatic and Consular Services were brought together as one organization. The Foreign Service was formed in anticipation of a trade war; security issues became the service's focus with World War II and remained so throughout the Cold War. With the end of the Cold War, protecting trade has once again come to the forefront of the service's concerns. The Foreign Service is made up of five foreign affairs agencies: the State Department, U.S. Agency for International Development, U.S. Information Agency (USIA), Foreign Commercial Service, and the Foreign Agricultural Service. The 1980 Foreign Service Act brought the personnel system of all five of these agencies under one legislative umbrella.

THE JOB

Foreign Service officers work in embassies and consulates throughout the world. Between foreign assignments, they may have duties in the Department of State in Washington, D.C., or they may be temporarily detailed to the Department of Defense, the Department of Commerce, or other government departments and agencies. Similarly, Foreign Service information officers serve abroad or may work in USIA headquarters in Washington.

James Prosser spent 36 years with the Foreign Service. Though he is retired, he visits academic and civic organizations to lecture about the history of the Foreign Service. As an officer, Prosser worked in the telecommunications and computer fields as an operator, engineer, manager, and international negotiator. He speaks German, French, and Italian. Among his experiences are the following: In the then Belgian Congo, he ran a communications center and shortwave radio station during the country's postcolonial struggle for independence, a time when many were losing their lives in the upheaval. In 1967, France expelled the North Atlantic Treaty Organization (NATO) headquarters and Prosser was placed in charge of moving the U.S. communications elements of NATO to Belgium, as well as designing the new communications facilities there. Prosser has served in Germany, Italy, Kenya, and other countries. "Being in charge of all U.S. government telecommunications facilities in Africa and the Indian Ocean was an especially gratifying challenge," Prosser says. He still visits Africa whenever possible.

The work of Foreign Service officers is divided into four broad areas: administration, consular affairs, economic and commercial affairs, and political affairs.

Administrative officers who work in embassies and consulates manage and administer the day-to-day operations of their posts. Some handle financial matters such as planning budgets and controlling expenditures. Others work in general services: They purchase and look after government property and supplies, negotiate leases and contracts for office space and housing, and make arrangements for travel and shipping. *Personnel officers* deal with assignments, promotions, and personnel relations affecting both U.S. and local workers. This includes hiring local workers and arranging labor and management agreements. Administrative officers based in Washington do similar work and act as liaison between the Department of State and their overseas colleagues.

Consular officers help and advise U.S. citizens abroad as well as foreigners wishing to enter the United States as visitors or residents. They provide medical, legal, personal, and travel assistance to U.S. citizens in cases of accidents or emergencies, such as helping those without money to return home, finding lost relatives, visiting and advising those in foreign jails, and distributing Social Security checks and other federal benefits to eligible people. They issue passports, register births and deaths and other information, serve as notaries public, and take testimony needed by courts in the United States. In addition, these officers issue visas to foreign nationals who want to enter the United States and decide which of them are eligible for citizenship. Consular officers located in the Bureau of Consular Affairs in Washington provide support and help for their fellow officers abroad.

Economic and commercial affairs may be handled by one officer at a small post or divided between two full-time officers at a large post. *Economic officers* study the structure of a country's economy and the way it functions to determine how the United States might be affected by trends, trade patterns, and methods of setting prices. Their analysis of the economic data, based on a thorough understanding of the international monetary system, is passed along to their counterparts in Washington. Economic officers in Washington write position papers for the State Department and the White House, suggesting U.S. policies to help improve economic conditions in foreign nations.

Commercial officers concern themselves with building U.S. trade overseas. They carry out marketing and promotion campaigns to encourage foreign countries to do business with the United States. When they learn of potential trade and investment opportunities abroad, they inform U.S. companies that might be interested. They then help the firms find local agents and advise them about local business practices. Most commercial officers are members of the Foreign Commercial Service of the U.S. Department of Commerce.

Political officers overseas convey the views and position of the United States to government officials of the countries where they are based. They also keep the United States informed about any political developments that may affect U.S. interests, and may negotiate agreements between the two governments. Political officers are alert to local developments and reactions to U.S. policy. They maintain close contact with foreign officials and political and labor leaders and try to predict changes in local attitudes or leadership that might affect U.S. policies. They report their observations to Washington and interpret what is happening.

Political officers in Washington study and evaluate the information submitted by their counterparts abroad. They keep State Department and White House officials informed of developments overseas and of the possible effects on the United States. They suggest revisions in U.S. policy and see that their fellow officers abroad carry out approved changes.

The U.S. Information Service assigns *information officers* and *cultural officers* to serve at diplomatic missions in foreign countries. Information officers prepare and disseminate information designed to help other countries understand the United States and its policies. They distribute press releases and background articles and meet with members of the local press, radio, television, and film companies to give them information about the United States. Cultural officers engage in activities that promote an understanding and appreciation of American culture and traditions. These activities may involve educational and cultural exchanges between the countries, exhibits, lectures, performing arts events, libraries, book translations, English teaching programs, and youth groups. Cultural officers deal with universities and cultural and intellectual leaders. Many officers work on both information and cultural programs.

REQUIREMENTS
High School

Those who work for the Foreign Service will need to call upon a great deal of general knowledge about the world and its history. Take courses such as social studies, history, American government, and English literature. English composition will help you develop writing and communication skills. Any foreign language course will give you a good foundation in language study—and good foreign language skills can help in getting a job with the Foreign Service and make you eligible for a higher starting salary. Take a journalism course in which you'll be following current events and world news, as well as developing your writing and editing skills. Accounting, math, business, and economics classes will give you a good background for dealing with foreign trade issues.

Postsecondary Training

Though the Foreign Service is open to any United States citizen between the ages of 21 and 59 who passes the written, oral, and physical examinations, you'll need at least a bachelor's degree to be competitive and to have the knowledge necessary for completing the exam. Most Foreign Service officers have graduate degrees. Regardless of the level of education, candidates are expected to have a broad knowledge of foreign and domestic affairs and to be well informed on U.S. history, government, economics, culture, literature, and business administration. The fields of study most often chosen by those with a higher education include history, international relations, political science, economics, law, English literature, and foreign languages. The Georgetown University School of Foreign Service (http://www.georgetown.edu/sfs) has undergraduate and graduate programs designed to prepare students for careers in international affairs. Many luminaries have graduated from the school, including Bill Clinton in 1968. Former Secretary of State Madeleine Albright served as a member of the school's faculty.

The Foreign Service has internship opportunities available to college students in their junior and senior years, and to graduate students. About half of these unpaid internships are based in Washington, D.C., while the other half are at U.S. embassies and consulates overseas. As an intern, you may write reports, assist with trade negotiations, or work with budget projects. You may be involved in visa or passport work. The Foreign Service also offers a

Foreign Affairs Fellowship Program, which provides funding to undergraduate and graduate students preparing academically to enter the Foreign Service.

Other Requirements

As you can tell from the education and examination requirements mentioned above, you must be very intelligent and a quick learner to be a successful Foreign Service officer. You should be flexible and adaptable to new cultures and traditions. You must be interested in the histories and traditions of foreign cultures and respectful of the practices of other nations. "Perhaps most important," James Prosser advises, "is a desire to communicate directly with foreign cultures and people. Start by learning their language and speak to them in it. That wins a lot of points in any discussion."

Good people skills are important because you'll be expected to work as a member of a team and deal diplomatically with people from other countries. But, you'll also be expected to work independently. You should be in good physical condition, so that your health can handle the climate variations of different countries.

EXPLORING

As a member of a foreign language club at your school, you may have the opportunity to visit other countries. If such programs don't exist at your school, check with your guidance counselor or school librarian about discounted foreign travel packages available to student groups. Also, ask them about student exchange programs if you're interested in spending several weeks in another country. There is also the People to People Student Ambassador Program, which offers summer travel opportunities to students in grades six through 12. To learn about the expenses, destinations, and application process, visit its website (http://www.studentambassadors.org).

James Prosser's interest in foreign cultures started when he was very young. "Back in the 1930s," he says, "I built a crystal radio set, which enabled me to listen to distant radio stations. That led me to discover shortwave listening, and soon I was listening to foreign countries."

The American Foreign Service Association (AFSA), a professional association serving Foreign Service officers, publishes the *Foreign Service Journal* (http://www.afsa.org/fsj). The journal features articles by Foreign Service officers and academics that can give you insight into the Foreign Service. AFSA offers a discount on student subscriptions.

It may be difficult finding part-time or summer jobs that are directly related to foreign service, but check with federal, state, and local government agencies and a local university. Some schools use volunteers or part-time employees to lead tours for foreign exchange students.

EMPLOYERS

The Foreign Service isn't a single organization. Prospective officers actually apply to join one of two different agencies: either the Department of State or the U.S. Information Agency (USIA). The Department of State is responsible for the development and implementation of foreign policy, while the USIA explains these policies and actions to the world by engaging in public diplomacy. When hired, officers are offered an appointment to one of these agencies. There's very little moving between agencies. Foreign Service officers work in Washington, D.C. or are stationed in one of the approximately 170 foreign countries that have U.S. embassies or consulates.

STARTING OUT

Many people apply to the Foreign Service directly after finishing graduate school, while others work in other government agencies or professions. Some serve with the Peace Corps or the military, gaining experience with foreign affairs before applying, or they work as teachers in American-sponsored schools overseas. Some work as Congressional aides or interns. James Prosser joined the Air Force with hopes of being sent overseas. "In the back of my mind, I thought this enlistment would be my best opportunity to go abroad and experience foreign cultures." However, he was stationed within the United States for his entire four years with the Air Force. Near the end of his enlistment, one of his Air Force instructors suggested the Foreign Service.

Before being offered a job with the Foreign Service, you must pass a series of tests. The written exam consists of multiple-choice questions and an essay, and tests your knowledge of history, foreign policy, geography, and other relevant subjects. The U.S. State Department offers a study guide to help applicants prepare for the exam. The number of positions available varies from year to year; typically, thousands of people apply for fewer than 100 positions. The Foreign Service has been known to cancel its annual exam because of too few job openings.

Those who pass the written exam move on to the oral interview and must pass a security clearance and a medical exam. But passing these tests doesn't necessarily mean employment; passing candidates are placed on a rank-order list based on their test scores. As jobs become available, offers are made to those at the top of the list.

ADVANCEMENT

New recruits are given a temporary appointment as career candidates, or junior officers. This probationary period lasts no longer than five years and consists of orientation and work overseas. During this time all junior officers must learn a foreign language. The candidate's performance will be reviewed after 36 months of service, at which time a decision on tenure (once tenured, an officer can't be separated from the service without written cause) and appointment as a career Foreign Service officer will be made. If tenure is not granted, the candidate will be reviewed again approximately one year later. Those who fail to show potential as career officers are dropped from the program.

Career officers are rated by their supervisors once a year. A promotion board decides who is eligible for advancement. Promotions are based on merit. Officers who do good work can expect to advance from Class 6 through Class 1 by the time they complete their careers. A very experienced career officer may have the opportunity to serve as a member of the Senior Foreign Service, which involves directing, coordinating, and implementing U.S. foreign policy.

EARNINGS

Foreign Service officers are paid on a sliding scale. The exact figures depend on their qualifications and experience. According to the U.S. State Department's information on Foreign Service officer benefits, starting salaries for new appointees without a bachelor's degree and six or fewer years professional experience and those appointees with a bachelor's degree and no experience were $35,819 in 2002. Applicants who either had a master's or law degree, a bachelor's degree and six or more years professional experience, or who had no college degree but 12 years of professional experience earned $40,067 in 2002. Junior officers make up to $49,123 a year. Career officers make between $50,960 and $100,897, while senior Foreign Service officers make $106,200–$118,400.

Benefits are usually generous, although they vary from post to post. Officers are housed free of charge or given a housing allowance. They receive a cost-of-living allowance, higher pay if they work in an area that imposes undue hardship on them, medical and retirement benefits, and an education allowance for their children.

Most officers overseas work regular hours. They may work more than 40 hours a week, though, because they are on call around the clock, seven days a week. Foreign Service officers receive paid vacation for anywhere from 13 to 26 days a year, depending on their length of service. They get three weeks of home leave for each year of duty overseas.

WORK ENVIRONMENT

Foreign Service officers may be assigned to work in Washington, D.C., or in any embassy or consulate in the world. They generally spend about 60 percent of their time abroad and are transferred every two to four years.

Foreign Service officers may serve tours of duty in such major world cities as London, Paris, Moscow, Tokyo, or in the less familiar locales of Iceland, Madagascar, Nepal, or the Fiji Islands. Environments range from elegant and glamorous to remote and primitive.

Most offices overseas are clean, pleasant, and well equipped. But Foreign Service officers sometimes have to travel into areas that may present health hazards. Customs may differ considerably, medical care may be substandard or nonexistent, the climate may be extreme, or other hardships may exist. In some countries there is the danger of earthquakes, typhoons, or floods; in others, the danger of political upheaval.

Although embassy hours are normally the usual office hours of the host country, other tasks of the job may involve outside activities, such as attending or hosting dinners, lectures, public functions, or other necessary social engagements.

OUTLOOK

There is heavy competition and extensive testing involved in obtaining Foreign Service positions. Approximately 250 posts abroad are staffed by Foreign Service officers and specialists representing four U.S. government agencies: the Department of State, the Agency for International Development, the Foreign Agricultural Service, and the Foreign Commercial Service.

The Foreign Service seeks candidates who can manage programs and personnel, as well as experts in transnational issues, such as science and technology; the fight against diseases, such as AIDS; efforts to save the environment; antinarcotics efforts; and trade. The U.S. Department of State also has an increasing need for candidates with training and experience in administration and management.

Those people interested in protecting diplomacy and the strength of the Foreign Service need to closely follow relevant legislation, as well as promote the importance of international affairs. "I personally believe," James Prosser says, "that retired Foreign Service officers have a duty to tell America what we are all about and how vital it is to the national interest that we continue to always have a complete and dedicated staff in the Foreign Service."

FOR MORE INFORMATION

This professional organization serving current and retired Foreign Service officers hosts an informative website and publishes career information, such as Inside a U.S. Embassy. Read sections of the book online or contact

American Foreign Service Association
2101 E Street, NW
Washington, DC 20037
Tel: 800-704-2372
http://www.afsa.org

The U.S. Department of State offers a wealth of information, including internship opportunities, the history of the Foreign Service, and current officers and embassies. Check out its website or contact

U.S. Department of State
2201 C Street, NW
Washington, DC 20520
Tel: 202-647-4000
http://careers.state.gov

GENEALOGISTS

QUICK FACTS

School Subjects History Journalism	**Certification or Licensing** Recommended
Personal Skills Communication/ideas Helping/teaching	**Outlook** Little change or more slowly than the average
Work Environment Primarily indoors Primarily multiple locations	**DOT** 211
	GOE 07.03.01
Minimum Education Level High school diploma	**NOC** N/A
Salary Range $15/hour to $45/hour to $100+/hour	**O*NET-SOC** N/A

OVERVIEW

Genealogists research their clients' ancestral background to help them discover and identify their personal and familial histories. They search back along family lines to create family trees. Genealogists also research medical histories, adoption records, and conduct period research for writers and filmmakers. The National Genealogical Society has over 17,000 members.

HISTORY

Genealogy, the study of the histories of families, has a long history of its own. The Bible records thousands of years of ancestry of the Hebrew people. In primitive tribes, young boys were taught to memorize and recite their lineage so they would be sure not to forget it. Today, genealogy is both a skilled profession and a hobby with many useful applications. Often the line of family descent must be known before a person can inherit title to land and property or be eligible for certain college scholarships. Membership in certain societies, such as the Daughters of the American Revolution and the Hereditary Order of the Descendants of Colonial Governors, requires a proper and verifiable family history. Most people, however, trace their genealogies for the sake of curiosity and enjoyment. In fact, genealogy has become the third most popular hobby in the United States, behind only coin and stamp collecting.

THE JOB

Genealogists trace family histories by examining historical and legal documents to answer questions about when and where people were born, married, lived, and died. It is like historical detective work, in which the genealogist fills in the missing facts through research and deduction.

Clients come to genealogists to have questions answered. They may want to know the lineage of their family since coming to America, or even further back into their country of origin, or they may wish to find out some facts about the lives of their ancestors. Clients must tell all the known information about their family tree, and back it up with documents, such as birth certificates, family Bibles, wedding licenses, and old letters when necessary.

Sometimes tracing a family history can be fairly straightforward, and research yields impressive results. At other times, genealogists may be thwarted by incomplete records, dead ends, and conflicting information. It is very difficult to know how long it will take to complete an assignment or how successfully a client's questions can be answered.

Barbara Hipp is a genealogist in Athens, Texas. Though she doesn't specialize, she has recently become interested in researching adoption records. "I have had many requests from people who were adopted overseas and are seeking birth parents," she says. "I also enjoy studying the migration routes of the late 1700s and 1800s. It is amazing how much the weather played a part in the transformation of this country."

Genealogists are familiar with many different sources of information and have the skills needed to do the right historical detective work. When researching, they often start in the public library, searching for names and dates in telephone directories, census records, military service records, newspaper clippings, letter files, diaries, and other sources. They may also contact local genealogical groups and historical societies to check for any relevant information that may be on hand. Visits to county courthouses can reveal a wealth of important data, including records of births, marriages, divorces, deaths, wills, tax records, and property deeds. A truly resourceful genealogist will also look for information in places other people might not think of, including the local newspaper's records, school board records, clubs, houses of worship, immigration bureaus, funeral homes, and cemeteries. A genealogist can never have too many sources of information, because each fact about a person's life and death should be authenticated in at least two different places for the research to be considered valid. Often two pieces of information will conflict, and a third source of validation must be found.

Once local sources of family information have been explored, genealogists must contact long-distance sources by mail, telephone, or email. One resource often used is the Genealogical Department of the National Archives and Records Service (http://www.archives. gov) in Washington, D.C. Here genealogists can find out about immigration records, passport applications, pension claims, and other data. They might also contact the Family History Library established and run by the leaders of the Church of Jesus Christ of Latter-Day Saints (http://www.familysearch.org). This library holds the world's largest collection of genealogical information. Genealogists might also need to gather information from records in other countries by contacting the genealogical societies and government agencies there.

"Belonging to historical societies and genealogical societies is a big asset in my work," Hipp says. "In these groups, you can gain moral support as well as great tips about areas to search." Historical societies help genealogists better understand the material they are researching. "Understanding the events and cultures of the era you're researching gives you a feeling for the trials and tribulations, joys, and sorrows the people lived with on a day-to-day basis."

Once the research has been completed, genealogists organize the pertinent family information in the manner requested by the client. From the raw information, they might prepare a basic family tree or other diagram to show births, marriages, and deaths. Genealogy reports can grow more detailed and informative. Some clients hire the genealogist to write a complete family history, which might include life stories of ancestors, portraits, pictures of homes and neighborhoods, maps, and anecdotes. Some people go so far as to have many copies of their family history printed and bound to be given as gifts to other family members, friends, libraries, and historical and genealogical societies.

Genealogists carefully record sources of all used information, as well as the time spent gathering each piece of data. It is important to have documented the exact title and page of each reference volume or record book, and the names and addresses of people interviewed in the course of research. Genealogists take photos of tombstones, monuments, or markers that give relevant data and make photocopies of official records, letters, and other printed matter when possible. All this extra information is important to show the accuracy of the research and may also help any genealogical work that someone might undertake in the future.

REQUIREMENTS
High School
If you are interested in a career in genealogy, you should study history, English literature and composition, geography, sociology, and psychology while in high school. Foreign languages and research and library skills are also valuable. Develop your computer knowledge, since libraries and document archives now have computerized catalogs and research systems. Because you may do genealogical work only on a part-time basis, you may wish to look into part-time work in related jobs, such as librarian, historian, and freelance writer, which will offer the free time to conduct genealogical research.

Postsecondary Training
There are no formal requirements for becoming a genealogist. Many competent genealogists are self-taught or have learned the trade from other established genealogists. However, a bachelor's degree in genealogy, history, English, or journalism can be a distinct advantage as it demonstrates your capacity for research and dedication to the profession. There are few colleges that offer major programs of study in this field. Brigham Young University in Provo, Utah, offers studies in family history; other institutions may offer similar credit or noncredit courses. In addition, many adult education programs and extension courses are available. The National Genealogical Society and the National Institute on Genealogical Research offer home study courses and seminars.

Certification or Licensing
Becoming certified, while not a requirement, may be a beneficial step for genealogists. Customers often ask for any professional certifications that testify to a person's qualifications and show that

work is done according to a code of ethics. The Board for Certification of Genealogists offers certification to qualified applicants under five different categories: certified genealogical records specialist, certified lineage specialist, certified genealogist, certified genealogical lecturer, and certified genealogical instructor. The Association of Professional Genealogists also has a credential program with similar requirements. The Genealogical Institute of the Maritimes grants genealogists working in Canada the following certifications: genealogical researcher (Canada) and certified genealogist (Canada). See the end of this article for contact information.

Other Requirements

Genealogists need an inquiring mind and an interest in history to do their work. They should also be patient, thorough, and well-organized when detailing documentation of facts and sources.

"You also have to be a people-person," Barbara Hipp says. "You'll do a lot of interviewing of family and friends." Genealogists spend many hours with librarians and other professionals while working on projects, so being outgoing and personable is a must. "But above all," Hipp says, "you must be a good listener."

EXPLORING

One of the best ways to explore the subject of genealogy is to discuss it with the staff of your local library. Librarians will be able to recommend good books on the subject and put you in touch with local genealogical societies, which often meet in public libraries. Most of these societies are open to anyone interested in the subject and welcome new members. Ask members about their genealogical work and ask if they recommend publications or other resources to learn more about the career. Professional, practicing genealogists can also give advice on good schools or training programs, opportunities for jobs, and some of the pitfalls of doing genealogical work full time.

Some community groups offer short educational courses in genealogy. Taking one of these courses will provide you with an opportunity to discover what resources and facilities are available locally for genealogical study, as well as learn beginning skills in the field.

Some websites provide resources to help you explore your own family lineage. Try filling out your own family tree at familytreemaker.com (http://www.familytreemaker.com). This site has free genealogy classes online, and offers tips on other ways to explore your own history, such as keeping a journal and looking over old family photographs. You may also find it helpful to read publications such as *Ancestry* magazine (http://www.ancestry.com).

EMPLOYERS
Many genealogists consider their research a hobby, but there are many opportunities for employment in genealogy and related fields. Self-employed genealogists work with individual families, with geneticists and physicians to research health data on a patient's ancestors, and with church groups and other organizations that research adoption records. Genealogists may also be able to find full-time work with professional family researchers, historical societies, libraries, and other research-oriented organizations. There are more than 17,000 members of the National Genealogical Society.

STARTING OUT
New genealogists have to work hard to drum up business. This may require advertising in the Yellow Pages, local newspapers, and genealogical magazines. They might also leave business cards with the local public or university library and historical society. As with any self-employed profession, steady work is never guaranteed, and genealogists may have to supplement their income. Many choose to do family history work only part time while holding other jobs, such as librarian, writer, teacher, and college professor.

"Make sure you have financial support before you start out," Barbara Hipp advises. "This is a challenging career, but not one that makes you a lot of money quickly. You should advertise on the Web and with genealogical and historical societies."

ADVANCEMENT
Self-employed genealogists advance their careers through their dedication to quality work, cleverness, and efforts to find new clients. Certification can help; professional societies publish lists of accredited members and distribute them to the public upon request. Genealogists can also diversify their skills, either by gaining more accreditation or by expanding services into related work, such as writing family histories and designing family crests and coats of arms. Other ways of expanding services might include conducting seminars or writing articles and how-to books to help amateurs.

EARNINGS

Because so many people in genealogy are hobbyists, and others work only part time, it is difficult to estimate annual salaries. Most genealogists, whether self-employed or working for a genealogy service company, charge by the hour. According to the Association of Professional Genealogists, self-employed genealogists charge between $15 and $100 an hour, with the average between $25 and $60. Some experienced genealogists specialize in difficult research and earn higher fees. For a larger project, like researching and writing an entire family history, a genealogist may charge a single fee, and may request it up front. Genealogists also charge for photocopies, postage, telephone calls, and other expenses incurred during research.

Because the work is not steady or guaranteed, genealogists usually develop ways to supplement their income. As noted earlier, they might write articles for magazines and journals or write a book on how to trace family history. Qualified genealogists might teach courses in family history at community colleges, public libraries, or other adult education venues.

WORK ENVIRONMENT

Because most genealogists are self-employed, they generally can set their own working hours and manage their own time. The profession is usually a solitary one, as genealogists spend much of their time looking through old records and searching library files, or working in their homes, organizing data and updating their records. Their search for information can take them into stuffy, badly lit archive vaults and basements, where they spend hours sifting through hundreds of documents looking for a single, vital piece of information. These documents can be crumbling and yellow, written in ink that is fading and hard to read. Hours or days of effort can produce nothing, or the genealogist can come upon rich treasures of previously undocumented and unused information.

Genealogy can require a good bit of legwork as well. Occasionally, a genealogist might be called on to travel to a distant city or abroad to complete research, take pictures of old family homes, or locate and interview distant relatives. More often, they are required to make trips to schools, cemeteries, churches, and homes for personal interviews. "You get to meet so many people," Barbara Hipp says. "You also acquire new friends. Finding lost relations has to be the best part of the job."

But one of the biggest disappointments in genealogy is the number of lost or destroyed records. "So much was lost during the Civil

War and to fires that plagued many areas in the 1920s. When records were destroyed, replacing them and collecting data were not priorities to most county officials," Hipp says. "One of the saddest events is when a county decides it no longer needs to store outdated records, and has them deliberately destroyed."

OUTLOOK

Despite the recent resurgence in popularity, genealogy holds limited prospects for growth in the future. Individuals researching their own families do the majority of genealogical work. People consult genealogists about how to get started and may seek professional help when they run into problems. Individuals also hire genealogists to help them research information in other parts of the country or the world.

Lawyers and people with legal claims sometimes employ genealogists to determine a person's right to a legacy, title, or family name. Societies whose members are required to prove a certain heritage, such as the Daughters of the American Revolution, employ genealogists to verify the ancestral claims made by prospective members. Physicians and medical researchers are also beginning to trace family histories of people with genetic predispositions for a specific illness and other hereditary maladies in hopes of finding a cure. Therefore, although much growth in the industry is unlikely, these needs should insure that work opportunities in the profession at least remain at the current level.

FOR MORE INFORMATION

For information on genealogical careers, publications, and conferences, contact

Association of Professional Genealogists
PO Box 745729
Arvada, CO 80006-5729
Tel: 303-422-9371
Email: admin@apgen.org
http://www.apgen.org

For information on becoming certified in one of the five categories of genealogical research, contact

Board for Certification of Genealogists
PO Box 14291
Washington, DC 20044
http://www.bcgcertification.org

For information on research trips, study courses, and resources in genealogy, contact
National Genealogical Society
4527 17th Street North
Arlington, VA 22207-2399
Tel: 800-473-0060
Email: ngs@ngsgenealogy.org
http://www.ngsgenealogy.org

For online links to genealogical sites ranging in topics, visit
Cyndi's List of Genealogy Sites on the Internet
http://www.CyndisList.com

HISTORIANS

QUICK FACTS

School Subjects
Foreign language
Geography
History

Personal Skills
Communication/ideas

Work Environment
Primarily indoors
Primarily multiple location

Minimum Education Level
Master's degree

Salary Range
$22,840 to $42,930 to
$74,449+

Certification or Licensing
Required (for secondary
school teachers)

Outlook
About as fast as the average

DOT
052

GOE
11.03.03

NOC
4169

O*NET-SOC
19-3093.00, 25-1125.00

OVERVIEW

Historians study, assess, and interpret the activities and conduct of individuals or social, ethnic, political, or geographical groups of the past.

HISTORY

Throughout the history of civilization some people have either recorded or passed along orally the significant events and ideas of their times. The Greek writer Herodotus generally is considered the first historian. Historical writings help us to know the people and leaders who lived centuries ago and how their actions may have influenced the development of modern civilization. It is the job of historians to analyze the past. Often, we can make better decisions and plan more carefully for the future if we are aware of the actions, judgments, precedents, and mistakes of the past.

Much of our knowledge of history had been gleaned by modern professional historians who have studied manuscripts, documents, artifacts, and other traces of earlier periods. Some of the manuscripts or writings they study were written as actual historical accounts; others may be letters, diaries, or fiction with some historical basis.

THE JOB

Modern *historians* are trained to gather, interpret, and evaluate the records of the past in order to describe and analyze past events, institutions, ideas, and people. Skill in research and writing is essential to their work, but scientific methods are also invaluable.

Some historians are college teachers; others write books and articles, do research, and lecture. Historians work for museums, special libraries, and historical societies, and they are often called on as advisers in such fields as politics, economics, law, and education. Most specialize in the history of a specific country or region or a specific period or industry.

Some historians research the accuracy of historical details in stage, motion picture, television, and radio presentations. They authenticate such things as customs, speech, costumes, architectural styles, modes of transportation, and other items peculiar to a particular period of history. A research director may head the research department of a film or television production company.

Historians who are called *archivists* are responsible for identifying, preserving, and cataloging historical documents of value to writing, researching, or teaching history. They are really history librarians who have learned the technique of selectivity; that is, they recognize which historical materials are worth preserving, since it would be impossible to save all material. Such historians may work in museums, libraries, historical societies, and also for the U.S. government, where they may collect materials, write about the activities of various departments, and prepare pamphlets, lectures, exhibits, or presentations on the Internet.

Curators work for a museum, special library, or historical society. They identify and preserve historical documents and other articles of the past. Often curators help scholars with research in the institution's collection. *Historical society directors* are curators who coordinate the activities of a historical society. They direct the research staff, review publications and exhibits, speak before various groups and organizations, and perform the administrative duties involved in running a historical institution.

Genealogists specialize in family histories. They use public records such as birth and death certificates, military records, census studies, and real estate deeds to trace connections between individuals. They are like detectives in a sense, but they must have the patience to continue following up leads in one historical record after another.

Biographers specialize in writing about the life of an individual, usually a famous one. Research from library sources and through personal interviews is an important first step. Biographers must have an in-depth knowledge not only of their subject's life but also of the particular era or field in which the person was important. They must write with careful attention to detail, but must also have a creative flair for making the subject interesting to the reader.

REQUIREMENTS
High School
If you are interested in becoming an historian, be sure to take college-preparatory courses in high school. Historians must be strong readers, writers, and speakers, so a strong background in English and speech will prepare you for further study in college. Knowledge of at least two foreign languages is also necessary for those who plan to earn a doctorate.

Postsecondary Training
The main educational requirement for an historian is graduate study. A master's degree in history is the minimum requirement for a college instructor's position, but a doctorate is much more desirable and is required by many colleges and universities. To become a professor or administrator, or to reach any other high level of employment, a doctorate is essential. Historians working for museums, historical societies, research councils, or the federal government generally have doctorates or the equivalent in training and experience. A person is rarely considered a professional historian without this educational background.

Some jobs for beginners with a bachelor's degree in history are available, usually with federal, state, or local governments. These jobs usually require knowledge of the archivist's work, but advancement without further education is not likely. A number of high school teaching positions are also available, provided the applicant meets state requirements for certification.

Certification or Licensing
Historians who work as public school teachers must be licensed under regulations established by the department of education of

the state in which they teach. Not all states require licensure for teachers in private or parochial schools. Contact you state's department of education for more information.

Other Requirements

To be a successful historian, you should have a real love for history and the past especially as you work long hours in research and writing. Historians need to have analytical minds capable of sifting facts scientifically. You must also be dedicated, self-motivated, and curious about the world around you. If you choose to become a history teacher, you should have good speaking skills, patience, and enjoy working with students.

EXPLORING

You can learn a great deal about a career as a historian by talking to your history teachers or arranging interviews with historians working in local museums or universities. You can experiment with research in the field of history by developing your own history projects, such as tracing the genealogy of your family, researching the history of your neighborhood, or analyzing the development of a favorite sports team. By seeking the advice of your history teacher while working on these projects, you will get a good feel for doing real research and drawing conclusions based on the historical information you have discovered.

EMPLOYERS

A large percentage of historians are employed at colleges and universities, while others teach at the middle or high school level. Historians are also employed in archives, historical societies, libraries, museums, nonprofit foundations, research councils, and large corporations. Others work for local, state, and the federal governments. Historians employed by the federal government often work at the National Archives and the Departments of Defense, Interior, and State. Some historians work in politics or journalism or serve as consultants to radio, television, or film producers.

STARTING OUT

Historians interested in becoming teachers enter the field after completing at least a master's degree in history. At this time, they may apply for an instructor's position at a college or university or they

Attention Future Historians

If you are interested in becoming an historian, you should read *Becoming a Historian: A Survival Manual*. This excellent guide, published by the American Historical Association (AHA), offers information on the graduate school decision and application process, coursework, academic relationships, funding graduate and postdoctorate study, finding a job, interviewing, analyzing job offers, and surviving your first year as a faculty member. For more information on *Becoming a Historian*, visit the AHA's website, http://www.theaha.org/pubs.

may seek employment as a history teacher at a middle school or high school.

Historians who are interested in nonacademic positions may learn about job leads through internships, professors, or from the career services office of their college or university. The American Historical Association also offers job listings to its student and professional members at its website. Many historians earn a doctorate before applying for nonteaching positions.

ADVANCEMENT

Historians advance in proportion to their level of education, experience, and personal qualities as writers, researchers, or teachers. University teachers usually begin as instructors. The next step is assistant professor, then associate professor, and finally full rank as a professor.

Historians in noneducational settings advance as they gain experience and contribute to their work. Historians who have earned a doctorate already have a competitive edge over workers with lesser degrees and, therefore, enjoy stronger advancement opportunities.

EARNINGS

In its 2001–02 salary survey, the College and University Personnel Association for Human Resources (CUPA-HR) reported that the average yearly income for historians at private colleges and universities was $58,050. Full professors of history at private institutions averaged $73,306; associate professors, $54,022; assistant professors, $42,921; and instructors, $34,511. The same CUPA-HR survey reports the following average salaries for historians at public institutions by professional level: professors, $74,449; associate professors, $54,171; assistant professors, $42,743; and instructors, $33,650. Average earnings for all history educators at public colleges and universities were $58,106.

The U.S. Department of Labor reports that historians earned average annual salaries of $42,930 in 2001. Salaries ranged from less than $22,840 to $70,050 or more annually.

WORK ENVIRONMENT

Historians employed in educational settings will enjoy clean, well-lighted, and pleasant work settings. College and university professors may have their own offices, or they may have to share an office with one or more colleagues. College professors enjoy a flexible schedule that allows them to arrange their schedule around class hours, academic meetings, and the established office hours when they meet with students. Although history professors may teach only two or three classes a semester, they spend a considerable amount of time preparing for lectures, examining student work, and conducting research.

Historians who teach at the middle- or high-school level will have more traditional hours. They may also be required to teach others types of classes and supervise extracurricular activities as part of their duties.

Historians who are employed in noneducational settings usually work in professional office settings. They may have to spend long hours in library stacks or searching electronic databases for the tiniest piece of information. Historians may be required to travel to conduct interviews or gather information at archives, museums, or other locations.

OUTLOOK

Competition for college faculty positions is so keen that many historians with doctorates have to accept part-time positions or find work in other occupations. Historians holding only master's degrees will also face much competition. Some history majors will be able to work as trainees in administrative and management positions in government agencies, nonprofit foundations, and civic organizations. The *Occupational Outlook Handbook* reports that overall employment of social scientists, including historians, is expected to grow about as fast as the average for all occupations over the next several years.

FOR MORE INFORMATION

For general information on the study of history, contact
American Association for State and Local History
1717 Church Street
Nashville, TN 37203-2991
Tel: 615-320-3203
Email: history@aaslh.org
http://www.aaslh.org

To learn more about the careers of historians, contact the following organizations:
American Historical Association
400 A Street, SE
Washington, DC 20003-3889
Tel: 202-544-2422
Email: aha@theaha.org
http://www.theaha.org

National Council for History Education
26915 Westwood Road, Suite B-2
Westlake, Ohio 44145
Tel: 440-835-1776
Email: nche@nche.net
http://www.history.org/nche

Organization of American Historians
112 North Bryan Avenue
Bloomington, IN 47408-4199
Tel: 812-855-7311
Email: oah@oah.org
http://www.oah.org

The following website was designed for high school and college teachers of U.S. history courses. It has a variety of interesting information and links.
History Matters: The U.S. Survey on the Web
http://www.historymatters.gmu.edu

INFORMATION BROKERS

QUICK FACTS

School Subjects Computer science English Journalism	**Certification or Licensing** None available
	Outlook Faster than the average
Personal Skills Communication/ideas Technical/scientific	**DOT** N/A
Work Environment Primarily indoors Primarily one location	**GOE** N/A
	NOC N/A
Minimum Education Level Bachelor's degree	**O*NET-SOC** N/A
Salary Range $20,000 to $54,500 to $100,000+	

OVERVIEW

Information brokers, sometimes called *online researchers* or *independent information professionals,* compile information from online databases and services. They work for clients in a number of different professions, researching marketing surveys, newspaper articles, business and government statistics, abstracts, and other sources of information. They prepare reports and presentations based on their research. Information brokers have home-based operations, or they work full time for libraries, law offices, government agencies, and corporations.

HISTORY

Strange as it may seem, some of the earliest examples of online researchers are the keepers of a library established by Ptolemy I in Egypt in the third century B.C. These librarians helped to build the first great library by copying and revising classical Greek texts. The monks of Europe also performed some of the modern-day researcher's tasks by building libraries and printing books. Despite their great efforts, libraries weren't used extensively until the 18th century, when literacy increased among the general population. In 1803, the first public library in the United States opened in Connecticut.

In the late 1800s and early 1900s, many different kinds of library associations evolved, reflecting the number of special libraries already established (such as medical and law libraries). With all the developments of the 20th century, these library associations helped to promote special systems and tools for locating information. These systems eventually developed into the online databases and Internet search engines used today. The Internet, although created in 1969 and subsidized by the government as a communication system for the Department of Defense, didn't become a significant source of information until relaxed government policies allowed for its commercial use in 1991.

THE JOB

An interest in the Internet and computer skills are important to success as an independent information broker, but this specialist needs to understand much more than just search engines. Information brokers need to master Dialog, Lexis/Nexis, and other information databases. They also have to compile information with fax machines, photocopiers, and telephones, as well as personal interviews. If you think this sounds like the work of a private eye, you are not far off; as a matter of fact, some information brokers have worked as private investigators.

A majority of research projects, however, are marketing based. Suppose a company wants to embark on a new, risky venture— maybe a fruit distribution company wants to make figs as popular as apples and oranges. First, the company's leaders might want to know some basic information about fig consumption. How many people have even eaten a fig? What articles about figs have been published in national magazines? What have been recent annual sales of figs, Fig Newtons, and other fig-based treats? What popular recipes include figs? The company hires consultants, marketing experts, and researchers to gather all this information.

Each researcher has his or her own approach to accomplishing tasks, but every researcher must first get to know the subject. A researcher who specializes in retail and distribution might already be familiar with the trade associations, publications, and other sources of industry information. Another researcher might have to learn as much as possible, as quickly as possible, about the lingo and organizations involved with the fruit distribution industry. This includes using the Internet's basic search engines to get a sense of what kind of information is available. The researcher then uses a database service, such as the Dialog system, which makes available billions of pages of text and images, including complete newspaper and magazine articles, wire service stories, and company profiles. Because database services often charge the user for the time spent searching or documents viewed, online researchers must know all the various tips and commands for efficient searching. Once the search is complete, and they've downloaded the information needed, online researchers must prepare the information for the company. They may be expected to make a presentation to the company or write a complete report that includes pie graphs, charts, and other illustrations to accompany the text.

The legal profession hires information brokers to search cases, statutes, and other sources of law; update law library collections; and locate data to support cases, such as finding expert witnesses, or researching the history of the development of a defective product that caused personal injury. The health care industry needs information brokers to gather information on drugs, treatments, devices, illnesses, or clinical trials. An information broker who specializes in public records researches personal records (such as birth, death, marriage, adoption, and criminal records), corporations, and property ownership. Other industries that rely on information brokers include banking and finance, government and public policy, and science and technology.

"This isn't the kind of profession you can do right out of high school or college," says Mary Ellen Bates, an independent information professional based in Washington, D.C. "It requires expertise in searching the professional online services. You can't learn them on your own time; you have to have real-world experience as an online researcher. Many of the most successful information brokers are former librarians." Her success in the business has led her to serve as president of the Association of Independent Information Professionals, to write and publish articles about the business, and to serve as a consultant to libraries and other organizations. Some of her projects have included research on the market for independent living facilities for senior citizens and the impact of large grocery chains on independent grocery stores. She's also been asked to find out what rental car companies do with cars after they're past their prime. "Keep in mind that you need a lot more than Internet research skills," Bates says. "You need the ability to run your business from the top to bottom. That means accounting, marketing, collections, strategic planning, and personnel management."

The expense of the commercial database services has affected the career of another online researcher, Sue Carver of Richland, Washington. Changes in Dialog's usage rates have forced her to seek out other ways to use her library skills. In addition to such services as market research and document delivery, Carver's Web page promotes a book-finding service, helping people to locate collectible and out-of-print books. "I have found this a fun, if not highly lucrative, activity which puts me in contact with a wide variety of people," she says. "This is a case where the Internet opens the door to other possibilities. Much of this business is repackaging information in a form people want to buy. This is limited only by your imagination." But she also emphasizes that the job of online researcher requires highly specialized skills in information retrieval. "Non-librarians often do not appreciate the vast array of reference material that existed before the Internet," she says, "nor how much librarians have contributed to the information age." Carver holds a master's degree in library science and has worked as a reference librarian, which involved her with searches on patents, molecular biology, and other technical subjects. She has also worked as an indexer on a nuclear engineering project and helped plan a search and retrieval system on a separate nuclear project.

REQUIREMENTS
High School
Take computer classes that teach word and data processing programs, presentation programs, and how to use Internet search engines. Any class offered by your high school or public library on information retrieval will familiarize you with database searches and such services as Dialog, Lexis/Nexis, and Dow Jones. English and composition courses will teach you to organize information and write clearly. Speech and theater classes will help you develop the skills to give presentations in front of clients. Journalism classes and working on your high school newspaper will involve you directly in information retrieval and writing.

Postsecondary Training
It is recommended that you start with a good liberal arts program in a college or university, then pursue a master's degree in either a sub-

ject specialty or in library and information science. Developing expertise in a particular subject will prepare you for a specialty in information brokering.

Many online researchers have master's degrees in library science. The American Library Association accredits library and information science programs and offers a number of scholarships. Courses in library programs deal with techniques of data collection and analysis, use of graphical presentation of sound and text, and networking and telecommunications. Internships are also available in some library science programs.

Continuing education courses are important for online researchers with advanced degrees. Because of the rapidly changing technology, researchers need to attend seminars and take courses through such organizations as the Special Libraries Association and the Information Professionals Institute (IPI). The IPI seminars, conducted in major cities across the country, deal with starting a business, finding clients, online searching, and other topics relevant to both the experienced and the inexperienced information brokers. Many online researchers take additional courses in their subject matter specialization. Mary Ellen Bates attends meetings of the Society of Competitive Intelligence Professionals, since a lot of her work is in the field of competitive intelligence.

Other Requirements

In addition to all the varied computer skills necessary to succeed as an information broker, you must have good communication skills. "You're marketing all the time," Bates says. "If you're not comfortable marketing yourself and speaking publicly, you'll never make it in this business." To keep your business running, you need persistence to pursue new clients and sources of information. You are your own boss, so you have to be self-motivated to meet deadlines. Good record-keeping skills will help you manage the financial details of the business and help you keep track of contacts.

Sue Carver advises that you keep up on current events and pay close attention to detail. You should welcome the challenge of locating hard-to-find facts and articles. "I have a logical mind," Carver says, "and love puzzles and mysteries."

EXPLORING

If you've ever had to write an extensive research paper, then you've probably already had experience with online research. In college, many of your term papers will require that you become familiar with Lexis/Nexis and other library systems. The reference librarians of your school and public libraries should be happy to introduce you to the various library tools available. On the Internet, experiment with the search engines; each service has slightly different features and capabilities. Visit Mary Ellen Bates' website at http://www.batesinfo.com for extensive information about the business and to read articles she's written. She's also the author of *Super Searchers Do Business* (Information Today, Inc., 1999) and a quarterly electronic newsletter called *For Your Information.* Also check out *Researching Online For Dummies,* 2nd edition (Wiley, 2000), by Bates and Reva Basch.

EMPLOYERS
A large number of information professionals are employed by colleges, universities, and corporations, and gain experience in full-time staff positions before starting their own businesses. Those who work for themselves contract with a number of different kinds of businesses and organizations. People seeking marketing information make the most use of the services of information professionals. Attorneys, consulting firms, public relations firms, government agencies, and private investigators also hire researchers. With the Internet, a researcher can work anywhere in the country, serving clients all around the world. However, living in a large city will allow an online researcher better access to more expansive public records when performing manual research.

STARTING OUT
People become researchers through a variety of different routes. They may go into business for themselves after gaining a lot of experience within an industry, such as in aviation or pharmaceuticals. Using their expertise, insider knowledge, and professional connections, they can serve as a consultant on issues affecting the business. Or they may become an independent researcher after working as a special librarian, having developed computer and search skills. The one thing most researchers have in common, however, is extensive experience in finding information and presenting it. Once they have the knowledge necessary to start their own information business, online researchers should take seminars offered by such organizations as the IPI. Amelia Kassel, president and owner of MarketingBase (http://www. marketingbase.com), a successful information brokering company,

offers a mentoring program via email. As mentor, she advises on such subjects as online databases, marketing strategies, and pricing.

Before leaving her full-time job, Mary Ellen Bates spent a year preparing for her own business. She says, "I didn't want to spend time doing start-up stuff that I could spend marketing or doing paying work." She saved business cards and established contacts. She saved $10,000 and set up a home-based office with a computer, desk, office supplies, fax, and additional phone lines. To help others starting out, Bates has written *Getting Your First Five Clients,* available through the Association of Independent Information Professionals.

ADVANCEMENT

The first few years of any business are difficult and require long hours of marketing, promotion, and building a clientele. Advancement will depend on the online researcher's ability to make connections and to broaden their client base. Some researchers start out specializing in a particular area, such as in telephone research or public record research, before venturing out into different areas. Once they're capable of handling projects from diverse sources, they can expand their business. They can also take on larger projects as they begin to meet other reliable researchers with whom they can join forces.

EARNINGS

Even if they have a great deal of research experience, self-employed information brokers' first few years in the business may be lean ones, and they should expect to make as little as $20,000. As with any small business, it takes a few years to develop contacts and establish a reputation for quality work. Independent information brokers usually charge between $45 and $100 an hour, depending on the project. Eventually, an online researcher should be able to make a salary equivalent to that of a full-time special librarian—a 2001 salary survey by the Special Libraries Association puts the national median at $54,500. Some very experienced independent researchers with a number of years of self-employment may make well over $100,000.

Helen Burwell, president of Burwell Enterprises, estimates that the average information broker charges $75 an hour. This hourly rate is affected by factors such as geographic location and the broker's knowledge of the subject matter. Information brokers can make more money in cities like New York and Washington, D.C., where their services are in higher demand. Also, someone doing high-level patent research, which requires a great deal of expertise, can charge more than someone retrieving public records.

Information brokers who work full-time for companies earn salaries comparable to other information technology (IT) professionals. According to a 2000 survey by the Society for Technical Communications, IT professionals' salaries can range from $36,000 for entry-level personnel to more than $90,000 for those with more than 10 years' experience. A full-time information broker who works for a large corporation primarily in the area of competitive intelligence can earn $100,000 annually.

WORK ENVIRONMENT

Most independent researchers work out of their own homes. This means they have a lot of control over their environment, but it also means they're always close to their workstations. As a result, online researchers may find themselves working longer hours than if they had an outside office and a set weekly schedule. "This is easily a 50- to 60-hour a week job," Mary Ellen Bates says. Online researchers are their own bosses, but they may work as a member of a team with other researchers and consultants on some projects. They will also need to discuss the project with their clients both before and after they've begun their research.

Information brokers employed by companies work in an office environment. Although most of their work takes place at a computer, they may have to make trips to libraries, government offices, and other places that hold information that's not available online. Whether self-employed or not, information brokers spend some time in boardrooms and conference situations making presentations of their findings.

OUTLOOK

Helen Burwell anticipates that independent information professionals will continue to find a great deal of work, but the growth of the industry won't be as rapid as in the past because of the increasing number of new information science graduates entering the field.

The Internet is making it easier for people and businesses to conduct their own online research; this is expected to help business for online researchers rather than hurt. Alex Kramer, past president of the Association of Independent Information Professionals, predicts that the more people recognize the vast amount of information available to them, the more they'll seek out the assistance of online researchers to efficiently compile that information. There will be continuing demand for information brokers in marketing, competitive intelligence, legal research, and science and technology.

Employment experts predict that with the growing reliance on computer technology, businesses will be willing to pay top dollar for employees and consultants who are flexible, mobile, and able to navigate the technology with ease.

FOR MORE INFORMATION

For information about library science programs and scholarships, contact
American Library Association
50 East Huron
Chicago, IL 60611
Tel: 800-545-2433
http://www.ala.org

To learn more about the benefits of association membership, contact
Association of Independent Information Professionals
7044 South 13th Street
Oak Creek, WI 53154-1429
Tel: 414-766-0421
Email: aiipinfo@aiip.org
http://www.aiip.org

For information about seminars and books on information brokers, contact
Information Professionals Institute
Burwell Enterprises
5619 Plumtree Drive
Dallas, TX 75252
Tel: 972-732-0160
http://www.burwellinc.com

For information on continuing education, contact
Special Libraries Association
1700 18th Street, NW
Washington, DC 20009-2514
Tel: 202-234-4700
Email: sla@sla.org
http://www.sla.org

INTELLIGENCE OFFICERS

QUICK FACTS

School Subjects Foreign language Government History	**Certification or Licensing** None available
	Outlook About as fast as the average
Personal Skills Communication/ideas Technical/scientific	**DOT** 059
Work Environment Indoors and outdoors Primarily one location	**GOE** 11.03.02
	NOC 0643
Minimum Education Level Bachelor's degree	**O*NET-SOC** N/A
Salary Range $29,037 to $51,508 to $105,000	

OVERVIEW

Intelligence officers are employed by the federal government to gather, analyze, and report information about the activities of domestic groups and the governments of foreign countries in order to protect the interests and security of the United States. Federal policy makers seek specific information, or strategic intelligence, on a variety of factors concerning foreign nations. These factors include political, economic, military, scientific and technical, geographic, and biographical data. The U.S. government then uses this intelligence, much of which is classified (secret), to help make decisions about its own military, economic, and political policies.

HISTORY

The concept of intelligence-gathering comes from ancient times. In a military treatise titled *Ping-fa* (*The Art of War*), written in about 400

B.C., the Chinese military philosopher Sun-Tzu mentions the use of secret agents and the importance of good intelligence. Knowledge of an enemy's strengths and weaknesses has always been important to a country's leaders, and so intelligence systems have been used for centuries.

Intelligence gathering has played a major role in contemporary military history. Both the British and the Americans used intelligence operatives during the Revolutionary War in an attempt to gain strategic advantage. The fledgling Continental Congress sent secret agents abroad in 1775, and Benedict Arnold will always be remembered as a spy who switched his allegiance from the colonists to the mother country. Some historians have suggested that World War I resulted from poor intelligence, since none of the countries involved had intended to go to war. With the rapid developments in technology that occurred in the early 20th century, especially in electronics and aeronautics, intelligence operations expanded in the decades after World War I. Operations escalated during World War II, when the U.S. Office of Strategic Services was in operation (1929–1945). The Central Intelligence Agency (CIA), established in 1947, developed out of this office. At that time, the U.S. government believed that espionage was necessary to combat the aggression of the Soviet Union. The CIA continued to expand its activities during the Cold War, when countries were, in essence, engaged in conflict, using intelligence agencies rather than armies.

Some CIA incidents have caused international embarrassment, such as when a Soviet missile shot down a U.S. spy plane that was flying over and photographing Soviet territory in 1960. A scandal involving illegal wiretaps of thousands of Americans who had opposed the Vietnam War caused the CIA to reduce its activities in the late 1970s, although it geared up again during the administration of President Ronald Reagan.

With the fall of Communism and the ending of the Cold War, the role of the CIA and intelligence officers changed. Emphasis is now placed on analyzing the constantly changing political and geographic situations in Eastern Europe, Asia, the Middle East, and other parts of the world. Intelligence officers are in demand to provide updated information and insight into how the political and economic circumstances of the world will affect the United States.

Today, the director of central intelligence advises the president and other policy makers and coordinates the activities of the entire national intelligence community. This community includes the CIA, the Defense Intelligence Agency (DIA), agencies from the military, the Department of State, the Department of Energy, the National Security Agency, the Federal Bureau of Investigation (FBI), the Department of Defense, and the Department of Homeland Security.

THE JOB
The goal of every intelligence service is to produce reports consisting of evaluated information and forecasts that political leaders can use in decision-making. Intelligence officers must first decide what information is needed, gather it efficiently, and then evaluate and analyze the information. Case officers stationed overseas are assigned to gather intelligence and then relay the information to analysts who interpret the data for their reports. Analysts' reports make predictions and forecasts about what is likely to happen in a foreign country. High-level managers review the reports and pass them along to clients, who may include the president of the United States. Specialized analysts include *technical analysts,* who may gather data from satellites, and *cryptographic technicians,* who are experts at coding, decoding, and sending secret messages.

Contrary to the impression given by spy movies such as the James Bond series, most intelligence is available from public sources, although some agents specialize in deciphering secret transmissions written in code. Intelligence is often misused as a synonym for espionage, which is only one means of collecting information. Ways of gathering information can be as simple and overt as reading a foreign newspaper, or as complicated and covert as eavesdropping on a telephone conversation. Sources of intelligence include foreign radio and television broadcasts, reports from diplomats and military attachés, public documents, interviews with tourists, air surveillance, and camera-loaded satellites. Aerial and space reconnaissance, electronic eavesdropping, and agent espionage are considered covert sources.

There are three categories of intelligence operations: strategic intelligence, tactical intelligence, and counterintelligence. *Strategic intelligence agents* keep track of world events, watch foreign leaders carefully, and study a foreign country's politics, economy, military status, and scientific advances. Political intelligence consists of determining which group holds power and looking at foreign policy, public opinion, and voting statistics. Economic factors include trade agreements, the gross national product, and possible famines, all of which can influence domestic and foreign policies. Military intelligence includes the types and number of weapons, troop deployment, and readiness for battle. Scientific and technological intelligence consists of noting recent discoveries and developments in electronics, nuclear physics, and chemical sciences. Geographic factors, such as border disputes, can affect economic and political decisions. Gathering biographical data on current government leaders and future candidates helps complete a country's political profile. Intelligence can be "hard" or "soft." "Hard" intelligence is quantifiable and verifiable—for example, military and technological information such as the number of active troops in North Korea. An example of "soft" intelligence would be attempting to predict who will be the next leader of Bolivia.

Tactical intelligence agents gather the same kind of information as described above, but they do so in combat areas or volatile political settings abroad, such as in a country about to undergo a military coup.

Counterintelligence agents are assigned to protect U.S. secrets, institutions, and intelligence activities from sabotage, and to identify and prevent enemy operations that would be harmful to the United States, its citizens, or its allies. Such enemy plots would include worldwide terrorism, drug trafficking, and the activities of extreme right-wing groups domestically and internationally.

Gathering information can be as routine as reading the local newspaper, or it can be an exciting or even dangerous job. Counterintelligence and tactical agents generally work undercover in secret operations. In less-developed countries, reporting is difficult because little statistical information is available. An officer might have to go into a mine, a refinery, or a wheat field to assess economic conditions. To be effective, an operative needs contacts and sources among government officials, politicians, businesspeople, newspaper reporters, importers, exporters, and ordinary citizens. Operatives often recruit foreign agents to supply intelligence about their native countries. They may also work undercover in a job or other occupation that provides a pretext for their being in a certain place or area.

The CIA and the DIA, both major employers of intelligence officers, gather political, economic, and military information about more than 150 foreign nations in order to protect national security. The director of the CIA reports directly to the president and to the National Security Council, while the head of the DIA reports to the Department of Defense. Congress reviews the activities of both agencies. The Senate and the House of Representatives each have a Committee on Intelligence that reviews CIA activities and approves the annual multibillion-dollar budget. However, many actions of the CIA are covert, and the role of the U.S. government is not acknowledged publicly until many years later. Examples include the overthrow of the Iranian prime minister in 1953 and of the Chilean government in 1973.

The DIA serves the military, but its officers are not military personnel. The DIA monitors foreign military affairs, weapons, and troops; tracks compliance with international arms agreements; answers questions about soldiers missing in action; and investigates the status of prisoners of war. It also keeps track of the activities of international terrorist organizations.

The Foreign Service, an arm of the State Department, employs men and women who represent the U.S. government through embassies and consulates to the governments of other nations all over the world. These Foreign Service officers keep the secretary of state informed about all aspects of the country in which they are stationed. Called "the eyes and ears" of the United States abroad, Foreign Service officers may be diplomats, consulates, or intelligence officers.

In the armed forces, communications and intelligence specialists serve as intelligence gatherers, interpreters, cryptologists, information analysts, and translators. Domestic intelligence activities usually fall under the command of the FBI or the Department of Homeland Security. In addition, the various intelligence agencies often coordinate their activities.

REQUIREMENTS
High School

If you are interested in becoming an intelligence officer, you can begin preparation in high school by taking courses in English, history, government, journalism, geography, social studies, and foreign languages. You should develop your writing and computer skills as well. Students with the highest grades have the best possibilities for finding employment as intelligence officers.

Postsecondary Training

You must earn at least a bachelor's degree to become an intelligence officer, and an advanced degree is desirable. Specialized skills are also needed for many intelligence roles. The ability to read and speak a foreign language is an asset, as is computer literacy. Intelligence officers must have excellent analytical as well as oral and written communication skills. An historian's skills are needed to analyze political, historical, cultural, and social institutions of other nations. An intelligence officer must examine the evolution of a country, analyzing how the trends and precedents of the past relate to current and future developments.

Other Requirements

Applicants must be U.S. citizens and at least 21 years old. High moral character, patriotism, discipline, and discretion are also essential. Because many officers are stationed abroad, they need to have the ability to adapt to changing living conditions and customs.

EXPLORING

Opportunities exist for paid and unpaid internships for college undergraduates and graduates at a number of agencies based in the Washington, D.C., area that deal with foreign and defense policy and other matters of interest to intelligence officers. The FBI, for example, runs the FBI Honors Internship Program during the summer.

The CIA runs a Student Trainee Program in Washington, D.C., which is open to "highly motivated undergraduates studying a wide variety of fields." Some of the undergraduate fields listed on the Student Trainee Program's website include engineering, computer science, mathematics, and finance. Students who are accepted to this program are expected to spend at least three semesters or four quarters on the job prior to graduation. You must apply six to nine months before you are available to work, and you must have at least a 3.0 grade point average. The CIA also has an internship program for students from many backgrounds, including political science and geography majors.

EMPLOYERS

Intelligence officers are federal employees and can work for any one of various agencies, such as the CIA, the FBI, the DIA, the military, and other organizations mentioned in this article.

STARTING OUT

Since intelligence officers work for the federal government, candidates usually must file a basic job application called Standard Form 171, which can be obtained from a local Federal Job Information Office. (One exception is the CIA, which has its own application process.) This form needs to be submitted together with an academic transcript. The applicant's qualifications are evaluated and given a numerical rating, placed on a register, and then submitted to the appropriate government office. Agencies generally seek the best students to fill intelligence positions, so high grades are essential. In addition, each intelligence agency recruits college graduates. Agencies send representatives to college campuses nationwide to interview interested students. Candidates must undergo a medical examination and a security check in addition to written and oral examinations. Those accepted into an agency generally receive one to two years of on-the-job training.

ADVANCEMENT

Extensive training programs are in place for entry-level personnel, and employees are encouraged to pursue specialized studies in foreign languages, engineering, or computer technology, for example. Entry-level employees generally are assigned to gather information. With experience and training, they can qualify as analysts. Advancement may include postings requiring more responsibility and assignments in foreign countries. Generally, officers advance according to a military schedule; they are promoted and given assignments according to the needs of the government. Further advancement leads to management positions, and all agencies aggressively follow an aggressive policy of advancement from within.

EARNINGS

Intelligence officers with bachelor's degrees generally start at levels equivalent to GS-7 to GS-11, which corresponded to a salary range of $29,037–$42,976 in 2003. Candidates with advanced degrees may start at the GS-12 level, which paid $51,508 in 2003. Those with an advanced degree in engineering or a physical science may be offered starting salaries of $55,000. Experience and additional qualifications, such as knowledge of a rare foreign language, bring higher salaries. Those in top management earn from $72,000 to $105,000 a year. Officers who work abroad receive free housing, special allowances, and other benefits. Those deployed in covert or hazardous situations also receive additional compensation. Overseas operatives and military intelligence personnel are generally allowed to retire earlier than civilian intelligence officers.

WORK ENVIRONMENT

Intelligence officers may find themselves in a laboratory, at a computer station, or in a jungle. Those working in counterintelligence and covert operations face danger on a daily basis. In addition to gathering information to protect the security of the United States, intelligence officers may be called upon to spy on the defenses of nations hostile to the United States or to prevent foreign spies from learning U.S. government secrets. They may work indoors or outdoors in a variety of climates and conditions. Many agents travel often, and travel may include everything from jet planes to small boats to traveling on foot. Most intelligence officers, however, are employed in offices in the Washington, D.C., area or other cities. Even those agents who are not working in the field generally work long and erratic hours to meet deadlines for filing reports, especially in times of crisis.

OUTLOOK

Intelligence operations are closely linked to the world political situation. In general, people with specialized skills or backgrounds in the languages and customs of certain countries will continue to be in high demand. In the past, more than half of all U.S. intelligence activities were focused on the Soviet Union. While the fall of Communism in Eastern Europe and in the former Soviet republics greatly reduced the number and intensity of intelligence operations in these countries, other parts of the world now demand more urgent attention from all agencies. For this reason, the outlook for intelligence jobs remains good, and new officers will be hired every year. The United States has become focused on terrorist activity, particularly from groups based in the Middle East, and remains concerned with the spread of nuclear, chemical, and biological weapons. As the number of countries with nuclear capabilities increases, and as economic, political, and technological changes worldwide become more frequent, strategic intelligence gathering becomes more and more important to governments all around the world. Increasingly, governments must be able to make decisions based on predictions beyond the foreseeable future. Intelligence has become one of the world's largest industries; in the United States alone, it is supported by a multibillion-dollar annual budget.

FOR MORE INFORMATION

In addition to sponsoring an annual award to a distinguished undergraduate student, the following organization also operates a placement service. For more information, contact

Association of Former Intelligence Officers
6723 Whittier Avenue, Suite 303A
McLean, VA 22101-4533

Tel: 703-790-0320
Email: afio@afio.com
http://www.afio.com

For career brochure, employment information, recruitment schedules, and other questions, contact
CIA Employment and Recruitment Center
PO Box 12727
Arlington, VA 22209-8727
Tel: 800-JOBS-CIA
http://www.odci.gov

The DIA accepts only employment-related correspondence at the following address (the telephone number given is a recorded job hotline)
Defense Intelligence Agency (DIA)
200 MacDill Boulevard
Civilian Personnel Division (DAH-2)
Washington, DC 20340-5100
Tel: 800-526-4629
http://www.dia.mil

For information on employment opportunities, contact
U.S. Department of State
Office of Recruitment, Examination and Employment
HR/REE, SA-1
2401 E Street, NW, 5th Floor Highrise
Washington, DC 20522-0151
Tel: 202-261-8888
http://www.state.gov

LAWYERS AND JUDGES

QUICK FACTS

School Subjects
English
Government
Speech

Personal Skills
Communication/ideas
Leadership/management

Work Environment
Primarily indoors
Primarily multiple locations

Minimum Education Level
Master's degree

Salary Range
$19,470 to $88,760 to
$1,000,000+

Certification or Licensing
Required by all states

Outlook
About as fast as the average
(lawyers)
More slowly than the
average (judges)

DOT
110 (lawyers), 111 (judges)

GOE
11.04.02 (lawyers),
11.04.01 (judges)

NOC
4112 (lawyers),
4111 (judges)

O*NET-SOC
23-1011.00 (lawyers),
23-1023.00 (judges)

OVERVIEW

Lawyers, or *attorneys,* serve in two ways in our legal system: as advocates and as advisers. As advocates, they represent the rights of their clients in trials and depositions or in front of administrative and government bodies. As advisers, attorneys counsel clients on how the law affects business or personal decisions, such as the purchase of property or the creation of a will. Lawyers represent individuals, businesses, and corporations. Approximately 681,000 lawyers work in the United States today, in various areas of the profession.

Judges are elected or appointed officials who preside over federal, state, county, and municipal courts. They apply the law to citizens and businesses and oversee court proceedings according to the established law. Judges also give new rulings on issues not previously decided. Over 43,000 judges work in all levels of the judiciary arm of the United States.

HISTORY

The tradition of governing people by laws has been established over centuries. Societies have built up systems of law that have been studied and drawn upon by later governments. The earliest known law is the Code of Hammurabi, developed about 1800 B.C. by the ruler of the Sumerians. Another early set of laws was the law of Moses, known as the Ten Commandments. Every set of laws, no matter when they were introduced, has been accompanied by the need for someone to explain those laws and help others live under them.

The great orators of ancient Greece and Rome set up schools for young boys to learn by apprenticeship the many skills involved in pleading a law case. Being an eloquent speaker was the greatest advantage. The legal profession has matured since those earlier times; a great deal of training and an extensive knowledge of legal matters are required of the modern lawyer and judge.

Much modern European law was organized and refined by legal experts assembled by Napoleon; their body of law was known as the Napoleonic Code. English colonists coming to America brought English common law, from which American laws have grown. In areas of the United States that were heavily settled by Spanish colonists, there are traces of Spanish law. As the population in the country grew, along with business, those who knew the law were in high demand. The two main kinds of law are *civil* and *criminal*, but many other specialty areas exist. When our country was young, most lawyers were general law practitioners—they knew and worked with all the laws for their clients' sakes. Today, there are many more lawyers who specialize in areas such as tax law, corporate law, and intellectual property law.

THE JOB

All lawyers may give legal advice and represent clients in court when necessary. No matter what their specialty, their job is to help clients know their rights under the law and then help them achieve these rights before a judge, jury, government agency, or other legal forum, such as an arbitration panel. Lawyers may represent businesses and individuals. For businesses, they manage tax matters, arrange for stock to be issued, handle claims cases, represent the firm in real estate dealings, and advise on all legal matters. For individuals they may be trustees, guardians, or executors; they may draw up wills or contracts or advise on income taxes or on the purchase or sale of a home. Some work solely in the courts; others carry on most of their business outside of court, doing such tasks as drawing up mortgages, deeds, contracts, and other legal documents or by handling the background work necessary for court cases, which might include researching cases in a law library or interviewing witnesses. A number of lawyers work to establish and enforce laws for the federal and state governments by drafting legislation, representing the government in court, or serving as judges.

Lawyers can also take positions as professors in law schools. Administrators, research workers, and writers are also important to the profession. Administrative positions in business or government may be of a nonlegal nature, but the qualities, background, and experience of a lawyer are often helpful in such positions.

Other individuals with legal training may choose not to practice but instead opt for careers in which their background and knowledge of law are important. These careers include tax collectors, credit investigators, FBI agents, insurance adjusters, process servers, and probation officers.

Some of the specialized fields for lawyers include the following:

Civil lawyers work in a field also known as private law. They focus on damage suits and breach-of-contract suits; prepare and draw up deeds, leases, wills, mortgages, and contracts; and act as trustees, guardians, or executors of an estate when necessary.

Criminal lawyers, also known as *defense lawyers,* specialize in cases dealing with offenses committed against society or the state, such as theft, murder, or arson. They interview clients and witnesses to ascertain facts in a case, correlate their findings with known cases, and prepare a case to defend a client against the charges made. They conduct a defense at the trial, examine witnesses, and summarize the case with a closing argument to a jury.

District attorneys, also known as *prosecuting attorneys,* represent the city, county, state, or federal government in court proceedings. They gather and analyze evidence and review legal material relevant to a lawsuit. Then they present their case to the grand jury, which decides whether the evidence is sufficient for an indictment. If it is not, the suit is dismissed and there is no trial. If the grand jury decides to indict the accused, however, the case goes to court, where the district attorney appears before the judge and jury to present evidence against the defendant.

Probate lawyers specialize in planning and settling estates. They draw up wills, deeds of trust, and similar documents for clients who want to plan the distribution of their belongings among their heirs when they die. Upon a client's death, probate lawyers vouch for the validity of the will and represent the executors and administrators of the estate.

Bankruptcy attorneys assist their clients, both individuals and corporations, in obtaining protection from creditors under existing bankruptcy laws and with financial reorganization and debt repayment.

Corporation lawyers advise corporations concerning their legal rights, obligations, or privileges. They study constitutions, statutes, previous decisions, ordinances, and decisions of quasi-judicial bodies that are applicable to corporations. They advise corporations on the pros and cons of prosecuting or defending a lawsuit. They act as agent of the corporation in various transactions and seek to keep clients from expensive litigation.

Maritime lawyers, sometimes referred to as *admiralty lawyers,* specialize in laws regulating commerce and navigation on the high seas and any navigable waters, including inland lakes and rivers. Although there is a general maritime law, it operates in each country according to that country's courts, laws, and customs. Maritime law covers contracts, insurance, property damage, and personal injuries.

Intellectual property lawyers focus on helping their clients with patents, trademarks, and copyright protection. *Patent lawyers* are intellectual property lawyers who specialize in securing patents for inventors from the United States Patent Office and prosecuting or defending suits of patent infringements. They prepare detailed specifications for the patent, may organize a corporation, or advise an existing corporation to commercialize on a patent. Biotechnology patent law is a further specialization of patent law. *Biotechnology patent lawyers* specialize in helping biotechnology researchers, scientists, and research corporations with all legal aspects of their biotechnology patents.

Elder law attorneys are lawyers who specialize in providing legal services for the elderly and, in some cases, the disabled.

Tax attorneys handle cases resulting from problems of inheritance, income tax, estate tax, franchises, and real estate tax, among other things.

Insurance attorneys advise insurance companies about legal matters pertaining to insurance transactions. They approve the wording of insurance policies, review the legality of claims against the company, and draw up legal documents.

An *international lawyer* specializes in the body of rules that are observed by nations in their relations with one another. Some of these laws have been agreed to in treaties, some have evolved from long-standing customs and traditions.

Securities and exchange lawyers monitor the activities of individuals and corporations involved in trading and oversee to make sure they comply with applicable laws. When corporations undergo takeovers and mergers, securities and exchange lawyers are there to represent the corporations' interests and fulfill all legal obligations involved in the transaction.

Real estate lawyers handle the transfer of property and perform such duties as searching public records and deeds to establish titles of property, holding funds for investment in escrow accounts, and acting as trustees of property. They draw up legal documents and act as agents in various real estate transactions.

Title attorneys deal with titles, leases, contracts, and other legal documents pertaining to the ownership of land, and gas, oil, and mineral rights. They prepare documents to cover the purchase or sale of such property and rights, examine documents to determine ownership, advise organizations about legal requirements concerning titles, and participate in the trial or lawsuits in connection with titles.

It is important to note that once you are licensed to practice law, you are legally qualified to practice any one or more of these and many other specialties. Some *general practitioners* handle both criminal and civil matters of all sorts. To become licensed, you must be admitted to the bar of that state. *Bar examiners* test the qualifications of applicants. They prepare and administer written exams covering legal subjects, examine candidates orally, and recommend admission of those who meet the prescribed standards.

Lawyers become judges by either election or appointment, and preside over federal, state, county, or municipal courts. Judges administer court procedures during trials and hearings and establish new rules on questions where standard procedures have not previously been set. They read or listen to claims made by parties involved in civil suits and make decisions based on facts, applicable statutes, and prior court decisions. They examine evidence in criminal cases to see if it supports the charges. Judges listen to the presentation of cases, rule on the admission of evidence and testimony, and settle disputes between attorneys. They instruct juries on their duties and advise them of laws that apply to the case. They sentence defendants found guilty of criminal charges and decide who is responsible in nonjury civil cases. Besides their work in the courtroom, judges also research legal matters, study prior rulings, write opinions, and keep abreast of legislation that may affect their rulings.

Some judges have other titles such as *magistrate* or *justice* and preside over a limited jurisdiction. Magistrates hear civil cases in which damages do not exceed a prescribed maximum, as well as minor misdemeanor cases that do not involve penitentiary sentences or fines that exceed a certain specified amount.

REQUIREMENTS
High School
A high school diploma, a college degree, and three years of law school are minimum requirements for a law degree. A high school diploma is a first step on the ladder of education that a lawyer must climb. If you are considering a career in law, courses such as government, history, social studies, and economics provide a solid background for entering college-level courses. Speech courses are also helpful to build strong communication skills necessary for the profession. Also take advantage of any computer-related classes or experience you can get, because lawyers and judges often use technology to research and interpret the law, from surfing the Internet to searching legal databases.

Postsecondary Training
To enter any law school approved by the American Bar Association, you must satisfactorily complete at least three, and usually four, years of college work. Most law schools do not specify any particular courses for prelaw education. Usually a liberal arts track is most advisable, with courses in English, history, economics, social sciences, logic, and public speaking. A college student planning on specialization in a particular area of law, however, might also take courses significantly related to that area, such as economics, agriculture, or political science. Those interested should write to several law schools to learn more about any requirements and to see if they will accept credits from the college the student is planning to attend.

Currently, over 185 law schools in the United States are approved by the American Bar Association; others, many of them night schools, are approved by state authorities only. Most of the approved law schools, however, do have night sessions to accommodate part-time students. Part-time courses of study usually take four years.

Law school training consists of required courses such as legal writing and research, contracts, criminal law, constitutional law, torts, and property. The second and third years may be devoted to specialized courses of interest to the student, such as evidence, business transactions and corporations, or admiralty. The study of cases and decisions is of basic importance to the law student, who will be required to read and study thousands of these cases. A degree of juris doctor (J.D.) or bachelor of laws (LL.B.) is usually granted upon graduation. Some law students considering specialization, research, or teaching may go on for advanced study.

Most law schools require that applicants take the Law School Admission Test (LSAT), where prospective law students are tested on their critical thinking, writing, and reasoning abilities.

Certification or Licensing

Every state requires that lawyers be admitted to the bar of that state before they can practice. They require that applicants graduate from an approved law school and that they pass a written examination in the state in which they intend to practice. In a few states, graduates of law schools within the state are excused from these written examinations. After lawyers have been admitted to the bar in one state, they can practice in another state without taking a written examination if the states have reciprocity agreements; however, they will be required to meet certain state standards of good character and legal experience and pay any applicable fees.

Other Requirements

Federal courts and agencies have their own rules regulating admission to practice. Other requirements vary among the states. For example, the states of Vermont, New York, Washington, Virginia, California, Maine, and Wyoming allow a person who has spent several years reading law in a law office but has no college training or who has a combination of reading and law school experience to take the state bar examination. Few people now enter law practice in this manner.

A few states accept the study of law by correspondence. Some states require that newly graduated lawyers serve a period of clerkship in an established law firm before they are eligible to take the bar examination.

Almost all judges appointed or elected to any court must be lawyers and members of the bar, usually with many years of experience.

Both lawyers and judges have to be effective communicators, work well with people, and be able to find creative solutions to problems, such as complex court cases.

EXPLORING

There are several ways in which you can learn more about a legal career. First, sit in on a trial or two at your local or state courthouse. Try to focus mainly on the judge and the lawyer and take note of what they do. Write down questions you have and terms or actions you don't understand. Then, talk to your guidance counselor and ask for help in setting up a telephone or in-person interview with a judge or lawyer. Prepare a list of questions before your conversation to help focus your thoughts. Also, talk to your guidance counselor or political science teacher about starting or joining a shadowing program. Shadowing programs allow you to follow a person in a certain career around for a day or two to get an idea of what goes on in a typical day. You may even be invited to help out with a few minor duties.

You can also search the World Wide Web for general information about lawyers and judges and current court cases. Read court transcripts and summary opinions written by judges on issues of importance today. After you've done some research and talked to a lawyer or judge and you still think you are destined for law school, try to get a part-time job in a law office. Ask your guidance counselor for help.

If you are already in law school, you might consider becoming a student member of the American Library Association. Student members receive *Student Lawyer,* a magazine that contains useful information for aspiring lawyers. Sample articles from the magazine can be read at http://www.abanet.org/lsd/stulawyer.

EMPLOYERS

About 75 percent of practicing lawyers in the United States work in private practice, either in law firms or alone. The others are employed in government, often at the local level. Lawyers working for the federal government hold positions in the Departments of Justice, Treasury, and Defense. Lawyers also hold positions as house counsel for public utilities, transportation companies, banks, insurance companies, real estate agencies, manufacturing firms, welfare and religious organizations, and other businesses and nonprofit organizations.

Judges and magistrates work for federal, state, and local levels of government.

STARTING OUT

The first steps in entering the law profession are graduation from an approved law school and passing a state bar examination. Usually beginning lawyers do not go into solo practice right away. It is often difficult to become established, and additional experience is helpful to the beginning lawyer. Also, most lawyers do not specialize in a particular branch of law without first gaining experience. Beginning lawyers usually work as assistants to experienced lawyers. At first they do mainly research and routine work. After a few years of successful experience, they may be ready to go out on their own. Other choices open to the beginning lawyer include joining an established law firm or entering into partnership with another lawyer. Positions are also available with banks, business corporations, insurance companies, private utilities, and with a number of government agencies at different levels.

Many new lawyers are recruited directly from law school. Recruiters from law firms and other organizations come to the school and interview possible hires. Other new graduates can get job leads from local and state bar associations.

ADVANCEMENT

Lawyers with outstanding ability can expect to go a long way in their profession. Novice lawyers generally start as law clerks, but as they prove themselves and develop their abilities, many opportunities for advancement will arise. They may be promoted to junior partner in a law firm or establish their own practice. Lawyers may enter politics and become judges, mayors, congressmen, or other government leaders. Top positions are also available in business for the qualified lawyer. Lawyers working for the federal government advance according to the civil service system. Judges usually advance from lower courts to higher courts either in terms of the matters that are decided or in terms of the level—local, state, or federal.

EARNINGS

Incomes generally increase as the lawyer gains experience and becomes better known in the field. The beginning lawyer in solo practice may barely make ends meet for the first few years. According to the National Association for Law Placement, 2002 median salaries for new lawyers ranged from $53,500 for lawyers employed by firms of two to 25 attorneys to $118,000 for lawyers employed by firms of 501 or more attorneys. Those working for the government made approximately $40,000. Starting salaries for lawyers in business were $60,000. Recent graduates entering private practice made the most, earning approximately $80,000.

Experienced lawyers earn salaries that vary depending on the type, size, and location of their employers. According to the U.S. Department of Labor, the 2001 median salary for practicing lawyers was $88,760, although some senior partners earned well over $1 million a year. Ten percent earned less than $43,000. General attorneys in the federal government received $87,080 in 2000. State and local government attorneys generally made less, earning $64,190 and $66,280, respectively, in 2000.

Judges earned median annual salaries of $87,260 in 2001, according to the U.S. Department of Labor. Salaries ranged from less than $19,470 to more than $139,130.

According to the Administrative Office of the U.S. Courts, federal district court judges earned an average of $145,100 in 2001. The chief justice of the United States earned $198,600, while associate justices of the Supreme Court earned $190,100 in 2002. A survey conducted by the National Center for State Courts reports the 2002 salary average for judges in the states' highest courts was $125,485. At the state level, judges serving in intermediate appellate courts averaged $116,064, and in general jurisdiction trial courts they earned an average of $109,811.

WORK ENVIRONMENT

Offices and courtrooms are usually pleasant, although busy, places to work. Lawyers also spend significant amounts of time in law libraries or record rooms, in the homes and offices of clients, and sometimes in the jail cells of clients or prospective witnesses. Many lawyers never work in a courtroom. Unless they are directly involved in litigation, they may never perform at a trial.

Some courts, such as small claims, family, or surrogate, may have evening hours to provide flexibility to the community. Criminal arraignments may be held at any time of the day or night. Court hours for most lawyers and judges are usually regular business hours, with a one-hour lunch break. Often lawyers have to work long hours, spending evenings and weekends preparing cases and materials and working with clients. In addition to the work, the lawyer must always keep up with the latest developments in the profession. Also, it takes a long time to become a qualified lawyer, and it may be difficult to earn an adequate living until the lawyer gets enough experience to develop an established private practice.

Lawyers who are employed at law firms must often work grueling hours to advance in the firm. Spending long weekend hours doing research and interviewing people should be expected.

OUTLOOK

According to the *Occupational Outlook Handbook*, employment for lawyers is expected to grow about as fast as the average through the next decade, but record numbers of law school graduates have created strong competition for jobs, even though the number of graduates has begun to level off. Continued population growth, typical business activities, and increased numbers of legal cases involving health care, environmental, intellectual property, international law, elder law, and sexual harassment issues, among others, will create a steady demand for lawyers. Law services will be more accessible to the middle-income public with the popularity of prepaid legal services and clinics. However, stiff competition has and will continue to urge lawyers to look elsewhere for jobs, in administrative, managerial, and business positions, where legal training is useful.

The top 10 percent of the graduating seniors of the country's best law schools will have more opportunities with well-known law firms and on legal staffs of corporations, in government agencies, and in law schools in the next few decades. Lawyers in solo practice will find it hard to earn a living until their practice is fully established. The best opportunities exist in small towns or suburbs of large cities, where there is less competition and new lawyers can meet potential clients more easily.

Graduates with lower class standings and from lesser known schools may have difficulty in obtaining the most desirable positions. Banks, insurance companies, real estate firms, government agencies, and other organizations often hire law graduates. Legal positions in the armed forces are also available.

Employment of judges is expected to grow more slowly than the average through the next decade. Judges who retire, however, will need to be replaced. There may be an increase in judges in cities with large population growth, but competition will be high for any openings.

FOR MORE INFORMATION

For information about law student services offered by the ABA, contact
American Bar Association (ABA)
Service Center
541 North Fairbanks Court
Chicago, IL 60611
Tel: 312-988-5522
Email: abasvcctr@abanet.org
http://www.abanet.org

For information on workshops and seminars, contact
Association of American Law Schools
1201 Connecticut Avenue, NW, Suite 800
Washington, DC 20036-2605
Tel: 202-296-8851
Email: aals@aals.org
http://www.aals.org

The FBA provides information for lawyers and judges involved in federal practice.
Federal Bar Association (FBA)
Student Services
2215 M Street, NW
Washington, DC 20037
Tel: 202-785-1614
Email: fba@fedbar.org
http://fedbar.org

For information on choosing a law school, law careers, salaries, and alternative law careers, contact
National Association for Law Placement
1025 Connecticut Avenue, NW, Suite 1110
Washington, DC 20036-5413
Tel: 202-835-1001
Email: info@nalp.org
http://www.nalp.org

LIBRARIANS

QUICK FACTS

School Subjects Computer science English	**Certification or Licensing** Required by certain states
Personal Skills Helping/teaching Leadership/management	**Outlook** About as fast as the average **DOT** 100
Work Environment Primarily indoors Primarily one location	**GOE** 11.02.04
Minimum Education Level Master's degree	**NOC** 5111
Salary Range $24,730 to $42,670 to $75,714+	**O*NET-SOC** 25-4021.00

OVERVIEW

As prominent professionals in the information services field, *librarians* help others find information and select materials best suited to their needs. Librarians work in public, academic, and special libraries; school library media centers; corporations, and government agencies. They are key personnel wherever books, magazines, audiovisual materials, and a variety of other informational materials are cataloged and kept. Librarians help make access to these reference materials possible. Approximately 149,000 librarians are employed in positions throughout the country.

HISTORY

Libraries were available only to the elite until the Middle Ages, when many private institutions were destroyed by wars. The preservation of many ancient library materials can be attributed to orders of monks who diligently copied ancient Greek and Roman texts, as well as the Bible and other religious texts, and protected materials in their monasteries. The invention of the printing press in the 15th century allowed books to be made more quickly and disseminated more widely. Books went from palaces and churches to the homes of the common people.

In 1638, John Harvard left his private collection of books to the Massachusetts Bay Colony's new college, which was later named for him; this collection became the foundation for the first library in the United States. In the 18th century, Benjamin Franklin initiated the idea of a library from which books could be borrowed. From these beginnings, thousands of public, private, and special libraries have grown, as has the need for trained professionals to manage the collections. The idea of a lending library brought librarians into a more public arena; they were no longer just the keepers of knowledge, but also the professionals who made information available to everyone.

Although the education and certification processes have changed drastically, the field of librarianship has been around for centuries. Long before formal courses of study were developed for the training of librarians, church and government leaders appointed educated, organized individuals to collect informational materials and store them in a manner that would enable materials to be found when needed. In the mid-1600s, Gabriel Naude wrote a practical guide on how to establish a library, offering advice on organizing and using collections of informational materials.

Over the years the duties of librarians have evolved along with the development of different kinds of libraries and the development of new technologies. In recent years libraries have expanded services and now distribute films, records and compact discs, digital video discs (DVDs), audio- and videotapes, Braille books, and talking books. A wealth of information is available through multimedia CD-ROMs, computer database vendors, and the Internet. Librarians are charged with effectively and efficiently utilizing—and teaching the public how to utilize—the information available to them.

THE JOB

Librarians perform a number of tasks depending on their specialties. Some librarians may focus entirely on user services while others are concerned with technical or administrative services. Depending on the needs of their departments or institutions, librarians may perform a combination of these tasks, or take care of even more specific duties within their specialty. Some specific types of librarians in each category are noted in the following paragraphs, but this is not an exhaustive list. If one of these areas interests you, be sure to contact a library school for information about additional opportunities.

The librarian working in user services helps patrons find materials and use resources effectively. This type of librarian must be thoroughly acquainted with all materials in the library, from card and online catalogs to reference books. *Reference librarians* advise users and help them find information they are seeking in encyclopedias, almanacs, reference books, computerized information databases, or other sources. They also have access to special materials that may be filed in areas not open to the public or kept off-site.

Often librarians in user services may choose to work with a special age group. *Children's librarians* help children select books, teach them about the library, and conduct story hours. *Young-adult librarians* perform similar services for junior and senior high school students. Instead of story hours, however, they plan programs of interest to young adults, such as creative writing workshops, film discussion groups, music concerts, or photography classes. *Adult services librarians* work with the adult population. They may help conduct education programs in community development, creative arts, public affairs, problems of the aging, and home and family.

Law librarians are professionally trained librarians who work in legal settings such as private law firms, government libraries, and law schools.

Medical librarians, also known as *information specialists,* help manage health information. They are employed in libraries or information centers in hospitals and other medical facilities, public libraries, government agencies, research centers, colleges and universities, and pharmaceutical, publishing, biotechnology, and insurance companies.

Music librarians perform many of the same duties as traditional librarians, but specialize in managing materials related to music. They are employed at large research libraries; colleges, universities, and conservatories; public libraries; radio and television stations; and musical societies and foundations. They also work for professional bands or orchestras and music publishing companies.

Library media specialists work with young people in school settings. They select materials useful to students in their class work, teach them to use the library media center effectively, help them with assignments, and work with teachers on research. Also known as *audiovisual librarians,* library media specialists (who must also be certified as teachers) select and maintain films, videotapes, slides, prints, records, cassettes, DVDs, compact discs, and other nonbook materials and supervise the purchase and maintenance of the equipment needed to use these materials.

Community outreach librarians or *bookmobile librarians* bring library services to outlying areas or to special communities such as nursing homes or inner-city housing projects. These librarians bring resources to communities that do not have easy access to library services.

The technical tasks of the librarian may include ordering, cataloging, and classifying materials according to the Dewey Decimal, Library of Congress, or other system, and librarians involved with these technical services might not deal with the public at all. These librarians select and order all books, periodicals, audiovisual materials, and other items for the library; this entails evaluating newly published materials as well as seeking out older ones. Many libraries now have added records, audio- and videotapes, compact discs, DVDs, films, filmstrips, slides, maps, art pieces, and photographs to their loan services. The selection and purchase of these is also the responsibility of the librarian. The librarian, therefore, considerably influences the quality and extent of a library collection.

All new additions to the library must be cataloged by title, author, and subject in either card or computerized catalog files. Labels and card pockets must be placed on the items, and they must then be properly shelved. Books and other materials must be kept in good condition and, when necessary, repaired or replaced. Librarians are also charged with purchasing, maintaining, and evaluating the circulation system. Considerable technical knowledge of computer systems may be necessary in deciding upon the extent and scope of the proper circulation for the library. The actual process of circulating books, such as stamping due dates, collecting fines, and tracking down overdue materials, however, is usually handled by nonprofessional library staff such as work-study students, part-time employees, or library technicians.

Acquisitions librarians choose and buy books and other media for the library. They must read product catalogs and reviews of new materials as part of the acquisitions decision process. They do not work with the public, but deal with publishers and wholesalers of new books, booksellers of out-of-print books, and distributors of audiovisual materials. When the ordered materials arrive, *catalog librarians*, with the aid of *classifiers*, classify the items by subject matter, assign classification numbers, and prepare cards or computer records to help users locate the materials. Since many libraries have computerized the acquisitions and cataloging functions, it is now possible for the user to retrieve materials faster. Many automated libraries are phasing out bulky card catalogs and providing users with small computer terminals instead.

Bibliographers usually work in research libraries, compiling lists of books, periodicals, articles, and audiovisual materials on selected topics. They also recommend the purchase of new materials in their special fields. *Information scientists,* or *technical librarians,* are specialists trained in computer sciences. More and more libraries today are tied into remote computer databases through their computer terminals, making it unnecessary for a library to house all the materials users may request. Information scientists design systems for storing and retrieving information. They also develop procedures for collecting, organizing, interpreting, and classifying information.

Circulation librarians, with the help of clerical workers and stack attendants, manage the records of books and materials that are borrowed and returned and make sure that the materials are returned to the appropriate place in the library. *Conservation librarians* are charged with protecting and lengthening the life of the library collection. These librarians plan for the future, preparing for circumstances that might threaten the collections.

Administrative services librarians watch over the management of all areas of the library. They supervise library personnel and prepare budgets. They are also responsible for public relations and represent the library within its community as well as in such policy-making organizations as state or national library associations. Ultimately, administrators make sure that the library is constantly cultivating and expanding its resources to best serve the needs of its community.

The *library director* is at the head of a typical library organizational scheme. This individual sets library policies and plans and administers programs of library services, usually under the guidance of a governing body, such as a board of directors or board of trustees. Library directors have overall responsibility for the operation of a library system. Among their many duties, they coordinate the activities of the *chief librarians,* who supervise branch libraries or individual departments, such as the circulation, general reference, or music departments; periodical reading room; or readers' advisory service. In a large public library a chief librarian supervises a staff of assistant librarians and division heads while administering and coordinating the functions of the library.

The *assistant librarians* often consult with (and report to) the chief librarian or library director regarding policy decisions for their area. They also train, schedule, and supervise *library technicians,* sometimes called *library assistants*. Library technicians work in all areas of library services. They assist patrons in the library or on the telephone, and they provide information on library services, facilities, and rules. They also catalog materials, prepare orders of materials and books, maintain files, work on checkouts, and perform many other varieties of jobs within specialized areas such as audiovisual or data processing.

REQUIREMENTS
High School

If you are interested in becoming a librarian, be sure to take a full college preparatory course load. Focus on classes in history, English, speech, and foreign languages if you are going into user services. If you plan on working in a special library, take classes related to that specialty. For instance, if science is your interest, take courses such as anatomy, biology, chemistry, and physics. Learning how to use a computer and conduct basic research in a library is essential. Developing these skills will not only aid in your future library work, but will also help you in college and in any other career options you might pursue.

Postsecondary Training

Consider enrolling in a liberal arts college to get a broad educational background, since librarians should be familiar with numerous subject areas. While an undergraduate, you can begin considering what area of librarianship you wish to pursue, and focus on those courses. Many library schools don't require specific undergraduate courses for acceptance, but a good academic record and reading knowledge of at least one foreign language is usually required. You should also consider taking classes that strengthen your skills in communications, writing, research methods, collection organization, and customer service, as well as maintenance and conservation. More than half of the accredited library schools do not require any introductory courses in library science while an undergraduate. It would be wise, though, to check with schools for specific requirements.

Upon receiving your bachelor's degree, you will need to earn a master's degree to become a librarian. The degree is generally known as the master of library science (MLS), but in some institutions it may be referred to by a different title, such as the master of library and information science (MLIS). You should plan to attend a graduate school of library and information science that is accredited by the American Library Association (ALA). Currently, there are over 55 ALA-accredited programs. Some libraries do not consider job applicants who attended a nonaccredited school.

During the year of graduate study, you will take courses in reference work, cataloging, classification, computers, library organizations, and administration. Other courses focus on the history of books and printing and on issues of censorship and intellectual freedom. Information scientists focus on courses in computer sciences, mathematics, and systems analysis. Many library schools have work-study programs where students take classes while gaining practical experience in a library.

Specialized librarians, such as law, pharmaceutical, or geology librarians, must have a very strong background in the subject in which they wish to work. Most have a degree in their subject specialization in addition to their MLS. In some cases, a graduate or professional degree in the subject is especially attractive to prospective employers. For work in research libraries, university libraries, or special collections, a doctorate may be required. A doctorate is commonly required for the top administrative posts of these types of libraries, as well as for faculty positions in graduate schools of library science.

Certification or Licensing

In many states, school librarians, also referred to as library media specialists, are required to earn teacher's certification in addition to preparation as a librarian. They may also be required to earn a master's degree in education. Various state, county, and local governments have set up other requirements for education and certification. You should contact the school board in the area in which you are interested in working for specific requirements. Your public library system should also have that information readily available.

The ALA is currently developing a voluntary certification program to recognize individuals who have demonstrated knowledge and skills in library science and promote professional development.

Other Requirements

Librarians are often expected to take part in community affairs, cooperating in the preparation of exhibits, presenting book reviews, and explaining library use to community organizations. You will need to be a leader in developing the cultural tastes of the library patrons. Librarians who deal with the public should have strong interpersonal skills, tact, and patience. An imaginative, highly motivated, and resourceful personality is very valuable. An affinity for problem solving is another desirable quality. Library specialists, too, must have particular personal qualifications; for example, young-adult librarians must have a real liking for teenagers, and bookmobile librarians should feel comfortable traveling to outlying areas and dealing with all sorts of people.

Librarians involved with technical services should be detail-oriented, have good planning skills, and be able to think analytically. All librarians should have a love for information and be willing to master the techniques for obtaining and presenting knowledge. They must also be prepared to master constantly changing technology.

EXPLORING

There are several ways you can explore the field of librarianship. First of all, high school students have their own personal experiences with the library: reading, doing research for class projects, or just browsing. If this experience sparks an interest in library work, you can talk with a school or community librarian whose own experiences in the field can provide a good idea of what goes on behind the scenes. Some schools may have library clubs you can join to learn about library work. If one doesn't exist, you could consider starting your own library club.

Once you know you are interested in library work, you might be able to work as an assistant in the school library media center or find part-time work in a local public library. Such volunteer or paid positions may provide you experience checking materials in and out at the circulation desk, shelving returned books, or typing title, subject, and author information on cards or in computer records. In college, you might be able to work as a technical or clerical assistant in one of your school's academic libraries.

Contact the American Library Association or another professional organization to inquire about student memberships. Most groups offer excellent mentoring opportunities as well. Finally, if you have an email account, sign up for one or more of the listservs offered by these groups. A listserv is an email list of professionals throughout the world who consult each other on special topics. ALA members monitor a number of listservs for members and nonmembers. By subscribing to a listserv, you can discover what matters concern professional librarians today. Before you post your own comment or query, however, be sure you know the rules and regulations created by the list's moderator and always be respectful of others.

EMPLOYERS

All types of libraries need library professionals. Public libraries, school libraries, library media centers, college or university libraries, research libraries, and other special libraries all employ librarians. Private industry and government departments have libraries that need staffing. Librarians also work outside of the traditional library setting.

A librarian can work for a small branch office of a major library, or in a large library that services many counties. A librarian in a smaller library may have duties in all areas of librarianship: ordering, cataloging, shelving, and circulating materials, as well as acting as reference librarian. On the other hand, a librarian at a larger institution has a more specialized venue, such as a history section or map room.

Many universities have multiple libraries that serve different groups of people. The University of Chicago library system, for example, has a separate law library, a general reading collection library, a humanities and social sciences repository, a social services administration division, and four science libraries. Librarians at such an institution might work in administration overseeing the branches of the entire system, or may deal with operations in one of the satellite areas.

Businesses and organizations also employ library professionals. Special librarians manage libraries for businesses, nonprofit corporations, and government agencies. The materials collected usually pertain to subjects of particular interest to the organization. *Institution librarians* plan and direct library programs for residents and staff of institutions such as prisons, hospitals, and other extended-care facilities.

As the field of library and information services grows, librarians can find more work outside of the traditional library setting. Experienced information scientists may advise libraries or other agencies on information systems, library renovation projects, or other information-based issues. In addition, librarians act as *trainers* and *service representatives* for online database vendors, helping users use the information from online services.

STARTING OUT

Generally, librarians must complete all educational requirements before applying for a job. In some cases part-time work experience while in graduate school may turn into a full-time position upon graduation. Some employers, too, may allow an especially promising applicant to begin learning on the job before the library degree is conferred.

Upon graduating, new librarians should consult the placement offices at their school. Employers seeking new graduates often recruit through library schools. Most professional library and information science organizations have job listings that candidates can consult. Also, many online job search engines can help librarians find an appropriate position. Newspaper classifieds may be of some help in locating a job, although other approaches may be more appropriate to the profession.

Many librarians entering the workforce today are combining their experience in another career with graduate library and information science education. For example, a music teacher who plays trumpet in a band could mix her part-time teaching experience and her hobby with a degree in library science to begin a full-time career as a music librarian. Almost any background can be used to advantage when entering the field of librarianship.

Since school library media specialists work in grammar schools and high schools, they must apply directly to school boards. Individuals interested in working in library positions for the federal government can contact the human resources department—or consult the website of the government agency where they are interested in working; for these government positions, applicants must take a civil service examination. Public libraries, too, are often under a civil service system of appointment.

ADVANCEMENT

The beginning librarian may gain experience by taking a job as an assistant. He or she can learn a lot from practical experience before attempting to manage a department or entire library. A librarian may advance to positions with greater levels of responsibility within the same library system, or a librarian may gain initial experience in a small library and then advance by transferring to a larger or more specialized library. Within a large library, promotions to higher positions are possible, for example, to the supervision of a department. Experienced librarians with the necessary qualifications may advance to positions in library administration. A doctorate is desirable for reaching top administrative levels, as well as for taking a graduate library school faculty position.

Experienced librarians, in particular those with strong administrative, computer, or planning backgrounds, may move into the area of information consulting. They use their expertise to advise libraries and other organizations on issues regarding information services.

Other experienced librarians, especially those with computer experience, may also go into specialized areas of library work, becoming increasingly valuable to business and industry, as well as other fields.

EARNINGS

Salaries depend on such factors as the location, size, and type of library, the amount of experience the librarian has, and the responsibilities of the position. According to the U.S. Department of Labor, median annual earnings of librarians in 2001 were $42,670. Salaries ranged from less than $24,730 to more than $65,240. Librarians working in elementary and secondary school earned $43,320 in 2000 and those in colleges and universities earned about $43,050. Librarians employed in local government earned $38,370 in 2000. In the federal government, the average salary for all librarians was about $63,651 in 2001.

The American Library Association's Survey of Librarian Salaries reports the following mean salaries for librarians and managers in 2002: library directors, $75,714; deputy/associate/assistant directors, $62,847; managers/supervisors of support staff, $44,549; librarians who do not supervise, $44,279; and beginning librarians, $35,051.

According to the Medical Library Association, the average starting salary (less than two years of experience) for medical librarians was $40,080 in 2001. The overall average salary for medical librarians was $49,955 in 2001.

Most librarians receive a full benefits package, which may include paid vacation time, holiday pay, compensated sick leave, various insurance plans, and retirement savings programs. Librarians who work in a college or university library may receive tuition waivers in order to earn advanced degrees in their field. Grade school or high school librarians may have shorter workdays or workweeks while school is out of session.

WORK ENVIRONMENT

Most libraries are pleasant and comfortable places in which to assist those doing research, studying, or reading for pleasure. Librarian must do a considerable amount of reading to keep informed in order to serve library patrons. They must also strive to stay abreast of constantly changing technology, which may seem overwhelming at times.

Some librarians, such as reference or special librarians, may find the work demanding and stressful when they deal with users who are working under deadline pressure. Librarians working in technical services may suffer eyestrain and headaches from working long hours in front of a computer screen.

On the average, librarians work between 35 and 40 hours per week. Since most libraries are open evenings and weekends to accommodate the schedules of their users, many librarians will have a nontraditional work schedule, working, for instance, from 11:00 A.M. to 9:00 P.M., or taking Monday and Tuesday as a weekend in lieu of Saturday and Sunday. Library media specialists usually work the same hours and have the same vacation schedule as teachers in the school system. Librarians working for the government or as special librarians usually work a 40-hour week during normal business hours. However, more and more librarians are finding it difficult to find full-time positions and are working in part-time positions instead.

There is, of course, some routine in library work, but the trend is to place clerical duties in the hands of library technicians and library assistants, freeing the professional librarian for administrative, research, personnel, and community services. For the most part, librarians tend to find the work intellectually stimulating, challenging, and dynamic. The knowledge that one is providing so many valuable services to the community can be extremely rewarding.

OUTLOOK

The American Library Association (ALA) predicts a serious shortage of librarians in the next five to 12 years. The Association reports that one in four librarians is expected to retire in the next five to seven years, and approximately half will retire within 12 years. Additionally, school and community libraries will be faced with escalating materials costs, tighter budgets, and increased circulation while having to rely more heavily on volunteers, part-time employees, and support staff. In some cases, libraries will hire a technician instead of a more highly paid librarian. According to the ALA, the states hardest hit by budget cuts are Illinois, Arizona, Massachusetts, and California. Librarians who are willing to relocate to states or districts facing fewer budget issues will have better employment opportunities.

Employment opportunities will be best in nontraditional library settings, such as information brokers, private corporations, and consulting firms. The outlook is good for those skilled in developing computerized library systems as well as for those with a strong command of foreign languages.

The expanding use of computers to store and retrieve information and to handle routine operations will require that librarians have strong computer skills, and in some cases these tasks, once performed solely by librarians, can now be performed by other library staff members. The automation of libraries will in no way replace librarians, however; personal judgment and knowledge will still be needed in libraries.

Employment opportunities will also arise for librarians who have a background in information science and library automation. The rapidly expanding field of information management has created a demand for qualified people to set up and maintain information systems for private industry and consulting firms. Many companies are also establishing in-house reference libraries to assist in research work. Some have developed full lending library systems for employees.

Many librarians will find employment as trainers, customer representatives, and sales representatives for information database vendors. The expansion of the Internet will create new occupational opportunities for librarians—opportunities with such titles as *Internet trainer, Internet consultant,* and *Internet coordinator.*

FOR MORE INFORMATION

For information on careers in law librarianship, contact
American Association of Law Libraries
53 West Jackson, Suite 940
Chicago, IL 60604
Tel: 312-939-4764
Email: aallhq@aall.org
Web: http://www.aallnet.org

For career information, a list of accredited schools, information on scholarships and grants, and college student membership, contact
American Library Association
50 East Huron Street
Chicago, IL 60611
Tel: 800-545-2433
Email: membership@ala.org
http://www.ala.org

For information on information science careers, contact
American Society for Information Science and Technology
1320 Fenwick Lane, Suite 510
Silver Spring, MD 20910

Tel: 301-495-0900
Email: asis@asis.org
http://www.asis.org

For information on careers in medical librarianship, contact
Medical Library Association
65 East Wacker Place, Suite 1900
Chicago, IL 60601-7298
Tel: 312-419-9094
Email: info@mlahq.org
http://www.mlanet.org

For information on careers in music librarianship, contact
Music Library Association
8551 Research Way, Suite 180
Middleton, WI 53562
Tel: 608-836-5825
Web: http://www.musiclibraryassoc.org

For information on working in a specialized library, contact
Special Libraries Association
1700 18th Street, NW
Washington, DC 20009-2514
Tel: 202-234-4700
Email: sla@sla.org
http://www.sla.org

To receive information on librarianship in Canada, write to
Canadian Library Association
328 Frank Street
Ottawa, ON K2P 0X8 Canada
Tel: 613-232-9625
Email: info@cla.ca
http://www.cla.ca

LINGUISTS

QUICK FACTS

School Subjects
  English
  Foreign language
  History
Personal Skills
  Communication/ideas
  Following instructions
Work Environment
  Indoors and outdoors
  One location with some
  travel
Minimum Education Level
  Bachelor's degree
Salary Range
  $30,000 to $60,000 to
  $130,000
	Certification or Licensing
	  None available
	Outlook
	  About as fast as the average
	DOT
	  059
	GOE
	  11.03.02
	NOC
	  4169
	O*NET-SOC
	  N/A

OVERVIEW

Linguists study the components and structure of the world's various languages, the relationships among them, and their effects on the societies that speak them. They teach, conduct research projects, and offer interpretation and translation services.

HISTORY

Language is a universal characteristic of the human species. Of all the creatures on earth, humans are the only ones that communicate with a true language. Around the world, there are between 3,000 and 4,000 different speech communities, or groups of people using a specific, unique language. These speech communities are divided still further by dialects. In America, people from various regions may speak with an accent, but many languages contain dialects that are so different from each other that it is often very difficult for one group of speakers to understand another.

The comparative study of languages began in the late 18th century, when scholars first began to study the similarities that existed between the ancient languages of Greek, Sanskrit, and Persian. In the 19th century, much work was accomplished in identifying and classifying languages into families, or groups of related languages. At that time, the Indo-European family of languages was first classified and studied.

In the 20th century, linguists began to study the structures on which languages are built. While this structure includes grammar and semantics, it also involves the way words change, compound, and sound to carry different meanings. In many ways, a language reflects the beliefs, values, and social interactions of the societies that speak it. Many linguists today are examining exactly how this works.

THE JOB

Linguists study and explore every aspect of spoken and written language: the sound, meaning, and origin of words; systems of grammar; semantics, or the way words combine to mean what they mean; the evolution of both individual languages and families of languages; and the sounds that are used in a language's vocabulary. Linguists study both "dead" languages (languages that are no longer spoken), such as Latin and Classical Greek, and modern languages. *Philologists* examine the structure, origin, and development of languages and language groups by comparing ancient and modern tongues. *Etymologists* specialize in the history and evolution of words themselves. *Scientific linguists* study the components of language to understand its social functioning, and they may apply linguistic theory to practical concerns and problems.

Other linguists, like Alexander Ivakhnenko of Chicago, are self-employed and work on a contract basis, offering their understanding of specific languages to organizations and institutions. Ivakhnenko has native fluency in Ukrainian and Russian, and near-native fluency in English. He has a background in teaching, interpretation, translation, and public relations. Ivakhnenko has also assisted with legal negotiations and has developed a legal dictionary in English-Ukrainian. "You have to be an extrovert to perform well in this environment," Ivakhnenko says, referring to classroom lectures and to projects that involve interpreting for large conferences and hearings. At the 1996 Democratic National Convention, Ivakhnenko interpreted for visiting dignitaries.

Some linguists study ancient languages from archaeological evidence such as the paintings and hieroglyphics inside the pyramids of

Egypt. Because this evidence is sometimes incomplete, linguists may need to reconstruct parts of the language and make assumptions based on accepted linguistic theory. Still, their work adds greatly to our knowledge of what daily life was like in these ancient cultures.

Other linguists choose to study languages being spoken today. Many of these are spoken by people in remote parts of the world, but they can also be close to home, such as the languages of Native American tribes. Because some of these languages have never been written down, a linguist may need to spend years talking to native speakers, living with them to gain a complete knowledge of their culture. Such work is valuable because many of these ancient languages, with their rich oral histories and traditions, are in danger of extinction due to electronic communications and the encroachment of modern civilizations. Some linguists may study how a modern language is changing and developing. For example, they may study changes in spoken American English in relation to the influences of immigration, slang, or the computer age.

Other work by linguists may have more immediate applications. For example, a linguist may study the physiology of language—that is, the ways in which the lips, tongue, teeth, and throat combine to make the sounds of language. This knowledge can have many applications. For example, knowledge of physiology can make it easier to teach foreign languages that contain unfamiliar sounds. The Japanese language, for example, does not contain a clear "l" sound, but linguists can develop methods of teaching English to native Japanese speakers that will overcome this. Knowledge of language physiology can also aid in the treatment of speech difficulties in children, disabled people, stroke victims, or people who have suffered brain damage.

Linguistic theory itself can have many practical applications. These include the development of improved methods of translation, such as computer-enhanced translation. Linguistic theory can help in the preparation of language-teaching textbooks, dictionaries, and audiotapes. Literacy programs, at home and abroad, also depend on the work of linguists. In other countries, these programs are often run by anthropologists and missionaries.

Linguists also study sign language, such as AMESLAN, or American Sign Language. In some interesting experiments, linguists and other scientists have taught simplified sign language to gorillas. Future experiments in communication with other species, such as dolphins, whales, and dogs, will also depend on the expertise of skilled linguists.

Outside the academic world, linguists are finding more and more applications for their talents. Computer experts and linguists work together in the development of new computer languages, based on the rules of human language, that will be more user-friendly. The development of voice-activated computers will also capitalize on the skill and efforts of linguists. This field, known as *computational linguistics,* is now offering many opportunities in the Internet industry, particularly with companies that build and operate search engines.

REQUIREMENTS
High School

A broadly based college prep curriculum will help you prepare for a linguistics program. You should take at least two years of a modern foreign language in addition to four years of English. Mathematics, logic, philosophy, and computer science will be helpful for college study in the field. History, psychology, sociology, and other social sciences are important, and the study of ancient languages such as Latin can also be useful.

Postsecondary Training

Employers require at least a bachelor's degree in linguistics, English, or a foreign language, although some will accept degrees in history, science, mathematics, or engineering. An advanced degree with some independent study in languages could be very helpful. To teach and work at university level, you will need a doctorate degree. In the United States, more than 150 universities and colleges offer degrees in linguistics, and more than 50 offer doctorate programs in the field. You can learn more about linguistics programs in the United States and Canada from the Linguistic Society of America (LSA). An electronic edition of the LSA directory of schools is available on its website (see the end of this article), along with links to the websites of individual colleges.

Other Requirements

"You should be meticulous, precise, and energetic," Alexander Ivakhnenko says. Linguistic work calls for people who are inquisitive and patient, and who truly enjoy working with words, language, and sound. Strong research, reading, and writing skills are also important. Over time, linguists develop a discerning ear that can identify the sounds of speech in any language. Linguists should also have an interest in people of other cultures and be able to relate to them well.

EXPLORING

You should become familiar with languages other than your own. Language clubs are a good way to do this, as is attending multicultural festivals and other events. You should take advantage of opportunities to travel to other countries and communicate with people of different language backgrounds in order to gain insight into how important language is to culture. If travel is not possible, you might discuss with your family the possibility of hosting a foreign exchange student.

If you live near a university, you may be able to arrange an appointment with a member of its linguistics department. This could offer insights into what a career in a university setting is like. In addition, university language departments often offer events, speakers, and films that focus on various languages and cultures.

EMPLOYERS

While some linguists are employed by private companies or the federal government, most linguists conduct their work at colleges and universities. In fact, colleges and universities employ more linguists than all other employers combined. Those without doctorate degrees can find work with community colleges and special programs offering English as a second language courses.

More of the jobs that linguists find outside of academia are as computational linguists for Internet companies. They build databases and lexicons and develop language-processing systems for websites to make it easier for people to navigate and get more precise answers to requests for information.

STARTING OUT

Professors often keep students aware of openings for graduate teaching assistantships and of campus recruiting visits by potential employers. In graduate school, students can find work tutoring undergraduate linguistics classes or assisting professors in their research or classroom work. Such experience is very important when it's time to look for employment.

Linguists interested in working for the federal government should look for civil service announcements and apply to the federal agency for which they want to work. The armed forces also sponsor the Defense Language Institute for military personnel. Admittance is based on scores from The Defense Language Aptitude Battery Test. Linguists who are attracted to missionary work should contact the representatives of the mission branch of their church or religious denomination.

ADVANCEMENT

Linguists working in a university setting will likely find advancement through promotions to associate and full professorships and, possibly, to department head. Advancement may also come in the form of grants that allow a linguist to establish a clinic, research program, or other special project.

Linguists working in the private sector may advance through promotion to an administrative job in publishing or the chance to write and market computer software. Depending on individual goals, a linguist working for a private firm may pursue a teaching position at a university, or a linguistics professor may leave to take a job with a firm. To promote his language services, Alexander Ivakhnenko relies on a variety of methods. "I use business cards," he says, "a Web page, word of mouth, and referrals from clients."

EARNINGS

A 2000–2001 salary survey by the American Association of University Professors found the average yearly income for all full-time faculty was $60,000. It also reports that professors by rank averaged the following salaries: full professors, $78,912; associate professors, $57,380; assistant professors, $47,358; and instructors, $35,790.

Linguistics professors tend to earn salaries lower than the average. Entry-level academics start around $30,000–$40,000.

The new field of computational linguistics offers an attractive alternative to academia. Computational linguists, who have a background in both linguistics and computer science, can earn $80,000–$130,000 with an advanced degree. Linguists with a master's degree can earn $40,000–$45,000 in this field. Computational linguists often receive stock options as well.

WORK ENVIRONMENT

Working conditions for linguists employed by colleges and universities are usually very good. Linguistics professors usually share a linguistics lab that has the sound spectrographs, tape recorders, computers, and other equipment they will need for their work. Linguistics professors commonly spend up to 12 hours a week in the classroom and divide the rest of their workweek between meeting students during office hours, doing research, preparing class materials, and writing. They often put in more than 35 or 40 hours a week, but they are able to structure their time to suit their interests and working habits. Also, because they work on the academic calendar, they receive ample vacation time, which they often use for study, research, and travel.

Linguists in the private sector generally work 35–40 hours per week, though they may have to work overtime to meet certain deadlines. Publishing firms and government agencies employing linguists generally have pleasant atmospheres and good equipment. Linguists involved in missionary work or overseas literacy programs generally live among the native people and adjust to their standard of living. Missionaries generally work long hours and receive no more than subsistence wages; however, their devotion to a higher cause enables them to adapt to uncomfortable surroundings.

Alexander Ivakhnenko cites traveling as a great benefit in his work. "I have to travel several times a year," he says. This gives him an opportunity to meet people, which he also enjoys. He also appreciates the flexible schedule that being self-employed allows, but the uneven income can be problematic.

Computational linguists work in a corporate environment with computers and database systems. They usually work 40 hours a week.

Ph.D. Program Rankings from a Different Perspective

You may be familiar with the annual rankings of college programs by *U.S. News & World Report* and other magazines, but you can also learn about Ph.D. programs from the 2000 National Doctorate Program Survey, which is conducted by the National Association of Graduate-Professional Students. Over 32,000 graduate students and recent Ph.D.'s were asked to grade their own doctorate programs. Visitors to http://survey.nagps.org can study report cards for more than 1,300 doctorate programs. You can search and prepare a report for programs using the following criterion: overall recommended practices, information for prospective students, preparation for a broad range of careers, teaching and TA preparation, professional development, career guidance and placement services, controlling time to degree, mentoring, program climate, and overall satisfaction.

OUTLOOK

While the employment outlook for linguists has improved over the past decade, it is still not good. There are more qualified linguists than there are jobs for them, and most openings will occur as other linguists retire or leave the field. The U.S. Department of Labor predicts faster than average employment growth for college and university professors over the next several years, but the field of linguistics is not a high-growth field.

As private companies expand and business becomes more international in scope, a knowledge of foreign language and culture may prove very beneficial to those linguists who develop additional business skills. Those people who do not limit themselves to strictly linguistic work and instead market their skills in other areas where they can be useful should be able to carve out their own employment niche.

More jobs for linguists are available today in the private sector. Computers and the Internet have created opportunities for linguists in developing computer languages and software that are more like human language. Some Internet companies are enticing linguistics students away from universities before they even finish their degrees with offers of high-paying positions.

FOR MORE INFORMATION

For information about linguistic programs at colleges and universities, contact

Linguistic Society of America
1325 18th Street, NW, Suite 211
Washington, DC 20036-6501
Email: lsa@lsadc.org
http://www.lsadc.org

For information about jobs and membership, contact

Modern Language Association of America
26 Broadway, 3rd Floor
New York, NY 10004-1789
Tel: 646-576-5000
Email: membership@mla.org
http://www.mla.org

LOBBYISTS

QUICK FACTS

School Subjects Government Journalism Speech	**Certification or Licensing** None available
	Outlook About as fast as the average
Personal Skills Communication/ideas Leadership/management	**DOT** 165
Work Environment Primarily indoors One location with some travel	**GOE** 11.09.03 **NOC** N/A
Minimum Education Level Bachelor's degree	**O*NET-SOC** N/A
Salary Range $20,000 to $100,000 to $500,000+	

OVERVIEW

A *lobbyist* works to influence legislation on the federal, state, or local level on behalf of clients. Nonprofit organizations, labor unions, trade associations, corporations, and other groups and individuals use lobbyists to voice concerns and opinions to government representatives. Lobbyists use their knowledge of the legislative process and their government contacts to represent their clients' interests. Though most lobbyists are based in Washington, D.C., many work throughout the country representing client issues in city and state government.

HISTORY

Lobbying has been a practice within government since colonial times. In the late 1700s, the term "lobbyist" was used to describe the special-interest representatives who gathered in the anteroom outside the legislative chamber in the New York state capitol. The term often had a negative connotation, with political cartoonists frequently portraying lobbyists as slick, cigar-chomping individuals attempting to buy favors. But in the 20th century, lobbyists came to be seen as experts in the fields that they represented, and members of Congress relied upon them to provide information needed to evaluate legislation. During the New Deal in the 1930s, government spending in Washington greatly increased, and the number of lobbyists proliferated proportionately. A major lobbying law was enacted in 1938, but it wasn't until 1946 that comprehensive legislation in the form of the Federal Regulation of Lobbying Act was passed into law. The act requires that anyone who spends or receives money or anything of value in the interests of passing, modifying, or defeating legislation being considered by the U.S. Congress be registered and provide spending reports. Its effectiveness, however, was reduced by vague language that frequently required legal interpretations. Further regulatory acts have been passed in the years since; most recently, the Lobbying Disclosure Act of 1995 has required registration of all lobbyists working at the federal level.

THE JOB

An example of effective lobbying concerns Medic Alert, an organization that provides bracelets to millions of people in the United States and Canada with health problems. Engraved on the bracelet is a description of the person's medical problem, along with Medic Alert's 24-hour emergency response phone number. The emergency response center is located in a part of California that considered changing its telephone area code. Medic Alert anticipated a lot of confusion—and many possible medical disasters—if the area code was changed from that which is engraved on the millions of bracelets. Medic Alert called upon doctors, nurses, and the media to get word out about the danger to lives. Through this lobbying, the public and the state's policy makers became aware of an important aspect of the area code change they may not have otherwise known.

The Medic Alert organization, like the thousands of associations, unions, and corporations in the United States, benefited from using lobbyists with an understanding of state politics and influence. The American Society of Association Executives estimates that the number of national trade and charitable associations is over 23,000. With 2,500 of these associations based in Washington, D.C., associations are the third-largest industry in the city, behind government and tourism. Lobbyists may work for one of these associations as directors of government relations, or they may work for an industry, company, or other organization to act on its behalf in government concerns. Lobbyists also work for lobbying firms that deal with many different clients on a contractual basis.

Lobbyists have years of experience working with the government, learning about federal and state politics, and meeting career politicians and their staffs. Their job is to make members of Congress aware of the issues of concern to their clients and the effect that legislation and regulations will have on them. They provide the members of Congress with research and analysis to help them make the most informed decisions possible. Lobbyists also keep their clients informed with updates and reports.

Tom McNamara is the president of a government relations firm based in Washington, D.C. He first became involved in politics by working on campaigns before he was even old enough to vote. Throughout his years in government work, he has served as the chief of staff for two different members of Congress and was active in both the Ronald Reagan and George H. Bush presidential campaigns. "Clients hire me for my advice," McNamara says. "They ask me to do strategic planning, relying on my knowledge of how Congress operates." After learning about a client's problem, McNamara researches the issue and develops a plan and a proposal to solve the problem. Some of the questions he must ask when seeking a solution are: What are our assets? Who can we talk to who has the necessary influence? Do we need the media? Do we need to talk to Congressional staff members? "With 22 years in the House of Representatives," McNamara says, "I have a tremendous base of people I know. Part of my work is maintaining these relationships, as well as developing relationships with new members and their staff."

Lobbying techniques are generally broken down into two broad categories: direct lobbying and indirect, or "grass roots," lobbying. Direct lobbying techniques include making personal contacts with members of Congress and appointed officials. It is important for lobbyists to know the key people who will be drafting legislation that is significant to their clientele. They hire technical experts to develop reports, charts, graphs, or schematic drawings that may help in the legislative decision-making process that determines the passage, amendment, or defeat of a measure. Sometimes a lobbyist with expertise on a particular issue works directly with a member of Congress in the drafting of a bill. Lobbyists also keep members of Congress tuned in to the voices of their constituents.

Indirect, or grass roots, lobbying involves persuading voters to support a client's view. If the Congress member knows that a majority of voters favor a particular point of view, he or she will support or fight legislation according to the voters' wishes. Probably the most widely used method of indirect lobbying is the letter-writing campaign. Lobbyists use direct mail, newsletters, media advertising, and other methods of communication to reach the constituents and convince them to write to their member of Congress with their supporting views. Lobbyists also use phone campaigns, encouraging the constituents to call their Congress member's office. Aides usually tally the calls that come in and communicate the volume to the legislator.

Indirect lobbying is also done through the media. Lobbyists try to persuade newspaper and magazine editors and radio and television news managers to write or air editorials that reflect the point of view of their clientele. They write op-ed pieces that are submitted to the media for publication. They arrange for experts to speak in favor of a particular position on talk shows or to make statements that are picked up by the media. As a persuasive measure, lobbyists may send a legislator a collection of news clippings indicating public opinion on a forthcoming measure, or provide tapes of aired editorials and news features covering a relevant subject.

REQUIREMENTS
High School
Becoming a lobbyist requires years of experience in other government and related positions. To prepare for a government job, take courses in history, social studies, and civics to learn about the structure of local, state, and federal government. English and composition classes will help you develop your communication skills. Work on the student council or become an officer for a school club. Taking journalism courses and working on the school newspaper will prepare you for the public relations aspect of lobbying. As a reporter, you'll research current issues, meet with policy makers, and write articles.

Postsecondary Training
As a rule, men and women take up lobbying after having left an earlier career. (Tom McNamara worked for over 20 years as a congressional staff member before moving on to this other aspect of government work.) Schools do not generally offer a specific curriculum that leads to a career as a lobbyist, thus your experience with legislation and policy making is what will prove valuable to

employers and clients. Almost all lobbyists have college degrees, and many have graduate degrees. Degrees in law and political science are among the most beneficial for prospective lobbyists, just as they are for other careers in politics and government. Journalism, public relations, and economics are other areas of study that would be helpful in the pursuit of a lobbying career.

Certification or Licensing

Lobbyists do not need a license or certification, but the Lobbying Disclosure Act of 1995 requires all lobbyists working on the federal level to register with the Secretary of the Senate and the Clerk of the House. You may also be required to register with the states in which you lobby and possibly pay a small fee.

There is no union available to lobbyists. Some lobbyists join the American League of Lobbyists, which provides a variety of support services for its members. Membership in a number of other associations, including the American Society of Association Executives and the American Association of Political Consultants, can also be useful to lobbyists.

Other Requirements

"I've had practical, everyday involvement in government and politics," McNamara says about the skills and knowledge most valuable to him as a lobbyist. "I know what motivates Congress members and staff to act."

In addition to this understanding, McNamara emphasizes that lobbyists must be honest in all their professional dealings with others. "The only way to be successful is to be completely honest and straightforward." Your career will be based on your reputation as a reliable person, so you must be very scrupulous in building that reputation.

You also need people skills to develop good relationships with legislators and serve your clients' interests. Your knowledge of the workings of government, along with good communication skills, will help you to explain government legislation to your clients in ways that they can clearly understand.

EXPLORING

To explore this career, become an intern or volunteer in the office of a lobbyist, legislator, government official, special interest group, or nonprofit institution (especially one that relies on government grants). Working in these fields will introduce you to the lobbyist's world and provide early exposure to the workings of government.

Other good ways to learn more about lobbying is to become involved in your school government; write for your school newspaper; perform public relations, publicity, and advertising work for school and community organizations; and take part in fund-raising drives. When major legislative issues are being hotly debated, you can write to your congressional representatives to express your views or even organize a letter writing or telephone campaign; these actions are forms of lobbying.

EMPLOYERS

Organizations either hire government liaisons to handle lobbying or they contract with law and lobby firms. Liaisons who work for one organization work on only those issues that affect that organization. Independent lobbyists work on a variety of different issues, taking on clients on a contractual basis. They may contract with large corporations, such as a pharmaceutical or communications company, as well as volunteer services to nonprofit organizations. Lobbying firms are located all across the country. Those executives in charge of government relations for trade associations and other organizations are generally based in Washington, D.C.

STARTING OUT

Lobbyist positions won't be listed in the classifieds. It takes years of experience and an impressive list of connections to find a government-relations job in an organization. Tom McNamara retired at age 50 from his work with the House of Representatives. "Lobbying was a natural progression into the private sector," he says. His love for public policy, campaigns, and politics led him to start his own lobbying firm. "I had an institutional understanding that made me valuable," he says.

Professional lobbyists usually have backgrounds as lawyers, public relations executives, congressional aides, legislators, government officials, or professionals in business and industry. Once established in a government or law career, lobbyists begin to hear about corporations and associations that need knowledgeable people for their government relations departments. The American Society of Association Executives (ASAE) hosts a website, http://www.asaenet.org, which lists available positions for executives with trade associations.

ADVANCEMENT

Lobbyists focus on developing long-standing relationships with legislators and clients and become experts on policy making and legislation. Association or company executives may advance from a position as director of government relations into a position as president or vice-president. Lobbyists who contract their services to various clients advance by taking on more clients and working for larger corporations.

EARNINGS

Because of the wide range of salaries earned by lobbyists, it is difficult to compile an accurate survey. The ASAE, however, regularly conducts surveys of association executives. According to ASAE's 2001 Association Executive Compensation Study, directors of government relations within trade associations earned an average of $93,666 annually. The report notes, however, that compensation varies greatly depending on location. Highest earnings of directors were reported in New York City ($185,300), Washington, D.C. ($174,000), and Chicago ($168,000). The size of an association's staff and budget also affects compensation levels.

Like lawyers, lobbyists are considered very well paid; also like lawyers, a lobbyist's income depends on the size of the organization he or she represents. Experienced contract lobbyists with a solid client base can earn well over $100,000 a year and some make more than $500,000 a year. Beginning lobbyists may make less than $20,000 a year as they build a client base. In many cases, a lobbyist may take on large corporations as clients for the bulk of the annual income, then volunteer services to nonprofit organizations.

WORK ENVIRONMENT

Lobbyists spend much of their time communicating with the people who affect legislation—principally the legislators and officials of federal and state governments. This communication takes place in person, by telephone, and by memoranda. Most of a lobbyist's time is spent gathering information, writing reports, creating publicity, and staying in touch with clients. They respond to the public and the news media when required. Sometimes their expertise is required at hearings or they may testify before a legislature.

Tom McNamara has enjoyed the change from congressional chief of staff to lobbyist. "I'm an integral part of the system of government," he says, "albeit in a different role." He feels that every day is different, and he has the opportunity to meet new and interesting people. "It's intellectually challenging," he says. "You have to stay on top of the issues, and keep track of the personalities as well as the campaigns."

OUTLOOK

The number of special-interest groups in the United States continues to grow, and as long as they continue to plead their causes before state and federal governments, lobbyists will be needed. However, lobbying cutbacks often occur in corporations. Because lobbying doesn't directly create a profit for a business, the government-relations department is often the first in a company to receive budget cuts. The American League of Lobbyists anticipates that the career will remain stable, though it is difficult to predict this with accuracy. In recent years, there has been a significant increase in registrations, but that is most likely a result of the Lobbying Disclosure Act of 1995 requiring registration.

The methods of grass roots advocacy will continue to be affected by the Internet and other new communication technology. Lobbyists and organizations use Web pages to inform the public of policy issues. These Web pages often include ways to immediately send email messages to state and federal legislators. Constituents may have the choice of composing their own messages or sending messages already composed. With this method, a member of Congress can easily determine the feelings of the constituents based on the amount of email received.

FOR MORE INFORMATION

For information about a lobbyist career, visit the following website or contact
American League of Lobbyists
PO Box 30005
Alexandria, VA 22310
Tel: 703-960-3011
Email: alldc.org@erols.com
http://www.alldc.org

For information about government relations and public policy concerns within trade associations, contact
American Society of Association Executives
1575 I Street, NW
Washington, DC 20005-1103
Tel: 202-626-2723
http://www.asaenet.or

MAGAZINE EDITORS

QUICK FACTS

School Subjects English Journalism	**Certification or Licensing** None available
Personal Interests Communication/ideas Helping/teaching	**Outlook** Faster than the average **DOT** 132
Work Environment Primarily indoors Primarily one location	**GOE** 01.01.01
Minimum Education Level Bachelor's degree	**NOC** 5122
Salary Range $14,000 to $39,960 to $75,000+	**O*NET-SOC** 27-3041.00

OVERVIEW

Magazine editors plan the contents of a magazine, assign articles and select photographs and artwork to enhance articles, and edit, organize, and sometimes rewrite the articles. They are responsible for making sure that each issue is attractive and readable and maintains the stylistic integrity of the publication. There are approximately 122,000 editors of all types employed in the United States.

HISTORY

The magazines that existed before the 19th century were designed primarily for small, highly educated audiences. In the early 19th century, however, inexpensive magazines that catered to a larger audience began to appear. At the same time, magazines began to specialize, targeting specific audiences. That trend continues today, with close to 20,000 magazines currently in production.

Beginning in the 19th century, magazine staffs became more specialized. Whereas in early publishing a single person would perform various functions, in 19th-century and later publishing, employees performed individual tasks. Instead of having a single editor, for example, a magazine would have an editorial staff. One person would be responsible for acquisitions, another would copyedit, another would be responsible for editorial tasks related to production, and so forth.

Starting with Gutenberg's invention of movable type, changes in technology have altered the publishing industry. The development of the computer has revolutionized the running of magazines and other publications. Editing, design, and layout programs have considerably shortened the time in which a publication goes to press. The worldwide scope of magazine reporting is now dependent upon technology that enables writers and editors to transmit stories and photographs almost instantaneously from one part of the world to another.

Finally, the Internet has provided an entirely new medium for magazine publishing, with many magazines maintaining both print and online versions. Online publishers avoid paper and printing costs, but still collect revenue from online subscriptions and advertising.

THE JOB

The duties of a magazine editor are numerous and unpredictable. The editor determines each article's placement in the magazine, working closely with the sales, art, and production departments to ensure that the publication's components complement one another and are appealing and readable.

Most magazines focus on a particular topic, such as fashion, news, or sports. Current topics of interest in the magazine's specialty area dictate a magazine's content. In some cases, magazines themselves set trends, generating interest in topics that become popular. Therefore, the editor should know the latest trends in the field that the magazine represents.

Depending on the magazine's size, editors may specialize in a particular area. For example, a fashion magazine may have a beauty editor, features editor, short story editor, and fashion editor. Each editor is responsible for acquiring, proofing, rewriting, and sometimes writing articles.

After determining the magazine's contents, the editor assigns articles to writers and photographers. The editor may have a clear vision of the topic or merely a rough outline. In any case, the editor supervises the article from writing through production and is assisted by copy editors, assistant editors, fact checkers, researchers, and editorial assistants. The editor also sets a department budget and negotiates contracts with freelance writers, photographers, and artists.

The magazine editor reviews each article, checking it for clarity, concision, and reader appeal. The editor may also edit the manuscript to highlight particular items. Sometimes the magazine editor writes an editorial to stimulate discussion or mold public opinion. The editor also may write articles on topics of personal interest.

Other editorial positions at magazines include the *editor in chief*, who is responsible for the overall editorial course of the magazine, the *executive editor*, who controls day-to-day scheduling and operations, and the *managing editor*, who coordinates copy flow and supervises production of master pages for each issue.

Some entry-level jobs in magazine editorial departments are stepping-stones to more responsible positions. *Editorial assistants* perform various tasks such as answering phones and correspondence, setting up meetings and photography shoots, checking facts, and typing manuscripts. *Editorial production assistants* assist in coordinating the layout of feature articles edited by editors and art designed by *art directors* to prepare the magazine for printing.

Many magazines hire *freelance writers* to write articles on an assignment or contract basis. Most freelance writers write for several different publications; some become *contributing editors* to one or more publications to which they contribute the bulk of their work.

Magazines also employ *researchers*, sometimes called *fact checkers*, to ensure the factual accuracy of an article's content. Researchers may be on staff or hired on a freelance basis.

REQUIREMENTS
High School
While in high school, develop your writing, reading, and analyzing skills through English and composition classes. Stay current with the latest news and events of the world and take several history and politics classes. Reading the daily newspaper and news magazines can also keep you fresh on current events and will help you to become familiar with different styles of journalistic writing.

If your school offers journalism classes or has a school newspaper, get involved. Any participation in the publishing process will be great experience, whether you are writing articles, proofreading copy, or laying out pages.

Postsecondary Training

A college degree is required for entry into this field. A degree in journalism, English, or communications is the most popular and standard degree for a magazine editor. Specialized publications prefer a degree in the magazine's specialty, such as chemistry for a chemistry magazine, and experience in writing and editing. A broad liberal arts background is important for work at any magazine.

Most colleges and universities offer specific courses in magazine design, writing, editing, and photography. Related courses might include newspaper and book editing.

Other Requirements

All entry-level positions in magazine publishing require a working knowledge of typing and word processing, plus a superior command of grammar, punctuation, and spelling. Deadlines are important, so commitment, organization, and resourcefulness are crucial.

Editing is intellectually stimulating work that may involve investigative techniques in politics, history, and business. Magazine editors must be talented wordsmiths with impeccable judgment. Their decisions about which opinions, editorials, or essays to feature may influence a large number of people.

EXPLORING

The best way to get a sense of magazine editing is to work on a high school or college newspaper or newsletter. You will probably start out as a staff writer, but with time and experience, you may be able to move into an editorial position with more responsibility and freedom to choose the topics to cover.

EMPLOYERS

Major magazines are concentrated in New York, Chicago, Los Angeles, Boston, Philadelphia, San Francisco, and Washington, D.C., while professional, technical, and union publications are located throughout the country.

STARTING OUT

Competition for editorial jobs can be fierce, especially in the popular magazine industry. Recent graduates hoping to break into the business should be willing to work other staff positions before moving into an editorial position.

Many editors enter the field as editorial assistants or proofreaders. Some editorial assistants perform only clerical tasks, whereas others may also proofread or perform basic editorial tasks. Typically, an editorial assistant who performs well will be given the opportunity to take on more and more editorial duties as time passes. Proofreaders have the advantage of being able to look at the work of editors, so they can learn while they do their own work.

Good sources of information about job openings are school placement offices, classified ads in newspapers and specialized publications such as *Publishers Weekly* (http://www.publishersweekly.com).

ADVANCEMENT

Employees who start as editorial assistants or proofreaders and show promise generally become copy editors. Copy editors work their way up to become senior editors, managing editors, and editors in chief. In many cases, magazine editors advance by moving from a position on one magazine to the same position with a larger or more prestigious magazine. Such moves often bring significant increases in both pay and status.

EARNINGS

According to the Magazine Publishers of America, the average salary for an editor who has four to 10 years of experience can range from $44,000 to $52,000. Entry-level editors earn from $14,000 to $30,000. Senior editors at large-circulation magazines average more than $75,000 a year. In addition, many editors supplement their salaried income by doing freelance work.

According to the Bureau of Labor statistics, the median annual earnings for salaried editors were $39,960 in 2001. The middle 50 percent earned between $29,740 and $54,930. Salaries ranged from less than $23,090 to more than $73,460.

Full-time editors receive vacation time, medical insurance, and sick time, but freelancers must provide their own benefits.

WORK ENVIRONMENT

Most magazine editors work in quiet offices or cubicles. However, even in relatively quiet surroundings, editors can face many distractions. An editor who is trying to copyedit or review the editing of others may, for example, have to deal with phone calls from reporters, questions from junior editors, meetings with members of the editorial and production staff, and questions from freelancers, among many other distractions.

An often stressful part of the magazine editor's job is meeting deadlines. Magazine editors work in a much more pressurized atmosphere than book editors because they face daily or weekly deadlines, whereas book production usually takes place over several months. Many magazine editors must work long hours during certain phases of the publishing cycle.

OUTLOOK

Magazine publishing is a dynamic industry. Magazines are launched every day of the year, although the majority fail. According to Magazine Publishers of America, 293 new magazines were introduced in 2001. The organization names the Internet, government affairs, and consumer marketing as some of the important issues currently facing the magazine publishing industry. The future of magazines is secure since they are a critical medium for advertisers.

A recent trend in magazine publishing is focus on a special interest. There is increasing opportunity for employment at special interest, trade, and association magazines for those whose backgrounds complement a magazine's specialty. Internet publishing will provide increasing job opportunities as more businesses develop online publications. Magazine editing is keenly competitive, however, and as with any career, the applicant with the most education and experience has a better chance of getting the job. The *Occupational Outlook Handbook* projects faster-than-average growth in employment for editors and writers.

FOR MORE INFORMATION

For general and summer internship program information, contact
Magazine Publishers of America
919 Third Avenue
New York, NY 10022
Tel: 212-872-3700
http://www.magazine.org

MARKETING RESEARCH ANALYSTS

QUICK FACTS

School Subjects
Business
Mathematics

Personal Skills
Following instructions
Technical/scientific

Work Environment
Primarily indoors
Primarily one location

Minimum Education Level
Bachelor's degree

Salary Range
$28,500 to $53,450 to
$96,980+

Certification or Licensing
None available

Outlook
Faster than the average

DOT
050

GOE
11.06.03

NOC
N/A

O*NET-SOC
19-3021.00

OVERVIEW

Marketing research analysts collect, analyze, and interpret data to determine potential demand for a product or service. By examining the buying habits, wants, needs, and preferences of consumers, research analysts are able to recommend ways to improve products, increase sales, and expand customer bases.

HISTORY

Knowing what customers want and what prices they are willing to pay have always been concerns of manufacturers and producers of goods and services. As industries have grown and competition for consumers of manufactured goods has increased, businesses have turned to marketing research as a way to measure public opinion and assess customer preferences.

Marketing research formally emerged in Germany in the 1920s and in Sweden and France in the 1930s. In the United States, emphasis on marketing research began after World War II. With a desire to study potential markets and gain new customers, U.S. firms hired marketing research specialists, professionals who were able to use statistics and refine research techniques to help companies reach their marketing goals. By the 1980s, research analysts could be found even in a variety of Communist countries, where the quantity of consumer goods being produced was rapidly increasing.

Today, the marketing research analyst is a vital part of the marketing team. By conducting studies and analyzing data, research professionals help companies address specific marketing issues and concerns.

THE JOB

Marketing researchers collect and analyze all kinds of information to help companies improve their products, establish or modify sales and distribution policies, and make decisions regarding future plans and directions. In addition, research analysts are responsible for monitoring both in-house studies and off-site research, interpreting results, providing explanations of compiled data, and developing research tools.

One area of marketing research focuses on company products and services. In order to determine consumer likes and dislikes, research analysts collect data on brand names, trademarks, product design, and packaging for existing products, items being test-marketed, and those in experimental stages. Analysts also study competing products and services that are already on the market to help managers and strategic planners develop new products and create appropriate advertising campaigns.

In the sales methods and policy area of marketing research, analysts examine firms' sales records and conduct a variety of sales-related studies. For example, information on sales in various geographical areas is analyzed and compared to previous sales figures, changes in population, and total and seasonal sales volume. By analyzing this data, marketing researchers can identify peak sales periods and recommend ways to target new customers. Such information helps marketers plan future sales campaigns and establish sales quotas and commissions.

Advertising research is closely related to sales research. Studies on the effectiveness of advertising in different parts of the country are conducted and compared to sales records. This research is helpful in planning future advertising campaigns and in selecting the appropriate media to use.

Marketing research that focuses on consumer demand and preferences solicits opinions of the people who use the products or services being considered. In addition to actually conducting opinion studies, marketing researchers often design the ways to obtain the information. They write scripts for telephone interviews, develop direct-mail questionnaires and field surveys, and design focus group programs.

Through one or a combination of these studies, market researchers are able to gather information on consumer reaction to the need for and style, design, price, and use of a product. The studies attempt to reveal who uses various products or services, identify potential customers, or get suggestions for product or service improvement. This information is helpful for forecasting sales, planning design modifications, and determining changes in features.

Once information has been gathered, marketing researchers analyze the findings. They then detail their findings and recommendations in a written report and often orally present them to management.

A number of professionals compose the marketing research team. The *project supervisor* is responsible for overseeing a study from beginning to end. The *statistician* determines the sample size—the number of people to be surveyed—and compares the number of responses. The project supervisor or statistician, in conjunction with other specialists (such as *demographers* and *psychologists*), often determines the number of interviews to be conducted as well as their locations. *Field interviewers* survey people in various public places, such as shopping malls, office complexes, and popular attractions. *Telemarketers* gather information by placing calls to current or potential customers, to people listed in telephone books, or to those who appear on specialized lists obtained from list houses. Once questionnaires come in from the field, *tabulators* and *coders* examine the data, count the answers, code non-categorical answers, and tally the primary counts. The marketing research analyst then analyzes the returns, writes up the final report, and makes recommendations to the client or to management.

Marketing research analysts must be thoroughly familiar with research techniques and procedures. Sometimes the research problem is clearly defined, and information can be gathered readily. Other times, company executives may know only that a problem exists as evidenced by a decline in sales. In these cases, the market research analyst is expected to collect the facts that will aid in revealing and resolving the problem.

REQUIREMENTS
High School

Most employers require their marketing research analysts to hold at least a bachelor's degree, so a college preparatory program is advised. Classes in English, marketing, mathematics, psychology, and sociology are particularly important. Courses in computing are especially useful, since a great deal of tabulation and statistical analysis is required in the marketing research field.

Postsecondary Training

A bachelor's degree is essential for careers in marketing research. Majors in marketing, business administration, statistics, computer science, or economics provide a good background for most types of research positions. In addition, course work in sociology and psychology is helpful for those who are leaning toward consumer demand and opinion research. Since quantitative skills are important in various types of industrial or analytic research, students interested in these areas should take statistics, econometrics, survey design, sampling theory, and other mathematics courses.

Many employers prefer that a marketing research analyst hold a master's degree as well as a bachelor's degree. A master's of business administration, for example, is frequently required on projects calling for complex statistical and business analysis. Graduate work at the doctorate level is not necessary for most positions, but it is highly desirable for those who plan to become involved in advanced research studies.

Other Requirements

To work in this career, you should be intelligent, detail oriented, and accurate; have the ability to work easily with words and numbers; and be particularly interested in solving problems through data collection and analysis. In addition, you must be patient and persistent, since long hours are often required when working on complex studies.

As part of the market research team, you must be able to work well with others and have an interest in people. The ability to communicate, both orally and in writing, is also important, since you will be responsible for writing up detailed reports on the findings in various studies and presenting recommendations to management.

EXPLORING

You can find many opportunities in high school to learn more about the necessary skills for the field of marketing research. For example, experiments in science, problems in student government, committee work, and other school activities provide exposure to situations similar to those encountered by marketing research analysts.

You can also seek part-time employment as a survey interviewer at local marketing research firms. Gathering field data for consumer surveys offers valuable experience through actual contact with both the public and marketing research supervisors. In addition, many companies seek a variety of other employees to code, tabulate, and edit surveys; monitor telephone interviews; and validate the information entered on written questionnaires. You can search for job listings in local newspapers and on the Web or apply directly to research organizations.

EMPLOYERS

Marketing research analysts are employed by large corporations, industrial firms, advertising agencies, data collection businesses, and private research organizations that handle local surveys for companies on a contract basis. While many marketing research organizations offer a broad range of services, some firms subcontract parts of an overall project out to specialized companies. For example, one research firm may concentrate on product interviews, while another might focus on measuring the effectiveness of product advertising. Similarly, some marketing analysts specialize in one industry or area. For example, agricultural marketing specialists prepare sales forecasts for food businesses, which use the information in their advertising and sales programs.

Although many smaller firms located all across the country outsource studies to marketing research firms, these research firms, along with most large corporations that employ marketing research analysts, are located in such big cities as New York or Chicago. Private industry employs about 90 percent of salaried marketing research analysts, but opportunities also exist in government and academia, as well as at hospitals, public libraries, and a variety of other types of organizations.

STARTING OUT

Students with a graduate degree in marketing research and experience in quantitative techniques have the best chances of landing jobs as marketing research analysts. Since a bachelor's degree in marketing or business is usually not sufficient to obtain such a position, many employees without postgraduate degrees start out as research assistants, trainees, interviewers, or questionnaire editors. In such positions, those aspiring to the job of research analyst can gain valuable experience conducting interviews, analyzing data, and writing reports.

Use your college placement office, the Web, and help wanted sections of local newspapers to look for job leads. Another way to get into the marketing research field is through personal and professional contacts. Names and telephone numbers of potential employers may come from professors, friends, or relatives. Finally, students who have participated in internships or have held marketing research-related jobs on a part-time basis while in school or during the summer may be able to obtain employment at these firms or at similar organizations.

ADVANCEMENT

Most marketing research professionals begin as junior analysts or research assistants. In these positions, they help in preparing questionnaires and related materials, training survey interviewers, and tabulating and coding survey results. After gaining sufficient experience in these and other aspects of research project development, employees are often assigned their own research projects, which usually involve supervisory and planning responsibilities. A typical promotion path for those climbing the company ladder might be from assistant researcher to marketing research analyst to assistant manager and then to manager of a branch office for a large private research firm. From there, some professionals become market research executives or research directors for industrial or business firms.

Since marketing research analysts learn about all aspects of marketing on the job, some advance by moving to positions in other departments, such as advertising or sales. Depending on the interests and experience of marketing professionals, other areas of employment to which they can advance include data processing, teaching at the university level, statistics, economics, and industrial research and development.

In general, few employees go from starting positions to executive jobs at one company. Advancement often requires changing employers. Therefore, marketing research analysts who want to move up the ranks frequently go from one company to another, sometimes many times during their careers.

EARNINGS

Beginning salaries in marketing research depend on the qualifications of the employee, the nature of the position, and the size of the firm. Interviewers, coders, tabulators, editors, and a variety of other employees usually get paid by the hour and may start at $6 or more per hour. The Bureau of Labor Statistics reported that in 2001, median annual earnings of market research analysts were $53,450. The middle 50 percent earned between $38,280 and $74,460. Salaries ranged from less than $28,500 to more than $96,980. Experienced analysts working in supervisory positions at large firms can have even higher earnings. Market research directors earn up to $200,000.

Because most marketing research workers are employed by business or industrial firms, they receive fringe benefit packages that include health and life insurance, pension plans, and paid vacation and sick leave.

WORK ENVIRONMENT

Marketing research analysts usually work a 40-hour week. Occasionally, overtime is necessary in order to meet project deadlines. Although they frequently interact with a variety of marketing research team members, analysts also do a lot of independent work, analyzing data, writing reports, and preparing statistical charts.

While most marketing research analysts work in offices located at the firm's main headquarters, those who supervise interviewers may go into the field to oversee work. In order to attend conferences, meet with clients, or check on the progress of various research studies, regular travel is required of many market research analysts.

OUTLOOK

The U.S. Department of Labor predicts that employment for marketing research analysts will grow faster than the average through the next decade. Increasing competition among producers of consumer goods and services and industrial products, combined with a growing awareness of the value of marketing research data, will contribute to opportunities in the field. Opportunities will be best for those with graduate degrees who seek employment in marketing research firms, financial services organizations, health care institutions, advertising firms, manufacturing firms producing consumer goods, and insurance companies.

While many new graduates are attracted to the field, creating a competitive situation, the best jobs and the highest pay will go to those individuals who hold a master's degree or doctorate in marketing research, statistics, economics, or computer science.

FOR MORE INFORMATION

For information on college chapters, internship opportunities, and financial aid opportunities, contact

American Advertising Federation
1101 Vermont Avenue, NW, Suite 500
Washington, DC 20005-6306
Tel: 202-898-0089
Email: aaf@aaf.org
http://www.aaf.org

For information on agencies, contact

American Association of Advertising Agencies
405 Lexington Avenue, 18th Floor
New York, NY 10174-1801
Tel: 212-682-2500
http://www.aaaa.org

For career resources and job listings, contact or check out the following website:

American Marketing Association
311 South Wacker Drive, Suite 5800
Chicago, IL 60606
Tel: 800-262-1150
Email: info@ama.org
http://www.marketingpower.com

MUSEUM DIRECTORS AND CURATORS

QUICK FACTS

School Subjects
Art
Business

Personal Skills
Communication/ideas
Leadership/management

Work Environment
Primarily indoors
One location with some travel

Minimum Education Level
Bachelor's degree

Salary Range
$18,910 to $60,000 to $500,000+

Certification or Licensing
None available

Outlook
About as fast as the average

DOT
102

GOE
N/A

NOC
0511

O*NET-SOC
25-4012.00

OVERVIEW

A *museum director* is equivalent to the chief executive officer of a corporation. The museum director is responsible for the daily operations of the museum, for long-term planning, policies, any research conducted within the museum, and for the museum's fiscal health. Directors must also represent the museum at meetings with other museums, business and civic communities, and the museum's governing body. Finally, directors ensure that museums adhere to state and federal guidelines for safety in the workplace and hiring practices, as well as industry recommendations concerning the acquisitions and care of objects within the museum.

Museum curators care for objects in a museum's collection. The primary curatorial activities are maintenance, preservation, archiving, cataloguing, study, and display of collection components. Curators must fund-raise to support staff in the physical care and study of collections. They also add to or alter a museum's collection by trading objects with other museums or purchasing new pieces. They educate others through scholarly articles and public programs that showcase the items.

HISTORY

More than any other museum workers, curators and directors are closely identified with the image and purposes of a museum, and the history of these positions has followed the fortunes of museums themselves. Over time, the goals of museums alternated between a professional concentration on acquiring and studying collections, with some indifference to the interests of the public, and a contrary focus on visitor education and entertainment that occasionally turned into spectacles and sideshows for profit. According to Joel Orosz, museum historian and author of *Curators and Culture,* the alternating between museum professionalism and public education marked the first long span of U.S. museum history, from about 1740 to 1870. By 1870, however, the two trends had blended together, which Orosz refers to as the American compromise: *both* popular education *and* scholarly research would be held as equal, coexisting goals. This achievement, the author asserts, arose out of uniquely American conditions, prior to several decades of efforts by British and European museums to instate a similar mixture of goals, and permanently shaped the rest of U.S. museum history.

At different times during the first century of U.S. museum history, new scientific inventions and technologies shifted the professional focus of museums, as many museums of this era were devoted to natural history. In addition, popular education benefited from improved mass transportation. Robert Fulton's design of the steamboat, the opening of the Erie Canal in 1825, and the rise of the railroads gave travelers an alternative to tiring and dusty journeys by horse-drawn coach; thus, people from states as far away as Ohio and Kentucky could include museums on the eastern seaboard in their travel plans. As distant travelers sought out museums, curators were gratified and responded with programs of more general, less scholarly interest. The concept of a national museum, free to all and representative of the nation as a whole, took root in the popular imagination and was finally achieved in 1846 with the opening of the Smithsonian Institution.

Following a period of national economic prosperity and intense museum-building activities in the years 1950–1980, the American

compromise has again reached center stage, this time in a controversial light. In a weakened economy, some museum directors
believe it is no longer economically viable to maintain to two separate enterprises under one roof. Because public service is at the forefront of a modern museum's mission, museums are focusing on
exhibits and programs for the public at the expense of support for
research. Few taxpayers are repeat visitors to museums in a given
year, and even fewer have any notion of what it is that museum
directors and curators do. The coming decade will likely see
increased revenue-generating activities for museums, a temporary
freeze on museum allocations for research areas, or both. The financial stress is not uniquely felt by museums, for other civic institutions, notably symphony orchestras, have folded or sharply
curtailed programs in the past few years. The American compromise
faces some restructuring, introducing a period of uncertainty for
many museum employees.

THE JOB

A museum director's most important duties are administrative,
including staff leadership, promoting fund-raising campaigns, and
ensuring that the museum's mission is carried out. Directors of large
museums may have the assistance of several divisional directors
with the authority for specific areas of museum management, such
as a director of finance, director of development, director of public
programs, director of research, director of education, director of
operations, and director of marketing and public relations. In recognition of the museum director's role as "director of directors," the
museum director sometimes has the title of *executive director.*

One unusual but not uncommon activity for a museum director
is the design of new facilities. A director may spend a year or more
working with architects and planners to reconfigure existing areas of
the museum, add a wing, or build a museum from the ground up.
Construction can draw resources away from other museum operations and may be accompanied by a massive capital campaign.

Every museum is unique in its mission, the community it serves,
its resources, and the way it operates. Therefore, the responsibilities
of museum directors vary widely. Directors of children's museums
typically have a background in education and apply educational
philosophies to the design of exhibits and programs suitable for
children. Interactive displays, live interpretation, and participatory
theater are frequent components of children's museums, and com-

munity outreach programs help ensure that children of all backgrounds benefit from the museum's programs.

A director of a natural history museum may have a background in science and manage a staff of scientists. Concern for the disturbance of regional habitats and species extinction has prompted some museums to replace traditional galleries exhibiting birds, mammals, or fish with conceptual exhibits emphasizing ecology and evolution. In museums with a strong anthropological component, returning religious objects or ancestral remains to the country or people of origin is an important and controversial area. Museum directors must have considerable intercultural understanding and knowledge of the state laws governing the disposition of materials in state-tax-funded museums.

Directors of art museums typically have academic credentials in a specific area of art history and have good financial and fund-raising skills to manage costly collections. The director may be personally involved in making acquisitions for the museum. Directors of museums reflecting a specific culture, such as Mexican, Asian, or Native American culture, need knowledge of that culture and diplomatic skills to arrange the exchange of exhibit material.

At science and technology museums, exhibits demonstrate basic physical or biological laws, such as those governing the workings of the human heart, or they may present historical or futuristic exhibits, displaying the actual spacecraft used in early flight or the technology of the future. Directors of science and technology museums place a high priority on instructing the young, and hands-on exhibits are a featured attraction.

A curator's chief responsibilities include study and preservation of the museum's collections. Depending on the museum's size, resources, and deployment of staff, those responsibilities can vary. In museums with a large curatorial staff, senior curators may function primarily as administrators, overseeing departmental budgets and hiring new curators. In a different employment environment, curators may focus closely on the study and shape of the collections, exchanging materials with other museums or acquiring new specimens and artifacts to create a representative study collection of importance to scholarly work. In a third type of environment, curators may be primarily educators who describe and present collections to the visiting public. At any time, museum administrators may ask curators to redirect efforts toward a different goal of priority to the museum. Thus, a curator develops or brings to the position substantial knowledge of the materials in the collection, and that knowledge is used by the museum for a changing mix of purposes over time.

Curators may also spend time in the field or as visiting scholars at other museums as a means of continuing research related to the home institution's collections. Fieldwork is usually supported by grants from external sources. As specialists in their disciplines, curators may teach classes in local schools and universities, sometimes serving as academic advisors to doctorate degree candidates whose research is based on museum holdings. Almost all curators supervise a staff ranging from volunteers, interns, and students to research associates, collections managers, technicians, junior curators, and secretarial staff. Some sort of written work, whether it is labeling exhibits, preparing brochures for museum visitors, or publishing in scholarly journals, is typically part of the position.

In related positions, *collections managers* and *curatorial assistants* perform many of the same functions as curators, with more emphasis on study and cataloguing of the collections and less involvement with administration and staff supervision. The educational requirements for these positions may be the same as for a curatorial position. A curatorial candidate may accept a position as collections manager while awaiting a vacancy on the curatorial staff, since the opportunity to study, publish research, and conduct fieldwork is usually equally available in both positions. In art, historical, and anthropological museums, *registrars* and *archivists* may act as collections managers by cataloguing and preserving documents and objects and making information on these items available for scholarly use.

Once hired, curators embark on what is essentially a lifelong program of continuing self-education in museum practices. Curators of large collections must remain current with preservation techniques, including climate control and pest control methods. The human working environment can affect collections in unpredictable ways. As an example, common fungi that afflict houseplants may degrade the preservation environment of a collection of amphibians and reptiles, which may mean that all staff in the area are prohibited from introducing house plants into their workstations.

An important development in collections management is computerized cataloguing of holdings for registry in national electronic databases. A number of larger museums and universities are working together to standardize data entry fields for these electronic registries, after which data on every item in a collection must be entered by hand and cross-checked for accuracy. Concurrently, there is a trend toward publishing through nonprint media, such as academic networks administered by the National Sciences Foundation. Continuing self-education in electronic technologies and participation in national conferences addressing these issues will be expected of curators throughout the upcoming decade and beyond, for electronic storage and retrieval systems have radically changed the face of collections management.

REQUIREMENTS
High School
Museum directors and curators need diverse educational backgrounds to perform well in their jobs. At the high school level, you should take courses in English, literature, creative writing, history, art, the sciences, speech, business, and foreign languages. These courses will give you the general background knowledge needed to understand both the educational and administrative functions of museums. Math and computer skills are also essential. Museum directors and curators are responsible for preparing budgets and seeking funds from corporations and federal agencies.

Postsecondary Training
Museum directors and curators must have a bachelor's degree. Some colleges and universities offer undergraduate degrees in museology, or the study of museums. Most museums require their directorial staff and chief curators to hold doctorate degrees. Directors and curators usually work in museums that specialize in art, history, or science. These individuals often have degrees in fields related to the museum's specialty. Directors often have advanced degrees in business management, public relations, or marketing. All curators must have a good working knowledge of the art, objects, and cultures represented in their collections.

Other Requirements
Excellent written and oral communication skills are essential. Directors have a primary responsibility to supervise museum staff members, relay information to museum board members, and acquire funding for all museum programming. Museum directors must have extraordinary people skills and feel at ease when soliciting funds. Curators must have excellent research skills. They must be able to meet deadlines, write scholarly articles, and give presen-

tations while managing their traditional museum duties. Museum directors and curators should be well organized and flexible.

Occasionally museums have specific requirements, such as foreign language fluency for an art or anthropology museum or practical computer skills for a science or natural history museum. A student usually acquires these skills as part of the background study within his or her area of concentration.

EXPLORING

Museum directorships and curatorial positions are highly competitive and reward high academic achievement. Outside of school, participation in clubs that involve fund-raising activities can serve as a strong introduction to one important aspect of a museum director's job. Becoming the president of one of these clubs can provide you with supervisory skills and experience with delegating authority.

Museums offer public programs for people of all ages. Field trips or tours introduce students to activities conducted by local museums. College-age students may work at museums as volunteers or perhaps as interns for course credit. Depending on the museum's needs, volunteers and interns may be placed anywhere in the museum, including administration, archives, and other areas where a student may observe staff functions firsthand.

EMPLOYERS

Museums as well as historical societies and state and federal agencies with public archives and libraries hire directors and curators. These institutions are located throughout the world, in both small and large cities, and are responsible for providing public access to their collections. Museums and similar institutions employ directors and curators to fulfill their educational goals through continued research, care of collections, and public programs.

STARTING OUT

As mentioned earlier, some U.S. colleges offer undergraduate programs in museology, but most museum workers at all levels enter museum work because they possess specific skills and a body of knowledge useful to a particular museum. For a museum director, as for a well-qualified curator, this translates into content knowledge, managerial and administrative skills, fund-raising ability, leadership ability, and excellent communication skills for effective interaction with the media and the board of trustees. While the role of a curator is focused primarily on collections and the role of director is often more administrative and interpersonal, the two positions both require a great degree of knowledge across the board regarding the museum's mission statement, acquisitions, and community involvement.

Museum directors typically move into their positions in one of three ways: laterally, from a previous directorship of another museum; vertically, from an administrative or curatorial position within the same museum; or laterally from a different sphere of employment, such as a university presidency, business management, government agency, or law practice.

A position as curator usually is not anticipated and prepared for in advance, but becomes available as an employment option following a long period of training in a discipline. College and advanced degree students who have identified a curatorial position as a career goal may be able to apply for curatorial internships of varying terms, usually a year or less. Interns typically work on a project identified by the museum, which may involve only one task or several different tasks. Additionally, museums thrive on a large base of volunteer labor, and this method of gaining museum experience should not be overlooked. Curators may ask volunteers to assist in a variety of tasks, ranging from clerical duties to conservation and computerized cataloguing. When funds are available, volunteer work may be converted to hourly paid work.

ADVANCEMENT
Museum directors typically succeed one another, moving from smaller museums to larger museums or from a general to a specialty museum. A museum directorship is a lifetime career goal and may be held for decades by the same person. A museum director who retires from the position is well prepared to sit on state or national advisory councils to the arts and sciences. Some return to academic life through teaching, research, or curricula development. Others provide oversight and guidance to large institutions, sit on corporate boards, or become involved in the start-up of new museums.

Curatorial positions follow the assistant, associate, and full (or senior) track of academic employment, with advancement depending on research and publishing, education, and service to the institution. A curator with a taste for and skill in administration may serve as departmental chair or may seek a higher administrative post.

In the course of their museum duties, curators may act as advisers to or principals in external nonprofit endeavors, such as setting up international ecological preserves or providing technical assistance and labor to aid a developing country in the study of its archaeological past. Many teach in local schools or universities. Curators who leave museum work may devote themselves full time to these or similar pursuits, although a university professorship as a second choice is difficult to achieve, for curators and professors are essentially competing for the same market position and have similar credentials. Occasionally curators find fieldwork so compelling that they leave not only the museum, but all formal employment, relying on grants and personal contributions from supporters to support their work. To maintain an independent life as a researcher without formal affiliation requires a high profile in the discipline, continuing demonstration of productivity in the form of new research and publications, and some skill in self-promotion.

EARNINGS

The salaries of museum directors and curators cover a broad range, reflecting the diversity, size, and budget of U.S. museums, along with the director or curator's academic and professional achievements. In general, museum workers' salaries are low compared to salaries for similar positions in the business world or in academia. This is due in part to the large number of people competing for the relatively small number of positions available. At the high end of the scale, museum directors at museums like the Whitney and the Metropolitan Museum of Art in New York City, or the Art Institute of Chicago earn more than $500,000 a year.

A survey of its members conducted by the Association of Art Museum Directors reported that the average salary of an art museum director is roughly $110,000. The average salary of a deputy director ranges from $65,000 to $123,000, while the average salary of an assistant to the director is roughly $31,000. The same study reported entry-level curatorial positions, often titled curatorial assistant or curatorial intern, as averaging $24,000, while assistant curator salaries average from $26,000 to $37,000 per year. Both the position of associate curator, a title with supervisory duties, and the position of curator of exhibitions average $34,000 to $53,000. Chief curator salaries average $57,000, but, as with many museum titles, may be considerably higher or lower depending on the demands of the job and the museum's overall budget. Curators directing an ongoing program of conservation and acquisitions in a large, national or international urban museum command the highest salaries and may earn as much as $152,000.

According to the Bureau of Labor Statistics, the median annual earnings of archivists, curators, museum technicians, and conservators were $34,190 in 2001. Salaries ranged from less than $18,910 to more than $63,870.

Fringe benefits, including paid vacations and sick leave, medical and dental insurance, and retirement plans, vary between museum directors and curators and according to each employing institution's policies.

WORK ENVIRONMENT

The directorship of a museum is an all-consuming occupation. Considerable travel, program development, fund-raising, and staff management may be involved. Evenings and weekends are often taken up by social activities involving museum donors or affiliates. A museum director must be willing to accept the pressure of answering to the museum's board of trustees while also overseeing museum staff and handling public relations.

As new issues affecting museums arise in the national consciousness and draw media attention, a director must be able to respond appropriately. The director must maintain the delicate balance in observing the museum's role as both public institution and research facility. Museum directors must juggle competing interests and requests for the museum's resources.

The office of a director is typically housed within the museum. Many directors have considerable staff support, to which they can delegate specific areas of responsibility, and thus must have strong interpersonal and diplomatic skills.

Curators typically have an office in a private area of the museum, but may have to share office space. Employment conditions and benefits are more like those of industry than academia, although the employment contract may stipulate that the curator is free to pursue a personal schedule of fieldwork for several weeks during the year.

A curatorial post and a directorship are typically nine-to-five jobs, but that does not take into account the long hours of study necessary to sustain scholarly research, weekend time spent on public programs, or evening meetings with donors, trustees, and museum affiliates. The actual hours spent on curatorial-related and directorship activities may be double those of the employment contract. Directors and curators must enjoy their work, be interested in museum operations and a museum's profile in the community, and willingly put in the necessary time.

OUTLOOK

There are few openings for directors and curators and competition for them is high. New graduates may have to start as interns, volunteers, assistants, or research associates before finding full-time curator or director positions. Turnover is very low in museum work, so museum workers may have to stay in a lower level position for some years before advancing to a director or curator position. The employment outlook for museum directors and curators is expected to increase about as fast as the average over the next several years, according to the *Occupational Outlook Handbook*. The best opportunities are in art, history, and technology museums.

Curators must be able to develop revenue-generating public programs based on the study collections and integrate themselves firmly into programs of joint research with area institutions (other museums or universities) or national institutions, ideally programs of some duration and supported by external funding. Museums are affected by economic conditions and the availability of grants and other charitable funding.

FOR MORE INFORMATION

For information on careers, education and training, and internships, contact
American Association of Museums
1575 Eye Street, NW, Suite 400
Washington, DC 20005
Tel: 202-289-1818
http://www.aam-us.org

This organization represents directors of the major art museums in North America. It sells a publication on professional practices, a salary survey, and a sample employment contract.
Association of Art Museum Directors
41 East 65th Street
New York, NY 10021
Tel: 212-249-4423
http://www.aamd.org

NEWSPAPER EDITORS

QUICK FACTS

School Subjects English Journalism	**Certification or Licensing** None available
Personal Interests Communication/ideas Helping/teaching	**Outlook** Faster than the average **DOT** 132
Work Environment Primarily indoors Primarily one location	**GOE** 11.08.01
Minimum Education Level Bachelor's degree	**NOC** 5122
Salary Range $23,090 to $39,960 to $73,460+	**O*NET-SOC** 27-3041.00

OVERVIEW

Newspaper editors assign, review, edit, rewrite, and lay out all copy in a newspaper except advertisements. Editors sometimes write stories or editorials that offer opinions on issues. Editors review the editorial page and copy written by staff or syndicated columnists. A large metropolitan daily newspaper staff may include various editors who process thousands of words into print daily. A small town staff of a weekly newspaper, however, may include only one editor, who might be both owner and star reporter. Large metropolitan areas, such as New York, Los Angeles, Chicago, and Washington, D.C., employ many editors. Approximately 122,000 editors work for publications of all types in the United States.

HISTORY

The primary function of the newspaper publishing industry is to inform the public. Newspapers provide details, eyewitness interviews, and interpretations of current events in all areas of our society, such as politics, entertainment, and international affairs, to name a few.

The first American newspaper, *Publick Occurrences Both Foreign and Domestick*, appeared in Boston in 1690 and lasted only one issue due to censorship by the British government. The first continuously published paper in America was the *Boston News-Letter*, first published in 1704. It appeared regularly until 1776. The first daily newspaper, the *Pennsylvania Evening Post and Daily Advertiser*, began publication in 1783.

Early newspaper publishers were jacks-of-all-trades. They interviewed newsmakers; researched, wrote, and edited stories; solicited advertising; and typeset and printed their publications. As newspapers became larger and circulation increased, one person alone could no longer handle all of these tasks. By the late 19th century, every newspaper employed full-time reporters and editors who were skilled at research, writing, and editing. Today, most large newspapers employ a wide range of editors.

Computer technology and the Internet have had a dramatic impact on the newspaper industry. Internet and email technology allow newspaper editors to research information, confirm stories, and communicate with reporters much faster than they have in the past. Most major newspapers publish online versions, which provide some or all of the information that appears simultaneously in print versions. The growth of the Internet as a publishing venue has created many new opportunities for newspaper editors and other professionals in the industry.

THE JOB

Newspaper editors are responsible for the paper's entire news content. The news section includes features, "hard" news, and editorial commentary. Editors of a daily paper plan the contents of each day's issue, assigning articles, reviewing submissions, prioritizing stories, checking wire services, selecting illustrations, and laying out each page with the advertising space allotted.

At a large daily newspaper, an *editor in chief* oversees the entire editorial operation, determines its editorial policy, and reports to the publisher. The *managing editor* is responsible for day-to-day operations in an administrative capacity. *Story editors,* or *wire editors,* determine which national news agency (or wire service) stories will be used and edit them. Wire services give smaller papers, without foreign correspondents, access to international stories.

A *city editor* gathers local and sometimes state and national news. The city editor hires copy editors and reporters, hands out assignments to reporters and photographers, reviews and edits stories, confers with executive editors on story content and space availability, and gives stories to copy editors for final editing.

A newspaper may have separate desks for state, national, and foreign news, each with its own head editor. Some papers have separate *editorial page editors*. The *department editors*, including *business editors, fashion editors, sports editors, book section editors,* and *entertainment editors,* oversee individual features. Department heads make decisions on coverage, recommend story ideas, and make assignments. They often have backgrounds in their department's subject matter and are highly skilled at writing and editing.

The copy desk, the story's last stop, is staffed by *copy editors,* who correct spelling, grammar, and punctuation mistakes; check for readability and sense; edit for clarification; examine stories for factual accuracy; and ensure the story conforms to editorial policy. Copy editors sometimes write headlines or picture captions and may crop photos. Occasionally they find serious problems that cause them to kick stories back to the editors or the writer.

Editors, particularly copy editors, base many of their decisions on a style book that provides preferences in spelling, grammar, and word usage; it indicates when to use foreign spellings or English translations and the preferred system of transliteration. Some houses develop their own style books, but often they use or adapt the *Associated Press Stylebook.*

After editors approve the story's organization, coverage, writing quality, and accuracy, they turn it over to the *news editors,* who supervise article placement and determine page layout with the advertising department. News and executive editors discuss the relative priorities of major news stories. If a paper is divided into several sections, each has its own priorities.

Modern newspaper editors depend heavily on computers. Generally, a reporter types the story directly onto the computer network, providing editors with immediate access. Some editorial departments are situated remotely from printing facilities, but computers allow the printer to receive copy immediately upon approval. Today, designers use computers to lay out pages. Many columnists send their finished columns from home computers to the editorial department via modem.

REQUIREMENTS
High School
English is the most important school subject for any future editor. You must have a strong grasp of the English language, including vocabulary, grammar, and punctuation, and you must be able to write well in various styles. Study journalism and take communications-related courses. Work as a writer or editor for your school paper or yearbook. Computer classes that teach word processing software and how to navigate the Internet will be invaluable in your future research. You absolutely must learn to type. If you cannot type accurately and rapidly, you will be at an extreme disadvantage in this profession.

Editors have knowledge in a wide range of topics, and the more you know about history, geography, math, the sciences, the arts, and culture, the better a writer and editor you will be.

Postsecondary Training
Look for a school with strong journalism and communications programs. Many programs require you to complete two years of liberal arts studies before concentrating on journalism studies. Journalism courses include reporting, writing, and editing; press law and ethics; journalism history; and photojournalism. Advanced classes include feature writing, investigative reporting, and graphics. Some schools offer internships for credit.

When hiring, newspapers look closely at a candidate's extracurricular activities, putting special emphasis on internships, school newspaper and freelance writing and editing, and part-time newspaper work (called *stringing*). Typing, computer skills, and knowledge of printing are helpful.

Other Requirements
To be a successful newspaper editor, you must have a love of learning, reading, and writing. You should enjoy the process of discovering information and presenting it to a wide audience in a complete, precise, and understandable way. You must be detail-oriented and care about the finer points of accuracy, not only in writing, but in reporting and presentation. You must be able to work well with coworkers, both giving and taking direction, and you must be able

to work alone. Editors can spend long hours sitting at a desk in front of a computer screen.

EXPLORING

One of the best ways to explore this job is by working on your school's newspaper or other publication. You will most probably start as a staff writer or proofreader, which will help you understand editing and how it relates to the entire field of publishing.

Keeping a journal is another good way to polish your writing skills and explore your interest in writing and editing your own work. In fact, any writing project will be helpful, since editing and writing are inextricably linked. Make an effort to write every day, even if it is only a few paragraphs. Try different kinds of writing, such as letters to the editor, short stories, poetry, essays, comedic prose, and plays.

EMPLOYERS

Generally, newspaper editors are employed in every city or town, as most towns have at least one newspaper. As the population multiplies, so do the opportunities. In large metropolitan areas, there may be one or two daily papers, several general-interest weekly papers, ethnic and other special-interest newspapers, trade newspapers, and daily and weekly community and suburban newspapers. All of these publications need managing and department editors. Online papers also provide opportunities for editors.

STARTING OUT

A typical route of entry into this field is by working as an editorial assistant or proofreader. Editorial assistants perform clerical tasks as well as some proofreading and other basic editorial tasks. Proofreaders can learn about editorial jobs while they work on a piece by looking at editors' comments on their work.

Job openings can be found using school placement offices, classified ads in newspapers and trade journals, and specialized publications such as *Publishers Weekly* (http://www.publishersweekly.com). In addition, many publishers have websites that list job openings, and large publishers often have telephone job lines that serve the same purpose.

ADVANCEMENT

Newspaper editors generally begin working on the copy desk, where they progress from less significant stories and projects to major news and feature stories. A common route to advancement is for copy editors to be promoted to a particular department, where they may move up the ranks to management positions. An editor who has achieved success in a department may become a city editor, who is responsible for news, or a managing editor, who runs the entire editorial operation of a newspaper.

EARNINGS

Salaries for newspaper editors vary from small to large communities, but editors generally are well compensated. Other factors affecting compensation include quality of education and previous experience, job level, and the newspaper's circulation. Large metropolitan dailies offer higher paying jobs, while outlying weekly papers pay less.

According to the Bureau of Labor Statistics, the median annual income for editors (including newspaper editors) was $39,960 in 2001. The lowest paid 10 percent of editors earned less than $23,090 annually. The highest paid 10 percent of all editors earned more than $73,460 per year.

On many newspapers, salary ranges and benefits, such as vacation time and health insurance, for most nonmanagerial editorial workers are negotiated by the Newspaper Guild.

WORK ENVIRONMENT

Editors work in a wide variety of environments. For the most part, publishers of all kinds realize that a quiet atmosphere is conducive to work that requires tremendous concentration. It takes an unusual ability to edit in a noisy place. Most editors work in private offices or cubicles. Even in relatively quiet surroundings, however, editors often have many distractions. In many cases, editors have computers that are exclusively for their own use, but in others, editors must share computers that are located in a common area.

Deadlines are an important issue for virtually all editors. Newspaper editors work in a much more pressured atmosphere than other editors because they face daily or weekly deadlines. To meet these deadlines, newspaper editors often work long hours. Some newspaper editors start work at 5:00 A.M., others work until 11:00 P.M. or even through the night. Those who work on weekly newspapers, including feature editors, columnists, and editorial page editors, usually work more regular hours.

Top 25 History Graduate Schools

U.S. News & World Report prepares annual ranking lists for graduate school programs. The following lists show the top-ranked history schools.

1. Princeton University (N.J.)
   http://history.princeton.edu

2. Yale University (Conn.)
   http://www.yale.edu/history

3. Stanford University (Calif.)
   http://history.stanford.edu

4. University of California—Berkeley
   http://history.berkeley.edu

5. Columbia University (N.Y.)
   http://www.columbia.edu/cu/history

6. University of Chicago
   http://history.uchicago.edu

7. University of Michigan-Ann Arbor
   http://www.lsa.umich.edu/history

8. Harvard University (Mass.)
   http://www.fas.harvard.edu/~history

9. University of California-Los Angeles
   http://www.sscnet.ucla.edu/history

10. Cornell University (N.Y.)
    http://falcon.arts.cornell.edu/History

11. Johns Hopkins University (MD)
    http://www.jhu.edu/~history

12. University of Wisconsin—Madison
    http://history.wisc.edu

13. University of North Carolina—Chapel Hill
    http://www.unc.edu/depts/history

14. University of Pennsylvania
    http://www.history.upenn.edu

15. Brown University (R.I.)
    http://www.brown.edu/Departments/History

16. Duke University (N.C.)
    http://www-history.aas.duke.edu

(continues)

Top 25 History Graduate Schools

(continued)

17 Northwestern University (Ill.)
http://www2.mmlc.northwestern.edu/history

18. University of Virginia
http://www.virginia.edu/history

19. Indiana University—Bloomington
http://www.indiana.edu/~histweb

20. Rutgers University—New Brunswick (N.J.)
http://history.rutgers.edu/undergrad/under_index.html

21. University of Minnesota—Twin Cities
http://www.hist.umn.edu

22. University of Illinois-Urbana-Champaign
http://www.history.uiuc.edu

23. University of Texas—Austin
http://www.utexas.edu/cola/depts/history

24. New York University
http://www.nyu.edu/gsas/dept/history

25. Emory University (GA)
http://www.emory.edu/history/graduate

Source: *U.S. News & World Report* (ranked in 2001)

OUTLOOK

According to the U.S. Department of Labor, employment for editors and writers, while highly competitive, should grow faster than the average. Opportunities will be better on small daily and weekly newspapers, where the pay is lower. Some publications hire freelance editors to support reduced full-time staffs. And as experienced editors leave the workforce or move to other fields, job openings will become available.

FOR MORE INFORMATION

The ASNE helps editors maintain the highest standards of quality, improve their craft, and better serve their communities. It preserves and promotes core journalistic values.

American Society of Newspaper Editors (ASNE)
11690B Sunrise Valley Drive
Reston, VA 20191-1409
Tel: 703-453-1122
http://www.asne.org

Founded in 1958 by The Wall Street Journal *to improve the quality of journalism education, this organization offers internships, scholarships, and literature for college students. For information on how to receive a copy of* The Journalist's Road to Success, *which lists schools offering degrees in newsediting, and financial aid to those interested in print journalism, contact*
Dow Jones Newspaper Fund
PO Box 300
Princeton, NJ 08543-0300
Tel: 609-452-2820
Email: newsfund@wsj.dowjones.com
http://djnewspaperfund.dowjones.com

This trade association for African-American owned newspapers has a foundation that offers a scholarship and internship program for inner-city high school juniors.
National Newspaper Publishers Association
3200 13th Street, NW
Washington, DC 20010
Tel: 202-588-8764
http://www.nnpa.org

This organization for journalists has campus and online chapters.
Society of Professional Journalists
Eugene S. Pulliam National Journalism Center
3909 North Meridian Street
Indianapolis, IN 46208
Tel: 317-927-8000
Email: questions@spj.org
http://spj.org

POLITICAL SCIENTISTS

QUICK FACTS

School Subjects Government Sociology	**Certification or Licensing** None available
Personal Skills Communication/ideas Helping/teaching	**Outlook** About as fast as the average **DOT** 051
Work Environment Primarily indoors Primarily one location	**GOE** 11.03.02
Minimum Education Level Doctorate degree	**NOC** 4169
Salary Range $21,900 to $81,040 to $100,000+	**O*NET-SOC** 19-3094.00, 25-1065.00

OVERVIEW

Political scientists study the structure and theory of government, usually as part of an academic faculty. They constantly seek both theoretical and practical solutions to political problems. They divide their responsibilities between teaching and researching. After compiling facts, statistics, and other research, they present their analyses in reports, lectures, and journal articles.

HISTORY

Political science is the oldest of the social sciences and is currently one of the most popular subjects of undergraduate study. The ideas of many early political scientists still influence current political theories. Machiavelli, the 16th-century Italian statesman and philosopher, believed that politics and morality are two entirely different spheres of human activity and that they should be governed by different standards and different laws. In the 17th century, Thomas Hobbes thought of government as a police force that prevented people from plundering their neighbors. John Locke was a 17th-century Englishman from whom we get the philosophy of "the greatest good for the greatest number." Some people call him the originator of "beneficent paternalism," which means that the state or ruler acts as a kindly leader to citizens, deciding what is best for them, then seeing that the "best" is put into effect, whether the citizens like it or not.

Common among theorists today is the assumption that politics is a process, the constant interaction of individuals and groups in activities that are directly or indirectly related to government. By 1945, political science in the United States was much more than the concern for institutions, law, formal structures of public government, procedures, and rules. It had expanded to include the dynamics of public governance. Instead of studying the rules of administrative procedure in a political group, for example, political scientists had begun to study the actual bureaucratic processes at work within the group. This signified the start of what would become systems theory in political science.

THE JOB
While many government careers involve taking action that directly impacts political policy, political scientists study and discuss the results of these actions. "You can look into just about anything that interests you," says Chris Mooney, an associate professor and director of graduate studies for the political science department of West Virginia University, "but you have to be able to argue that it's relevant to some basic theory in political science."

Political scientists may choose to research political lyrics in rock music, or study how teenagers form their political ideas. They may research the history of women in politics, the role of religion in politics, and the political histories of other countries. For example, in addition to his teaching responsibilities, Mooney is currently researching the reasons why some states have the death penalty. Many political scientists specialize in one area of study, such as public administration, history of political ideas, political parties, public law, American government, or international relations.

About 80 percent of all political scientists are employed as college and university professors. Depending on the institution for which they work, political scientists divide their time between teaching and researching. Mooney estimates that 45 percent of his time is devoted to teaching, 45 percent to research, and the remaining time is for service to the university, such as committee work. Though he works for a research-oriented university, "teaching drives everything," he says.

In addition to teaching and researching, political scientists write books and articles based on their studies. A number of political science associations publish journals, and there are small presses devoted to publishing political theory. Mooney has published two books, and many scholarly articles in such journals as *Policy Studies Journal, Health Economics,* and the *American Journal of Political Science.* His area of study is behavioral political science. For his current study of the death penalty, he is compiling economic, social, and demographic facts. This data is then fed into the computer, and Mooney attempts to draw conclusions. Sometimes graduate students are involved with the research; they assist with the collection of data, computer work, and copyediting.

In researching policy issues, political scientists use a variety of different methods. They work with historians, economists, policy analysts, demographers, and statisticians. The Internet has become a very important resource tool for political scientists. The federal government has been dedicated to expanding the World Wide Web, including making available full text of legislation, recent Supreme Court decisions, and access to the Library of Congress. Political scientists also use the data found in yearbooks and almanacs, material from encyclopedias, clippings from periodicals or bound volumes of magazines or journals. They refer to law books, to statutes, to records of court cases, to the *Congressional Record,* and to other legislative records. They consult census records, historical documents, personal documents such as diaries and letters, and statistics from public opinion polls. They use libraries and archives to locate rare and old documents and records. For other information, political scientists use the "participant observer" method of research. In this method, they become part of a group and participate in its proceedings, while carefully observing interaction. They may also submit questionnaires. Questions will be carefully worded to elicit the facts needed, and the questionnaire will be administered to a selected sample of people.

When conducting research, political scientists must avoid letting their own biases distort the way in which they interpret the gathered facts. Then, they must compare their findings and analyses with those of others who have conducted similar investigations. Finally, they must present the data in an objective fashion, even though the findings may not reveal the kinds of facts they anticipated.

Those political scientists who are not employed as teachers work for labor unions, political organizations, or political interest groups. Political scientists working for government may study organizations ranging in scope from the United Nations to local city councils. They may study the politics of a large city like New York or a small town in the Midwest. Their research findings may be used by a city's mayor and city council to set public policy concerning waste management or by an organization, such as the National Organization for Women, to decide where to focus efforts on increasing the participation of women in local politics. Political scientists who work for the U.S. Department of State in either this country or in the foreign service use their analyses of political structures to make recommendations to the U.S. government concerning foreign policy.

Political scientists may also be employed by individual members of Congress. In this capacity, they might study government programs concerned with low-income housing and make recommendations to help the member of Congress write new legislation. Businesses and industries also hire political scientists to conduct polls on political issues that affect their operations. A tobacco company might want to know, for example, how the legislation restricting advertising by tobacco companies affects the buying habits of consumers of tobacco products.

REQUIREMENTS
High School

Take courses in government, American history, and civics to gain insight into politics. Math is also important because, as a political scientist, you'll be evaluating statistics, demographics, and other numerical data. English and composition classes will help you develop the writing and communication skills you'll need for teaching, publishing, and presenting papers. Take a journalism course and work for your high school newspaper to develop research, writing, and editing skills. Join a speech and debate team to gain experience researching current events, analyzing data, and presenting the information to others.

Postsecondary Training

Though you'll be able to find some government jobs with a bachelor's degree in political science, you won't be able to pursue work in major academic institutions without a doctorate.

The American Political Science Association (APSA) publishes directories of undergraduate and graduate political science programs. An undergraduate program requires general courses in English, economics, statistics, and history, as well as courses in American politics, international politics, and political theory. Look for a school with a good internship program through which you can become involved with the U.S. Congress or state legislature. *U.S. News & World Report* publishes rankings of graduate schools. In 2001, Harvard was deemed the top-ranked political science department. Stanford, University of California (Berkeley), and University of Michigan (Ann Arbor) all tied for second place, and Yale came in fifth place.

Your graduate study will include courses in political parties, public opinion, comparative political behavior, and foreign policy design. You'll also assist professors with research, attend conferences, write articles, and teach undergraduate courses.

Other Requirements

Because you'll be compiling information from a number of different sources, you must be well-organized. You should also enjoy reading and possess a curiosity about world politics. "You have to really enjoy school," Chris Mooney says, "but it should all be fairly fascinating. You'll be studying and telling people about what you're studying." People skills are important, as you'll be working closely with students and other political scientists.

EXPLORING

Write to college political science departments for information about their programs. You can learn a lot about the work of a political scientist by looking at college course lists and faculty bios. Political science departments also have Web pages with information, and links to the curricula vitae (C.V.) of faculty. A C.V. is an extensive resume including lists of publications, conferences attended, and other professional experience. A C.V. can give you an idea of a political scientist's career and education path.

Contact the office of your state's senator or representative in the U.S. Congress about applying to work as a page. Available to students at least 16 years old, the highly competitive page positions allow students to serve members of Congress, running messages across Capitol Hill in Washington, D.C. This experience would be very valuable to you in learning about the workings of government.

EMPLOYERS

Political science is a popular major among undergraduates, so practically every college and university has a political science department. Political scientists find work at public and private universities, and at community colleges. They teach in undergraduate, master's, and doctorate programs. Teaching jobs at doctorate institutions are usually better paying and more prestigious. The most sought after positions are those that offer tenure.

STARTING OUT

"Go to the best school you can," Chris Mooney advises, "and focus on getting into a good graduate school." Most graduate schools accept a very limited number of applicants every semester, so there's a lot of competition for admittance into some of the top programs. Applicants are admitted on the basis of grade point averages, test scores, internships performed, awards received, and other achievements.

Once you're in graduate school, you'll begin to perform the work you'll be doing in your career. You'll teach undergraduate classes, attend conferences, present papers, and submit articles to political science journals. Your success as a graduate student will help you in your job search. After completing a graduate program, you'll teach as an adjunct professor or visiting professor at various schools until you can find a permanent tenure-track position.

Membership in APSA and other political science associations entitles you to job placement assistance. APSA can also direct you to a number of fellowship and grant opportunities. Michigan State University posts job openings on its H-Net (Job Guide for the Humanities and Social Sciences) Web page at http://www.matrix. msu.edu/jobs. Due to the heavy competition for these jobs, you'll need an impressive C.V., including a list of publications in respected political science journals, a list of conferences attended, and good references attesting to your teaching skills.

ADVANCEMENT

In a tenure-track position, political scientists work their way up through the ranks from assistant professor, to associate professor, to full professor. They will probably have to work a few years in temporary, or visiting, faculty positions before they can join the permanent faculty of a political science department. They can then expect to spend approximately seven years working toward tenure. Tenure provides political scientists with job security and prominence within their department, and is awarded on the basis of publications, research performed, student evaluations, and teaching experience.

EARNINGS

The *Occupational Outlook Handbook* reports that median annual earnings for social scientists in 2000 were $81,040. In 2001 starting federal government salaries for political scientists with a bachelor's degree and no experience were $21,900 or $27,200, depending on academic record. Those with a master's degree earned an average starting salary of $33,300, while those with a Ph.D. averaged $40,200.

The American Association of University Professors (AAUP) conducts an annual survey of the salaries of college professors. With the 2001–2002 survey, the AAUP found that full professors (with varying educational backgrounds) received an average of $83,282 a year, and associate professors received an average of $59,496 annually.

WORK ENVIRONMENT

Political scientists who work as tenured faculty members enjoy pleasant surroundings. Depending on the size of the department, they will have their own office and be provided with a computer, Internet access, and research assistants. With good teaching skills, they will earn the respect of their students and colleagues. Political science professors are also well-respected in their communities.

Political science teachers work a fairly flexible schedule, teaching two or three courses a semester. The rest of their 40–50-hour workweek will be spent meeting individually with students, conducting research, writing, and serving on committees. Some travel may be required, as teachers attend a few conferences a year on behalf of their department, or as they take short-term assignments at other institutions. Teachers may teach some summer courses, or have the summer off. They will also have several days off between semesters.

OUTLOOK

Overall employment of social scientists is expected to grow about as fast as the average over the next several years, according to the *Occupational Outlook Handbook*.

The survival of political science departments depends on continued community and government support of education. The funding of humanities and social science programs is often threatened, resulting in budget cuts and hiring freezes. This makes for heavy competition for the few graduate assistantships and new faculty positions available. Also, there's not a great deal of mobility within the field; professors who achieve tenure generally stay in their positions until retirement.

The pay inequity between male and female professors is of some concern. In the workplace in general, women are paid less than men, but this inequity is even greater in the field of academics. The AAUP is fighting to correct this, and female professors are becoming more cautious when choosing tenure-track positions.

More and more professors are using computers and the Internet, not just in research, but in conducting their classes. According to an annual survey conducted by the Campus Computing Project, computers and CD-ROMs are used increasingly in the lecture hall, and many professors use Web pages to post class materials and other resources.

FOR MORE INFORMATION

For more information on a political science career, contact
American Political Science Association
1527 New Hampshire Avenue, NW
Washington, DC 20036-1206
Tel: 202-483-2512
Email: apsa@apsanet.org
http://www.apsanet.org

For employment opportunities, mail resume and cover letters to
U.S. House of Representatives
Office of Human Resources
175 Ford House Office Building
Washington, DC 20515-6610
Tel: 202-225-2450
http://www.house.gov

U.S. Senate Placement Office
Room SH-142B
Washington, DC 20510
Tel: 202-224-9167
http://www.senate.gov

REGIONAL AND LOCAL OFFICIALS

QUICK FACTS

School Subjects Economics Government History **Personal Skills** Communication/ideas Leadership/management **Work Environment** Primarily indoors One location with some travel **Minimum Education Level** Bachelor's degree **Salary Range** $0 to $40,000 to $100,000+	**Certification or Licensing** None available **Outlook** Little or no change **DOT** 188 **GOE** 11.05.03 **NOC** 0011 **O*NET-SOC** 11-1031.00

OVERVIEW

Regional and local officials hold positions in the legislative, executive, and judicial branches of government at the local level. They include mayors, commissioners, and city and county council members. These officials direct regional legal services, public health departments, and police protection. They serve on housing, budget, and employment committees and develop special programs to improve communities.

HISTORY

The framers of the U.S. Constitution didn't make any specific provisions for the governing of cities and counties. This allowed state governments to compose their own definitions; when drawing up their own constitutions, the states essentially considered county governments to be extensions of the state government.

City governments, necessary for dealing with increased industry and trade, evolved during the 19th century. Population growth and suburban development helped to strengthen local governments after World War I. The county governments grew even stronger after World War II, due to rising revenues and increased independence from the states.

THE JOB

There are a variety of different forms of local government across the country, but they all share similar concerns. County and city governments make sure that the local streets are free of crime as well as free of potholes. They create and improve regional parks and organize music festivals and outdoor theater events to be staged in these parks. They identify community problems and help to solve them in original ways. For example, in an effort to solve the problem of unemployment among those recently released from jail, King County, Washington, developed a baking training program for county inmates. The inmates' new talents with danishes and bread loaves opened up well-paying job opportunities in grocery store bakeries all across the county. King County also has many youth programs, including the Paul Robeson Scholar-Athlete Award to recognize students who excel in both academics and athletics.

The Innovative Farmer Program in Huron County, Michigan, was developed to introduce new methods of farming to maintain the role of agriculture as part of the county's economy. The program is studying new cover-crops, tillage systems, and herbicides. In Onondaga County, New York, the public library started a program of basic reading instruction for deaf adults. In Broward County, Florida, a program provides a homelike setting for supervised visitation and parenting training for parents who are separated from their children due to abuse or domestic violence.

The needs for consumer protection, water quality, and affordable housing increase every year. Regional or local officials are elected to deal with issues such as public health, legal services, housing, and budget and fiscal management. They attend meetings and serve on committees. They know about the industry and agriculture of the area as well as the specific problems facing constituents, and they offer educated solutions, vote on laws, and generally represent the people in their districts.

There are two forms of county government: the *commissioner/administrator form*, in which the county board of commissioners appoints an administrator who serves the board, and the *council/executive form*, in which a county executive is the chief administrative officer of the district and has the power to veto ordinances enacted by the county board. A county government may include a *chief executive*, who directs regional services; *council members*, who are the county legislators; a *county clerk*, who keeps records of property titles, licenses, etc.; and a *county treasurer*, who is in charge of the receipt and disbursement of money.

A county government doesn't tax its citizens, so its money comes from state aid, fees, and grants. A city government funds its projects and programs with money from sales and other local taxes, block grants, and state aid. Elected executives direct these funds and services. *Mayors* serve as the heads of city governments and are elected by the general populace. Their specific functions vary depending on the structure of their government. In mayor-council governments, both the mayor and the city council are popularly elected. The council is responsible for formulating city ordinances, but the mayor exercises control over the actions of the council. In such governments, the mayor usually plays a dual role, serving not only as chief executive officer but also as an agent of the city government responsible for such functions as maintaining public order, security, and health. In a commission government, the people elect a number of *commissioners*, each of whom serves as head of a city department. The presiding commissioner is usually the mayor. The final type of municipal government is the council/manager form. Here, the council members are elected by the people, and one of their functions is to hire a *city manager* to administer the city departments. A mayor is elected by the council to chair the council and officiate at important municipal functions.

REQUIREMENTS
High School

Courses in government, civics, and history will give you an understanding of the structure of government. English courses are important because you will need good writing skills to communicate with constituents and other government officials. Math, accounting, and economics will help you develop analytical skills for examining statistics and demographics. Journalism classes will develop research and interview skills for identifying problems and developing programs.

Postsecondary Training

To serve on a local government, your experience and understanding of the city or county are generally more important than your educational background. Some mayors and council members are elected to their positions because they've lived in the region for a long time and have had experience with local industry and other concerns. For example, someone with years of farming experience may be the best candidate to serve a small agricultural community. Voters in local elections may be more impressed by a candidate's previous occupations and roles in the community than they are by a candidate's postsecondary degrees.

That said, most regional and local officials still hold an undergraduate degree, and many hold a graduate degree. Popular areas of study include public administration, law, economics, political science, history, and English. Regardless of your major as an undergraduate, you are likely to be required to take classes in English literature, statistics, foreign language, western civilization, and economics.

Other Requirements

To be successful in this field, you must understand deeply the city and region you serve. You need to be knowledgeable about the local industry, private businesses, and social problems. You should also have lived for some time in the region in which you hope to hold office.

You also need good people skills to be capable of listening to the concerns of constituents and other officials and exchanging ideas with them. Other useful qualities are problem-solving skills and creativity to develop innovative programs.

EXPLORING

Depending on the size of your city or county, you can probably become involved with your local government at a young age. Your council members and other government officials should be more accessible to you than state and federal officials, so take advantage of that. Visit the county court house and volunteer in whatever capacity you can with county-organized programs, such as tutoring in a literacy program or leading children's reading groups at the public library. Become involved with local elections.

Many candidates for local and state offices welcome young people to assist with campaigns. As a volunteer, you may make calls, post signs, and get to see a candidate at work. You will also have the opportunity to meet others who have an interest in government, and the experience will help you to gain a more prominent role in later campaigns.

Another way to learn about government is to become involved in an issue that interests you. Maybe there's an old building in your neighborhood you'd like to save from destruction, or maybe you have some ideas for youth programs or programs for senior citizens. Research what's being done about your concerns and come up with solutions to offer to local officials.

EMPLOYERS

Every city in the United States requires the services of local officials. In some cases, the services of a small town or suburb may be overseen by the government of a larger city or by the county government. According to the National Association of Counties, 48 states have operational county governments—a total of over 3,000 counties. (Connecticut and Rhode Island are the only two states without counties.) The counties with the largest populations are Los Angeles County, California; Cook County, Illinois; and Harris County, Texas. There are also 31 governments that are consolidations of city and county governments; New York, Denver, and San Francisco are among them.

STARTING OUT

There is no direct career path for gaining public office. The way you pursue a local office will be greatly affected by the size and population of the region in which you live. When running for mayor or council of a small town, you may have no competition at all. On the other hand, to become mayor of a large city, you need extensive experience in the city's politics. If you're interested in pursuing a local position, research the backgrounds of your city mayor, county commissioner, and council members to get an idea of how they approached their political careers.

Some officials stumble into government offices after some success with political activism on the grass roots level. Others have had success in other areas, such as agriculture, business, and law enforcement, and use their particular understanding of an area to help improve the community. Many local politicians started their careers by assisting in someone else's campaign or advocating for an issue.

ADVANCEMENT

Some successful local and regional officials maintain their positions for many years. Others hold local office for only one or two terms, then return full time to their businesses and other careers. You might also choose to use a local position as a stepping stone to a position of greater power within the region or to a state office. Many mayors of the largest cities run for governor or state legislature and may eventually move into federal office.

EARNINGS

In general, salaries for government officials tend to be lower than what the official could make working in the private sector. In many local offices, officials volunteer their time or work only part time. According to a salary survey published in 2001 by the International City/County Management Association, the chief elected official of a city makes an average salary of $20,719 a year. The average salary for city managers was $85,587. A county's chief elected official averages $35,118 a year. County clerks average about $44,680, and treasurers earn $43,985.

A job with a local or regional government may or may not provide benefits. Some positions may include accounts for official travel and other expenses.

WORK ENVIRONMENT

Most government officials work in a typical office setting. Some may work a regular 40-hour week, while others work long hours and weekends. Though some positions may only be considered part time, they may take up nearly as many hours as full-time work. Officials have the opportunity to meet with the people of the region, but they also devote a lot of time to clerical duties. If serving a large community, they may have assistants to help with phones, filing, and preparing documents.

Because officials must be appointed or elected in order to keep their jobs, determining long-range career plans can be difficult. There may be extended periods of unemployment, where living off of savings or other jobs may be necessary. Because of the low pay of some positions, officials may have to work another job even while they serve in office. This can result in little personal time and the need to juggle many different responsibilities at once.

OUTLOOK

Though the form and structure of state and federal government are not likely to change, the form of your local and county government can be altered by popular vote. Every election, voters somewhere in the country are deciding whether to keep their current forms of government or to introduce new forms. But these changes don't greatly affect the number of officials needed to run your local government. The chances for holding office are greater in small communities. The races for part-time and nonpaying offices are also less competitive.

The issues facing a community will have the most effect on the jobs of local officials. In a city with older neighborhoods, officials deal with historic preservation, improvements in utilities, and water quality. In a growing city of many suburbs, officials have to make decisions regarding development, roads, and expanded routes for public transportation.

The federal government has made efforts to shift costs to the states. If this continues, states may offer less aid to counties. A county government's funds are also affected by changes in property taxes.

FOR MORE INFORMATION

For information about the forms of city and county governments around the country and to learn about programs sponsored by local and regional governments, contact the following organizations:

International City/County Management Association
777 North Capitol Street, NE, Suite 500
Washington, DC 20002
Tel: 202-289-4262
http://www.icma.org

National Association of Counties
440 First Street, NW, Suite 800
Washington, DC 20001
Tel: 202-393-6226
http://www.naco.org

RESEARCH ASSISTANTS

QUICK FACTS

School Subjects
English
History
Journalism

Personal Skills
Communication/ideas
Following instructions

Work Environment
Primarily indoors
Primarily multiple locations

Minimum Educational Level
Bachelor's degree

Salary Range
$12,000 to $26,000 to $74,000

Certification or Licensing
None available

Outlook
About as fast as the average

DOT
109

GOE
11.03.03

NOC
4122

O*NET-SOC
N/A

OVERVIEW

Research assistants work to help writers, scientists, radio, film, and television producers, marketing and advertising executives, attorneys, professors, publishers, politicians, museum curators, and a wide variety of other professionals with their jobs. They are information specialists who find the facts, data, and statistics that their employers need, leaving the employers free to pursue the larger task at hand.

HISTORY

Although the job of the research assistant has changed little over the years, the tools used to gather information have changed dramatically. An assistant to a doctor a hundred years ago would have had to travel to libraries and other information centers to gather data on a disease from books and then laboriously take down notes on paper. Today that same research assistant could do an Internet search and print the findings in only a few minutes. As technology becomes more advanced, research assistants will have the convenience of using new methods to complete their research, but they will also bear the burden of having to master the techniques to get the information they need.

THE JOB

Although the fields in which they work may differ greatly, all research assistants work to help their employers complete a job more easily and more thoroughly. A research assistant may work for one person, such as a university professor, or for a team of people, such as the writers of brochures, newsletters, and press releases at a large nonprofit organization. If the research assistant works for more than one person, he or she needs to follow a system to determine whose work will be done when. Sometimes the team assigning the work determines the order in which jobs should be done; other times, research assistants keep sign-up sheets and perform the research requests in the order they are listed. An urgent job often necessitates that the research assistant disregard the sheet and jump quickly to the new task. Sometimes research assistants help with clerical duties, such as transcription, word processing, and reception, or, in the case of scientific research assistants, with cleaning and maintaining laboratories and equipment.

After receiving a research assignment from the person or people they assist, research assistants must first determine how to locate the desired information. This can entail a single phone call or anywhere from hours to weeks of research in libraries, archives, museums, laboratories, and on the Internet until all of the necessary information is compiled and consolidated. Research assistants must then prepare the material for presentation to the person who requested it. If specific brochures or catalogs are requested, the research assistant need only hand them over when they arrive. More often than not, however, the research assistant has to write up notes or even a report outlining the research efforts and presenting the information they were asked to locate. These reports may include graphs, charts, statistics, and drawings or photographs. They include a listing of sources and the exact specifications of any interviews conducted, surveys taken, or experiments performed. Sometimes research assistants are asked to present this information verbally as well.

Research assistants work for writers in a wide variety of circumstances. They may work for commercial magazines and newspapers, where they might locate possible interview candidates, conduct surveys, scan other periodicals for relevant articles and features, or help a writer gather information for an article. For example, a writer doing an article on the history of rap music might send a research assistant to compile statistics on rap music sales from over the years or create a comprehensive list of artists signed by a specific record label. Some research assistants working for periodicals and other publications do nothing but confirm facts, such as dates, ages, and statistics. These researchers are called *fact checkers*. Research assistants who work in radio, film, or television often help locate and organize historical facts, find experts to be interviewed, or help follow up on ideas for future programs.

Many large companies, agencies, and organizations hire research assistants to help their in-house writing staff produce brochures, newsletters, and press releases. Research assistants may gather facts and statistics, retrieve applicable quotes, and conduct preliminary phone interviews.

Advertising and marketing agencies hire research assistants to help them discover consumer desires and the best ways to advertise and market products. Imagine that a small toy company is considering marketing a new toy. Research assistants for the company might be assigned to help find out how much it would cost to make the toy, whether or not there is already a similar toy on the market, who might buy the toy, and who might sell the toy. This would help the marketing department decide in what ways the toy should be marketed. In advertising, research assistants may be asked to provide executives with statistics and quotes so that the executives may determine whether a product is appealing to a certain portion of the population.

University professors hire research assistants to help them in their research in all fields. For example, a history professor working on a paper about the Italian military might send a research assistant to the library to uncover everything possible about the Italian military presence in Greece during World War II. A research assistant in microbiology will help a biologist prepare and perform experiments and record data. Often, professors hire graduate students as research assistants, either during the summer or in addition to the student's regular course load. Sometimes a research assistantship is part of a financial aid package; this ensures that the professor has help with research and gives the students an opportunity to earn money while learning more about their chosen field.

Politicians hire research assistants to help find out how a campaign is succeeding or failing, to find statistics on outcomes of past elections, and to determine the issues that are especially important to the constituents, among other things. Research assistants who work for politicians may also follow the opponent's campaign, trying to find ways to win over new supporters.

Some research assistants work for museums where they try to determine ways to add to a collection, develop signs and explanations for public education, and keep an inventory of all collection pieces. Research assistants may also do research to help curators learn more about the pieces in the museum's collection.

REQUIREMENTS
High School
Requirements for becoming a research assistant vary depending upon the field in which you hope to work. In high school, take a wide variety of college preparatory courses, including English, history, mathematics, and the sciences. Knowledge of at least one foreign language can be extremely helpful in gaining employment as a research assistant, especially in the fields of marketing, publishing, and the arts. Since writing and presenting research are important aspects of the research assistant's work, you should take classes that strengthen these skills, such as public speaking, journalism, and statistics. Knowledge of computers and excellent library skills are absolutely vital to this profession. If you will be working in the hard sciences or engineering, laboratory skills are essential.

Postsecondary Training
In college you should begin thinking about a specific field you are interested in and take courses in that field. If you are interested in advertising research but your college does not offer an advertising degree, you should plan to major in English or psychology but take a large concentration of communications, business, and economics courses. Often, English and journalism are good majors for the research assistant career, as the work requires so much reading, researching, and writing. Some employers prefer research assistants to have a degree in library science.

Some fields require degrees beyond a bachelor's degree for research assistants. This is often true in the hard sciences, engineering, medicine, and law. Depending on the field, some employers require a master's degree, or some advanced study in the area. For instance, an insurance company that hires a research assistant may require the employee to take insurance courses in order to become more knowledgeable about the industry. Research assistants in the social sciences or arts will find more high-paying employment opportunities with a master's in library science.

Other Requirements

To succeed as a research assistant, you must be naturally curious and enjoy doing research, finding and organizing facts, working with other people, and handling a variety of tasks. You should also be self-motivated, take instruction well, and be resourceful. For example, a research assistant assigned by an attorney to research marriage records at the county clerk's office should not be calling the law firm every few minutes to ask for further direction. A good research assistant must be able to take an assignment, immediately ask any questions necessary to clarify the task, and then begin retrieving the requested information.

EXPLORING

You can begin exploring this career while working on your own school assignments. Use different types of resources, such as newspapers, magazines, library catalogs, computers, the Internet, and official records and documents. If you are interested in becoming a research assistant in the sciences or medicine, pay close attention to procedures and methods in your laboratory classes.

Consider joining groups in your school devoted to research or fieldwork. Work as a reporter for your school newspaper, or volunteer to write feature articles for your yearbook. Both of these positions will provide you with experience in research and fact-finding. You can also create your own research opportunities. If you are a member of the marching band, for instance, you could research the history of the clarinet and write an article for the band newsletter.

Occasionally, small newspapers, nonprofit groups, political campaigns, and other organizations will accept student interns, volunteers, or even summer employees to help out with special projects. If you obtain such a position, you may have the opportunity to help with research, or at least, to see professionals in action, learn valuable work skills, and help support a good cause.

There are many books available describing the techniques of basic research skills. Ask a librarian or bookstore worker to help you locate them, or better yet, begin developing your research skills by tracking down materials yourself. The Internet is also full of helpful information on all subjects. To get tips on designing research surveys and analyzing data, visit http://www.hostedsurvey.com.

EMPLOYERS

All types of companies, organizations, and private individuals employ research assistants. Most college and university professors have a research assistant on staff to help them with articles and books they are writing. Newspapers and magazines use research assistants to find information for articles and verify facts. Museums employ research assistants to find information to add to museum collections, as well as to search museum archives for information requested by outside historians, scientists, writers, and other scholars. Companies in all fields need people to help find information on products, ingredients, production techniques, and competitors.

The government is a major employer of research assistants. Local, state, and federal government offices often hire research assistants to conduct interviews, gather statistics, compile information, and synthesize data. Research assistants for the government work for the U.S. Census Bureau, the U.S. Bureau of Labor Statistics, and the Library of Congress, among other divisions.

STARTING OUT

How you begin a career as a research assistant depends largely upon the field in which you are interested in working. In college, you may wish to pursue an assistantship with a professor. He or she can act as a mentor while you are earning your degree and offer valuable advice and feedback on your research techniques.

After receiving a bachelor's degree, you might begin by contacting agencies, firms, or companies where you'd like to work. For example, if you are interested in doing research to support writers, you might apply to newspapers, magazines, and large companies that produce their own publications. Also, some college and university career offices have listings of job openings in the research fields; occasionally these jobs are advertised in newspapers and magazines.

There may also be freelance opportunities for the beginning research assistant. Try marketing your services in the school newspaper or bulletin boards of your alma mater. You can also set up a Web page that lists your qualifications and the services you offer. Ask for referrals from professors with whom you have studied or worked. If you do a thorough, competent job on research assignments, you can use positive word-of-mouth to get more work.

ADVANCEMENT

A research assistant who gains a high skill level and demonstrates dedication to the employer and the field may earn the opportunity to lead other assistants on a special project. Some research assistants who work for writers and prove to have excellent writing skills themselves may get hired to write newsletter articles or brochures for publications. Depending on departmental needs, research assistants who work for a university while earning a degree may be offered a full-time position upon completion of their studies. Research assistants who work for clients on a freelance basis may find that they get more assignments and can command higher fees as they gain experience and a good reputation.

Advancement in this field is usually up to the individual. You will need to seek out opportunities. If you are interested in getting better assignments, you will probably need to ask for them. If you would like to supervise a newsletter or brochure project within your company, try making a proposal to your manager. With a proven track record and a solid idea of how a project can be accomplished, you will likely receive increased responsibility.

EARNINGS

Earnings vary widely, depending on field, level of education, and employer. Generally, large companies pay their research assistants more than smaller businesses and nonprofit organizations do. Research assistants with advanced degrees make more than those with bachelor's degrees only. Research assistants who work for large pharmaceutical companies or engineering laboratories and have advanced science degrees make some of the highest wages in the field.

Each college and university has its own salary budget for graduate student research assistants. There are often set minimum salaries for academic year employment and for full 12-month employment. Most student research assistants work part time and receive a percentage of these minimums based on the number of hours they work (usually 50 percent, 25 percent, or 33 percent). Some schools have an hourly rate that averages about $10–$15. Annual salaries for university research assistants can range from $12,000 to $42,000.

According to *The Scientist* and Abbott, Langer & Associates, Inc., senior researchers in the life sciences who work in academia earn from $30,000 to $74,000 annually, and postdoctorate researchers earn from $26,000 to $39,000. In industry, senior researchers earn from

$30,000 to $72,000, and junior/postdoctorate researchers earn from $26,000 to $44,000.

Self-employed research assistants are paid by the hour or by assignment. Depending on the experience of the research assistant, the complexity of the assignment, and the location of the job, pay rates may be anywhere from $7 to $25 per hour, although $10–$12 is the norm.

Benefits such as health insurance, vacation, and sick leave vary by field and employer. Universities generally provide health care coverage, paid vacations, sick time, and a pension plan for full-time employees. Research assistants employed full-time by a private company are also eligible for similar benefits; some companies may provide benefits to part-time or contract workers. Freelancers must provide their own benefits.

Research assistants who work in some fields may receive additional bonuses. A person working on a research project about movies, for instance, may receive free passes to a local theater. A woman's magazine may send research assistants cosmetics samples so they can test different lipsticks for staying power. Research assistants charged with finding information about another country's economy may even be sent abroad. All of these perks, of course, vary depending on the needs of the employer and the experience of the researcher.

WORK ENVIRONMENT

Most research assistants work indoors in clean, climate-controlled, pleasant facilities. Many spend most of their time at the business that employs them, checking facts over the phone, finding data on a computer, searching the company's records, writing up reports, or conducting laboratory research. Others spend a great deal of time in libraries, government offices, courthouses, museums, archives, and even in such unlikely places as shopping malls and supermarkets. Research assistants go wherever they must to obtain the information requested.

Most assignments require that research assistants do their work on their own, with little direct supervision. Research assistants need to be very self-motivated in order to get the work done since they often do not have someone readily available to support them. It is important for research assistants who leave their offices for work to remember that they are representatives of their company or employer and to act and dress according to the employer's standards.

Full-time research assistants work 35–40 hours a week. They may have to work overtime or on weekends right before deadlines or when involved in special projects. Some research assistants, especially those who work for smaller organizations or for professors or private employers, work only part time. They may work as little as 10 hours a week. These research assistants are usually graduate students or freelancers who have a second job in a related field.

OUTLOOK
The outlook for the research assistant career generally depends upon the outlook for the field in which the researcher works. That is, a field that is growing quickly will usually need many new researchers, whereas a field with little growth will not. A researcher with a good background in many fields will be in higher demand, as will a researcher with specialized knowledge and research techniques specific to a field.

Although definite statistical data as to the present and future of all researchers is sketchy at best, as technology becomes more advanced

Opening Doors: The Graduate Degree

A graduate degree opens many doors for an undergraduate history major. Consider the following:

- A graduate degree in education, anthropology, linguistics, archaeology, English, history, political science, and other liberal arts fields will give you the qualifications to work as a college professor.

- A graduate degree in law (called juris doctor or bachelor of laws) will allow you to become a lawyer or judge—both high-prestige and lucrative careers.

- A graduate degree in library science will allow you to become a librarian. Your background in history will make you an appealing candidate to work in historical libraries and archives.

- A graduate degree in a foreign language will make you an excellent candidate for employment as a cultural adviser, FBI agent, book editor who specializes in bilingual editing, foreign correspondent, intelligence officer, or linguist.

and the amount of information available through newer media like the Internet increases, knowledgeable research assistants will be essential to find, sort, compile, present, and analyze this information. As a result of technological advancements, a new career niche has developed for *information brokers*, who compile information from online databases and services.

Since many people take research assistant positions as stepping-stones to positions with more responsibility or stability, positions are often available to beginning researchers. Research assistants with good experience, excellent work ethics, and the drive to succeed will rarely find themselves out of work. Jobs will be available, but it may take some creative fact finding for research assistants to locate positions that best meet their needs and interests.

FOR MORE INFORMATION

To find out about health care research projects and opportunities with the U.S. Department of Health and Human Services, contact

Agency for Healthcare Research and Quality
2101 East Jefferson Street, Suite 501
Rockville, MD 20852
Tel: 301-594-1364
Email: info@ahrq.gov
http://www.ahcpr.gov

For a list of research opportunities and student internships with National Institutes of Health, contact

National Institutes of Health
Office of Human Resources Management
6100 Executive Boulevard, Room 3E01 MSC 7509
Bethesda, MD 20892-7509
http://ohrm.cc.nih.gov

For information on research assistant positions with the U.S. Census Bureau, contact

U.S. Census Bureau
Washington, DC 20233
Tel: 301-457-4608
Email: recruiter@ccmail.census.gov
http://www.census.gov

SECONDARY SCHOOL TEACHERS

QUICK FACTS

School Subjects
English
Psychology

Personal Skills
Communication/ideas
Helping/teaching

Work Environment
Primarily indoors
Primarily one location

Minimum Education Level
Bachelor's degree

Salary Range
$27,980 to $43,280 to
$67,940+

Certification or Licensing
Required by all states

Outlook
About as fast as the average

DOT
091

GOE
11.02.01

NOC
4141

O*NET-SOC
25-2022.00, 25-2023.00,
25-2031.00, 25-2032.00

OVERVIEW

Secondary school teachers teach students in grades 7–12. Specializing in one subject area, such as art or math, these teachers work with five or more groups of students during the day. They lecture, direct discussions, and test students' knowledge with exams, essays, and homework assignments. There are close to 1 million secondary school teachers employed in the United States.

HISTORY

Early secondary education was typically based upon training students to enter the clergy. Benjamin Franklin pioneered the idea of a broader secondary education with the creation of the academy, which offered a flexible curriculum and a wide variety of academic subjects.

It was not until the 19th century, however, that children of different social classes commonly attended school into the secondary grades. The first English Classical School, which was to become the model for public high schools throughout the country, was established in 1821 in Boston. An adjunct to the high school, the junior high school was conceived by Dr. Charles W. Eliot, president of Harvard University. In a speech before the National Education Association in 1888, he recommended that secondary studies be started two years earlier than was the custom. The first such school opened in 1908, in Columbus, Ohio. Another opened a year later in Berkeley, California. By the early 20th century, secondary school attendance was made mandatory in the United States.

THE JOB

Many successful people credit secondary school teachers with helping guide them into college, careers, and other endeavors. The teachers' primary responsibility is to educate students in a specific subject. But secondary teachers also inform students about colleges, occupations, and such varied subjects as the arts, health, and relationships.

Secondary school teachers may teach in a traditional area, such as science, English, history, and math, or they may teach more specialized classes, such as information technology, business, and theater. Many secondary schools are expanding their course offerings to better serve the individual interests of their students. "School-to-work" programs, which are vocational education programs designed for high school students and recent graduates, involve lab work and demonstrations to prepare students for highly technical jobs. Though secondary teachers are likely be assigned to one specific grade level, they may be required to teach students in surrounding grades. For example, a secondary school mathematics teacher may teach algebra to a class of ninth-graders one period and trigonometry to high school seniors the next.

In the classroom, secondary school teachers rely on a variety of teaching methods. They spend a great deal of time lecturing, but they also facilitate student discussion and develop projects and activities to interest the students in the subject. They show films and videos, use computers and the Internet, and bring in guest speakers. They assign essays, presentations, and other projects. Each subject calls upon particular approaches and may involve laboratory experiments, role-playing exercises, shop work, and field trips.

Outside of the classroom, secondary school teachers prepare lectures, lesson plans, and exams. They evaluate student work and calculate grades. In the process of planning their class, secondary school teachers read textbooks, novels, and workbooks to determine reading assignments; photocopy notes, articles, and other handouts; and develop grading policies. They also continue to study alternative and traditional teaching methods to hone their skills. They prepare students for special events and conferences and submit student work to competitions. Many secondary school teachers also serve as sponsors to student organizations in their field. For example, a French teacher may sponsor the French club and a journalism teacher may advise the yearbook staff. Some secondary school teachers also have the opportunity for extracurricular work as athletic coaches or drama coaches. Teachers also monitor students during lunch or break times and sit in on study halls. They may also accompany student groups on field trips, competitions, and events. Some teachers also have the opportunity to escort students on educational vacations to foreign countries, to Washington, D.C., and to other major U.S. cities. Secondary school teachers attend faculty meetings, meetings with parents, and state and national teacher conferences.

Some teachers explore their subject area outside of the requirements of the job. *English* and *writing teachers* may publish in magazines and journals, *business* and *technology teachers* may have small businesses of their own, *music teachers* may perform and record their music, *art teachers* may show work in galleries, and *sign-language teachers* may do freelance interpreting.

REQUIREMENTS
High School
You should follow your guidance counselor's college preparatory program and take advanced classes in such subjects as English, science, math, and government. You should also explore an extracurricular activity, such as theater, sports, and debate, so that you can offer these additional skills to future employers. If you're already aware of which subject you'd like to teach, take all the available courses in that area. You should also take speech and composition courses to develop your communication skills.

Postsecondary Training
There are over 500 accredited teacher education programs in the United States. Most of these programs are designed to meet the certification requirements for the state in which they're located. Some

states may require that you pass a test before being admitted to an education program. You may choose to major in your subject area while taking required education courses, or you may major in secondary education with a concentration in your subject area. You'll probably have advisers (both in education and in your chosen specialty) to help you select courses.

In addition to a degree, a training period of student teaching in an actual classroom environment is usually required. Students are placed in schools to work with full-time teachers. During this period, undergraduate students observe the ways in which lessons are presented and the classroom is managed, learn how to keep records of such details as attendance and grades, and get actual experience in handling the class, both under supervision and alone.

Besides licensure and courses in education, prospective high school teachers usually need 24–36 hours of college work in the subject they wish to teach. Some states require a master's degree; teachers with master's degrees can earn higher salaries. Private schools generally do not require an education degree.

Certification or Licensing

Public school teachers must be licensed under regulations established by the department of education of the state in which they teach. Not all states require licensure for teachers in private or parochial schools. When you've received your teaching degree, you may request that a transcript of your college record be sent to the licensure section of the state department of education. If you have met licensure requirements, you will receive a certificate and thus be eligible to teach in the public schools of the state. In some states, you may have to take additional tests. If you move to another state, you will have to resubmit college transcripts, as well as comply with any other regulations in the new state to be able to teach there.

Other Requirements

Working as a secondary school teacher, you'll need to have respect for young people and a genuine interest in their success in life. You'll also need patience; adolescence can be a troubling time for children, and these troubles often affect behavior and classroom performance. Because you'll be working with students who are at very impressionable ages, you should serve as a good role model. You should also be well organized, as you'll have to keep track of the work and progress of many students.

EXPLORING

By going to high school, you've already gained a good sense of the daily work of a secondary school teacher. But the requirements of a teacher extend far beyond the classroom, so ask to spend some time with one of your teachers after school, and ask to look at lecture notes and record-keeping procedures. Interview your teachers about the amount of work that goes into preparing a class and directing an extracurricular activity. To get some firsthand teaching experience, volunteer for a peer tutoring program. Other teaching opportunities that may exist in your community are coaching an athletic team at the YMCA, counseling at a summer camp, teaching an art course at a community center, or assisting with a community theater production.

EMPLOYERS

Secondary school teachers are needed at public and private schools, including parochial schools, juvenile detention centers, vocational schools, and schools of the arts. They work in middle schools, junior high schools, and high schools. Though some rural areas maintain schools, most secondary schools are in towns and cities of all sizes. Teachers are also finding opportunities in charter schools, which are smaller, deregulated schools that receive public funding.

STARTING OUT

After completing the teacher certification process, including your months of student teaching, you'll work with your college's placement office to find a full-time position. The departments of education of some states maintain listings of job openings. Many schools advertise teaching positions in the classifieds of the state's major newspapers. You may also directly contact the principals and superintendents of the schools in which you'd like to work. While waiting for full-time work, you can work as a substitute teacher. In urban areas with many schools, you may be able to substitute full time.

ADVANCEMENT

Most teachers advance simply by becoming more of an expert in their jobs. There is usually an increase in salary as teachers acquire experience. Additional training or study can also bring an increase in salary.

A few teachers with management ability and interest in administrative work may advance to the position of principal. Others may advance into supervisory positions, and some may become *helping teachers* who are charged with the responsibility of helping other teachers find appropriate instructional materials and develop certain phases of their courses of study. Others may go into teacher education at a college or university. For most of these positions, additional education is required. Some teachers also make lateral moves into other education-related positions such as guidance counselor or resource room teacher.

EARNINGS

Most teachers are contracted to work nine months out of the year, though some contracts are made for 10 or a full 12 months. (When regular school is not in session, teachers are expected to conduct summer teaching, planning, or other school-related work.) In most cases, teachers have the option of prorating their salary up to 52 weeks.

According to the Bureau of Labor Statistics, the median annual salary for secondary school teachers was $43,280 in 2001. The lowest 10 percent earned $27,980; the highest 10 percent earned $67,940 or more.

The American Federation of Teachers reports that the national average salary for all teachers was 43,250 during the 2000–2001 school year. Beginning teachers earned approximately $28,986 a year.

Teachers can also supplement their earnings through teaching summer classes, coaching sports, sponsoring a club, or other extracurricular work.

On behalf of the teachers, unions bargain with schools over contract conditions such as wages, hours, and benefits. A majority of teachers join the American Federation of Teachers or the National Education Association. Depending on the state, teachers usually receive a retirement plan, sick leave, and health and life insurance. Some systems grant teachers sabbatical leave.

WORK ENVIRONMENT

Although the job of the secondary school teacher is not overly strenuous, it can be tiring and trying. Secondary school teachers must stand for many hours each day, do a lot of talking, show energy and enthusiasm, and handle discipline problems. But they also have the reward of guiding their students as they make decisions about their lives and futures.

Secondary school teachers work under generally pleasant conditions, though some older schools may have poor heating and electrical systems. Though violence in schools has decreased in recent years, media coverage of the violence has increased, along with student fears. In most schools, students are prepared to learn and to perform the work that's required of them. But in some schools, students may be dealing with gangs, drugs, poverty, and other problems, so the environment can be tense and emotional.

School hours are generally 8:00 A.M.–3:00 P.M., but teachers work more than 40 hours a week teaching, preparing for classes, grading papers, and directing extracurricular activities. As a coach, or as a music or drama director, teachers may have to work some evenings and weekends. Many teachers enroll in master's or doctorate programs and take evening and summer courses to continue their education.

OUTLOOK

The U.S. Department of Education predicts that employment for secondary teachers will grow by 16.6 percent through 2010 to meet rising enrollments and to replace the large number of retiring teachers. The National Education Association believes this will be a challenge because of the low salaries that are paid to secondary school teachers. Higher salaries will be necessary to attract new teachers and retain experienced ones, along with other changes such as smaller classroom sizes and safer schools. Other challenges for the profession involve attracting more men into teaching. The percentage of male teachers at this level continues to decline.

In order to improve education for all children, changes are being considered by some districts. Some private companies are managing public schools. Though some believe that a private company can afford to provide better facilities, faculty, and equipment, this is not a proven fact. Teacher organizations are concerned about taking school management away from communities and turning it over to remote corporate headquarters. Charter schools and voucher programs are two other controversial alternatives to traditional public education. Charter schools, which are small schools that are publicly funded but not guided by the rules and regulations of traditional public schools, are viewed by some as places of innovation and improved educational methods; others see charter schools as ill-equipped and unfairly funded with money that could better benefit local school districts. Vouchers, which exist only in a few cities, allow students to attend private schools courtesy of tuition vouchers; these vouchers are paid for with public tax dollars. In theory, the vouchers allow for more choices in education for poor and minority students, but private schools still have the option of being highly selective in their admissions. Teacher organizations see some danger in giving public funds to unregulated private schools.

FOR MORE INFORMATION

For information about careers and current issues affecting teachers, contact or visit the websites of the following organizations:

American Federation of Teachers
555 New Jersey Avenue, NW
Washington, DC 20001
Tel: 202-879-4400
Email: online@aft.org
http://www.aft.org

National Education Association
1201 16th Street, NW
Washington, DC 20036
Tel: 202-833-4000
http://www.nea.org

For information on accredited teacher education programs, contact

National Council for Accreditation of Teacher Education
2010 Massachusetts Avenue, NW, Suite 500
Washington, DC 20036-1023
Tel: 202-466-7496
Email: ncate@ncate.org
http://www.ncate.org

TOUR GUIDES

QUICK FACTS

School Subjects Foreign language History Speech	**Certification or Licensing** Recommended **Outlook** About as fast as the average
Personal Skills Communication/ideas Leadership/management	**DOT** 353
Work Environment Indoors and outdoors Primarily multiple locations	**GOE** 07.05.01 **NOC** 6441
Minimum Education Level Some postsecondary training	**O*NET-SOC** 39-6021.00, 39-6022.00
Salary Range $20,000 to $31,000 to $65,000+	

OVERVIEW

Tour guides plan and oversee travel arrangements and accommodations for groups of tourists. They assist travelers with questions or problems, and they may provide travelers with itineraries of their proposed travel route and plans. Tour guides research their destinations thoroughly so that they can handle any unforeseen situation that may occur. There are approximately 44,000 tour and travel guides employed in the United States.

HISTORY

People have always had a certain fascination with the unknown. Curiosity about distant cities and foreign cultures was one of the main forces behind the spread of civilization. Traveling in the ancient world was an arduous and sometimes dangerous task. Today, however, travel is commonplace. People travel for business, recreation, and education. Schoolchildren may take field trips to their state's capitol, and some college students now have the opportunity to study in foreign countries. Recreation and vacation travel account for much of people's spending of their disposable income.

Early travelers were often accompanied by guides who had become familiar with the routes on earlier trips. When leisure travel became more commonplace in the 19th century, women and young children were not expected to travel alone, so relatives or house servants often acted as companions. Today, tour guides act as escorts for people visiting foreign countries and provide them with additional information on interesting facets of life in another part of the world. In a way, tour guides have taken the place of the early scouts, acting as experts in settings and situations that other people find unfamiliar.

THE JOB

Acting as knowledgeable companions and chaperons, tour guides escort groups of tourists to different cities and countries. Their job is to make sure that the passengers in a group tour enjoy an interesting and safe trip. To do this, they have to know a great deal about their travel destination and about the interests, knowledge, and expectations of the people on the tour.

One basic responsibility of tour guides is handling all the details of a trip prior to departure. They may schedule airline flights, bus trips, or train trips as well as book cruises, houseboats, or car rentals. They also research area hotels and other lodging for the group and make reservations in advance. If anyone in the group has unique requirements, such as a specialized diet or a need for wheelchair accessibility, the tour guide will work to meet these requests.

Tour guides plan itineraries and daily activities, keeping in mind the interests of the group. For example, a group of music lovers visiting Vienna may wish to see the many sites of musical history there as well as attend a performance by that city's orchestra. In addition to sightseeing tours, guides may make arrangements in advance for special exhibits, dining experiences, and side trips. Alternate outings are sometimes planned in case of inclement weather conditions.

The second major responsibility of tour guides is, of course, the tour itself. Here, they must make sure all aspects of transportation, lodging, and recreation meet the itinerary as it was planned. They must see to it that travelers' baggage and personal belongings are loaded and handled properly. If the tour includes meals and trips to local establishments, the guide must make sure that each passenger is on time for the various arrivals and departures.

Tour guides provide the people in their groups with interesting information on the locale and alert them to special sights. Tour guides become familiar with the history and significance of places through research and previous visits and endeavor to make the visit as entertaining and informative as possible. They may speak the native language or hire an interpreter in order to get along well with the local people. They are also familiar with local customs so their group will not offend anyone unknowingly. They see that the group stays together so that members do not miss their transportation arrangements or get lost. Guides may also arrange free time for travelers to pursue their individual interests, although time frames and common meeting points for regrouping are established in advance.

Even with thorough preparation, unexpected occurrences can arise on any trip and threaten to ruin everyone's good time. Tour guides must be resourceful to handle these surprises, such as when points of interest are closed or accommodations turn out to be unacceptable. They must be familiar with an area's resources so that they can help in emergencies such as passenger illness or lost personal items. Tour guides often intercede on their travelers' behalf when any questions or problems arise regarding currency, restaurants, customs, or necessary identification.

REQUIREMENTS
High School
Although as a tour guide you will not necessarily need a college education, you should at least have a high school diploma. Courses such as speech, communications, art, sociology, anthropology, political science, and literature often prove beneficial. Some tour guides study foreign languages and cultures as well as geography, history, and architecture.

Postsecondary Training
Some cities have professional schools that offer curricula in the travel industry. Such training may take nine to 12 months and offer job placement services. Some two- and four-year colleges offer tour guide training that lasts six to eight weeks. Community colleges may offer programs in tour escort training. Programs such as these

often may be taken on a part-time basis. Classes may include world geography, psychology, human relations, and communication courses. Sometimes students go on field trips themselves to gain experience. Some travel agencies and tour companies offer their own training so that their tour guides may receive instruction that complements the tour packages the company offers.

Certification or Licensing

The National Tour Association offers the certified tour professional designation to candidates who complete 200 education credits in two areas: professional study and professional activity. Candidates must also have a minimum of five years of employment in the travel industry, unless they have an industry-specific degree from an accredited college or university. Candidates with a college degree must have a minimum of three years of industry employment.

Other Requirements

To be a tour guide, you should be an outgoing, friendly, and confident person. You must be aware of the typical travelers' needs and the kinds of questions and concerns travelers might have. As a tour guide, you should be comfortable being in charge of large groups of people and have good time-management skills. You also need to be resourceful and be able to adapt to different environments. Tour guides are fun-loving and know how to make others feel at ease in unfamiliar surroundings. Tour guides should enjoy working with people as much as they enjoy traveling.

EXPLORING

One way to become more familiar with the responsibilities of this job is to accompany local tours. Many cities have their own historical societies and museums that offer tours as well as opportunities to volunteer. To appreciate what is involved with speaking in front of groups and the kind of research that may be necessary for leading tours, you can prepare speeches or presentations for class or local community groups. You may also find it helpful to read publications such as *Courier*, the National Tour Association's (http://www.ntaonline.com) monthly travel magazine.

EMPLOYERS

The major employers of tour guides are, naturally, tour companies. Many tour guides work on a freelance basis, while others may own their own tour businesses. Approximately 44,000 tour and travel guides are employed in the United States.

STARTING OUT

If you are interested in a career as a tour guide, you may begin as a guide for a museum or state park. This would be a good introduction to handling groups of people, giving lectures on points of interest or exhibits and developing confidence and leadership qualities. Zoos, theme parks, historical sites, or local walking tours often need volunteers or part-time employees to work in their information centers, offer visitors directions, and answer a variety of inquiries. When openings occur, it is common for part-time workers to move into full-time positions.

Travel agencies, tour bus companies, and park districts often need additional help during the summer months when the travel season is in full swing. Societies and organizations for architecture and natural history, as well as other cultural groups, often train and employ guides. If you are interested in working as a tour guide for one of these types of groups, you should submit your application directly to the directors of personnel or managing directors.

ADVANCEMENT

Tour guides gain experience by handling more complicated trips. Some workers may advance through specialization, such as tours to specific countries or to multiple destinations. Some tour guides choose to open their own travel agencies or work for wholesale tour companies, selling trip packages to individuals or retail tour companies.

Some tour guides become *travel writers* and report on exotic destinations for magazines and newspapers. Other guides may decide to work in the corporate world and plan travel arrangements for company executives. With the further development of the global economy, many different jobs have become available for people who know foreign languages and cultures.

EARNINGS

Tour guides may find that they have peak and slack periods of the year that correspond to vacation and travel seasons. Many tour guides, however, work eight months of the year. Salaries range from $9.75 per hour to $20 per hour. Experienced guides with managerial responsibilities can earn up to $65,000 a year, including gratuities. According to the National Tour Association's *2000 Wage and Benefits Survey*, the average daily rate of compensation for tour directors/escorts was $113, which is a 25 percent increase since 1995.

Guides receive their meals and accommodations free while conducting a tour, in addition to a daily stipend to cover their personal expenses. Salaries and benefits vary, depending on the tour operators that employ guides and the location they are employed in. Generally, the Great Lakes, mid-Atlantic, southeast, and southern regions of the United States offer the highest compensation.

Tour guides often receive paid vacations as part of their fringe benefits package; some may also receive sick pay and health insurance. Some companies may offer profit sharing and bonuses. Guides often receive discounts from hotels, airlines, and transportation companies in appreciation for repeat business.

WORK ENVIRONMENT

The key word in the tour guide profession is *variety*. Most tour guides work in offices while they make travel arrangements and handle general business, but once on the road, they experience a wide range of accommodations, conditions, and situations. Tours to distant cities involve maneuvering through busy and confusing airports. Side trips may involve bus rides, train transfers, or private car rentals, all with varying degrees of comfort and reliability. Package trips that include seeing a number of foreign countries may require the guide to speak a different language in each city.

The constant feeling of being on the go, plus the responsibility of leading a large group of people, can sometimes be stressful. Unexpected events and uncooperative people have the capacity to ruin part of a trip for everyone involved, including the guide. However, the thrill of travel, discovery, and meeting new people can be so rewarding that all the negatives can be forgotten (or eliminated by preplanning on the next trip).

OUTLOOK

Because of the many different travel opportunities for business, recreation, and education, there will be a steady need for tour guides over the next several years. Tours for special interests, such as to ecologically significant areas and wilderness destinations, continue to grow in popularity. Although certain seasons are more popular for travel than others, well-trained tour guides can keep busy all year long.

Another area of tourism that is on the upswing is inbound tourism. Many foreign travelers view the United States as a dream destination, with tourist spots such as New York, Disney World, and the national park system drawing millions of foreign visitors each year. Job opportunities in inbound tourism will likely be more plentiful than those guiding Americans in foreign locations. The best opportunities in inbound tourism are in large cities with international airports and in areas with a large amount of tourist traffic. Opportunities will also be better for those guides who speak foreign languages.

Aspiring tour guides should keep in mind that this field is highly competitive. Tour guide jobs, because of the obvious benefits, are highly sought after, and the beginning job seeker may find it difficult to break into the business. It is important to remember that the travel and tourism industry is affected by the overall economy. When the economy is depressed, people have less money to spend and, therefore, they travel less. Recent terrorist attacks have also adversely affected the travel and tourism industry. If the public perceives that travel is risky, they will travel less and, as a result, tour guides may see reduced employment opportunities.

FOR MORE INFORMATION

For information on the travel industry and the related career of travel agent, contact

American Society of Travel Agents
1101 King Street, Suite 200
Alexandria, VA 22314
Tel: 703-739-2782
Email: askasta@astahq.com
http://www.astanet.com

For information on internships, scholarships, the certified tour professional designation, and a list of colleges and universities that offer tourism-related programs, contact

National Tour Association
546 East Main Street
PO Box 3071
Lexington, KY 40508
Tel: 800-682-8886
Email: questions@ntastaff.com
http://www.ntaonline.com

WRITERS

QUICK FACTS

School Subjects English Journalism	**Certification or Licensing** None available
Personal Skills Communication/ideas Helping/teaching	**Outlook** Faster than the average **DOT** 131
Work Environment Primarily indoors Primarily one location	**GOE** 01.01.02 **NOC** 5121
Minimum Education Level Bachelor's degree	
Salary Range $20,570 to $42,450 to $83,180+	**O*NET-SOC** 27-3042.00, 27-3043.01, 27-3043.02, 27-3043.03, 27-3043.04

OVERVIEW

Writers are involved with expressing, editing, promoting, and interpreting ideas and facts in written form for books, magazines, trade journals, newspapers, technical studies and reports, company newsletters, radio and television broadcasts, and advertisements.

Writers develop fiction and nonfiction ideas for plays, novels, poems, and other related works; report, analyze, and interpret facts, events, and personalities; review art, music, drama, and other artistic presentations; and persuade the general public to choose or favor certain goods, services, and personalities. There are approximately 183,000 salaried writers, authors, and technical writers employed in the United States.

HISTORY

The skill of writing has existed for thousands of years. Papyrus fragments with writing by ancient Egyptians date from about 3000 B.C., and archaeological findings show that the Chinese had developed books by about 1300 B.C. A number of technical obstacles had to be overcome before printing and the profession of writing evolved. Books of the Middle Ages were copied by hand on parchment. The ornate style that marked these books helped ensure their rarity. Also, few people were able to read. Religious fervor prohibited the reproduction of secular literature.

Two factors helped create the publishing industry: the invention of the printing press by Johannes Gutenberg in the middle of the 15th century and the liberalism of the Protestant Reformation, which helped encourage a wider range of publications, greater literacy, and the creation of a number of works of literary merit. The first authors worked directly with printers.

The modern publishing age began in the 18th century. Printing became mechanized, and the novel, magazine, and newspaper developed. The first newspaper in the American colonies appeared in the early 18th century, but it was Benjamin Franklin, who, as editor and writer, made the *Pennsylvania Gazette* one of the most influential by setting a high standard for his fellow American journalists. Franklin also published the first magazine in the colonies, *The American Magazine*, in 1741.

Advances in the printing trades, photoengraving, retailing, and the availability of capital produced a boom in newspapers and magazines in the 19th century. Further mechanization in the printing field, such as the use of the Linotype machine, high-speed rotary presses, and special color reproduction processes, set the stage for still further growth in the book, newspaper, and magazine industry.

In addition to the print media, the broadcasting industry has contributed to the development of the professional writer. Film, radio, and television are sources of entertainment, information, and education that provide employment for thousands of writers.

THE JOB

Writers work in the field of communications. Specifically, they deal with the written word, whether it is destined for the printed page, broadcast, computer screen, or live theater. The nature of their work is as varied as the materials they produce: books, magazines, trade journals, newspapers, technical reports, company newsletters and other publications, advertisements, speeches, scripts for motion picture and stage productions, and scripts for radio and television broadcast. Writers develop ideas and write for all media.

Prose writers for newspapers, magazines, and books share many of the same duties. First they come up with an idea for an article or book from their own interests or are assigned a topic by an editor. The topic is of relevance to the particular publication; for example, a writer for a magazine on parenting may be assigned an article on car seat safety. Then writers begin gathering as much information as possible about the subject through library research, interviews, the Internet, observation, and other methods. They keep extensive notes from which they will draw material for their project. Once the material has been organized and arranged in logical sequence, writers prepare a written outline. The process of developing a piece of writing is exciting, although it can also involve detailed and solitary work. After researching an idea, a writer might discover that a different perspective or related topic would be more effective, entertaining, or marketable.

When working on assignment, writers submit their outlines to an editor or other company representative for approval. Then they write a first draft of the manuscript, trying to put the material into words that will have the desired effect on their audience. They often rewrite or polish sections of the material as they proceed, always searching for just the right way of imparting information or expressing an idea or opinion. A manuscript may be reviewed, corrected, and revised numerous times before a final copy is submitted. Even after that, an editor may request additional changes.

Writers for newspapers, magazines, or books often specialize in their subject matter. Some writers might have an educational background that allows them to give critical interpretations or analyses. For example, a health or science writer for a newspaper typically has a degree in biology and can interpret new ideas in the field for the average reader.

Columnists or *commentators* analyze news and social issues. They write about events from the standpoint of their own experience or opinion. *Critics* review literary, musical, or artistic works and performances. *Editorial writers* write on topics of public interest, and their comments, consistent with the viewpoints and policies of their employers, are intended to stimulate or mold public opinion. *Newswriters* work for newspapers, radio, or TV news departments, writing news stories from notes supplied by reporters or wire services.

Corporate writers and writers for nonprofit organizations have a wide variety of responsibilities. These writers may work in such places as a large insurance corporation or for a small nonprofit religious group, where they may be required to write news releases, annual reports, speeches for the company head, or public relations materials. Typically they are assigned a topic with length requirements for a given project. They may receive raw research materials, such as statistics, and they are expected to conduct additional research, including personal interviews. These writers must be able to write quickly and accurately on short deadlines, while also working with people whose primary job is not in the communications field. The written work is submitted to a supervisor and often a legal department for approval; rewrites are a normal part of this job.

Copywriters write copy that is primarily designed to sell goods and services. Their work appears as advertisements in newspapers, magazines, and other publications or as commercials on radio and television broadcasts. Sales and marketing representatives first provide information on the product and help determine the style and length of the copy. The copywriters conduct additional research and interviews; to formulate an effective approach, they study advertising trends and review surveys of consumer preferences. Armed with this information, copywriters write a draft that is submitted to the account executive and the client for approval. The copy is often returned for correction and revision until everyone involved is satisfied. Copywriters, like corporate writers, may also write articles, bulletins, news releases, sales letters, speeches, and other related informative and promotional material. Many copywriters are employed in advertising agencies. They also may work for public relations firms or in communications departments of large companies.

Technical writers can be divided into two main groups: those who convert technical information into material for the general public, and those who convey technical information between professionals. Technical writers in the first group may prepare service manuals or handbooks, instruction or repair booklets, or sales literature or brochures; those in the second group may write grant proposals, research reports, contract specifications, or research abstracts.

Screenwriters prepare scripts for motion pictures or television. They select or are assigned a subject, conduct research, write and submit a plot outline and narrative synopsis (treatment), and confer with the producer and/or director about possible revisions. Screenwriters may adapt books or plays for film and television dramatizations. They often collaborate with other screenwriters and may specialize in a particular type of script or writing.

Playwrights do similar writing for the stage. They write dialogue and describe action for plays that may be tragedies, comedies, or dramas, with themes sometimes adapted from fictional, historical, or narrative sources. Playwrights combine the elements of action, conflict, purpose, and resolution to depict events from real or imaginary life. They often make revisions even while the play is in rehearsal.

Continuity writers prepare the material read by radio and television announcers to introduce or connect various parts of their programs.

Novelists and *short story writers* create stories that may be published in books, magazines, or literary journals. They take incidents from their own lives, from news events, or from their imaginations and create characters, settings, actions, and resolutions. *Poets* create narrative, dramatic, or lyric poetry for books, magazines, or other publications, as well as for special events such as commemorations. These writers may work with literary agents or editors who help guide them through the writing process, which includes research of the subject matter and an understanding of the intended audience. Many universities and colleges offer graduate degrees in creative writing. In these programs, students work intensively with published writers to learn the art of storytelling.

Writers can be employed either as in-house staff or as freelancers. Pay varies according to experience and the position, but freelancers must provide their own office space and equipment such as computers and fax machines. Freelancers also are responsible for keeping tax records, sending out invoices, negotiating contracts, and providing their own health insurance.

REQUIREMENTS
High School
While in high school, build a broad educational foundation by taking courses in English, literature, foreign languages, general science, social studies, computer science, and typing. The ability to type is almost a requisite for all positions in the communications field, as is familiarity with computers.

Postsecondary Training
Competition for writing jobs almost always demands the background of a college education. Many employers prefer you have a broad liberal arts background or majors in English, literature, history, philosophy, or one of the social sciences. Other employers desire communications or journalism training in college. Occasionally a master's degree in a specialized writing field may be required. A number of schools offer courses in journalism, and some of them

offer courses or majors in book publishing, publication management, and newspaper and magazine writing.

In addition to formal course work, most employers look for practical writing experience. If you have served on high school or college newspapers, yearbooks, or literary magazines, you will make a better candidate, as well as if you have worked for small community newspapers or radio stations, even in an unpaid position. Many book publishers, magazines, newspapers, and radio and television stations have summer internship programs that provide valuable training if you want to learn about the publishing and broadcasting businesses. Interns do many simple tasks, such as running errands and answering phones, but some may be asked to perform research, conduct interviews, or even write some minor pieces.

Writers who specialize in technical fields may need degrees, concentrated course work, or experience in specific subject areas. This applies frequently to engineering, business, or one of the sciences. Also, technical communications is a degree now offered at many universities and colleges.

If you wish to enter positions with the federal government, you will have to take a civil service examination and meet certain specified requirements, according to the type and level of position.

Other Requirements

To be a writer, you should be creative and able to express ideas clearly, have a broad general knowledge, be skilled in research techniques, and be computer literate. Other assets include curiosity, persistence, initiative, resourcefulness, and an accurate memory. For some jobs—on a newspaper, for example, where the activity is hectic and deadlines are short—the ability to concentrate and produce under pressure is essential.

EXPLORING

As a high school or college student, you can test your interest and aptitude in the field of writing by serving as a reporter or writer on school newspapers, yearbooks, and literary magazines. Various writing courses and workshops will offer you the opportunity to sharpen your writing skills.

Small community newspapers and local radio stations often welcome contributions from outside sources, although they may not have the resources to pay for them. Jobs in bookstores, magazine shops, and even newsstands will offer you a chance to become familiar with various publications.

You can also obtain information on writing as a career by visiting local newspapers, publishers, or radio and television stations and interviewing some of the writers who work there. Career conferences and other guidance programs frequently include speakers on the entire field of communications from local or national organizations.

EMPLOYERS

There are approximately 126,000 writers and authors, and 57,000 technical writers currently employed in the United States. Nearly a fourth of salaried writers and editors work for newspapers, magazines, and book publishers, according to the *Occupational Outlook Handbook*. Writers are also employed by advertising agencies and public relations firms, in radio and television broadcasting, and for journals and newsletters published by business and nonprofit organizations, such as professional associations, labor unions, and religious organizations. Other employers are government agencies and film production companies.

STARTING OUT

A fair amount of experience is required to gain a high-level position in the field. Most writers start out in entry-level positions. These jobs may be listed with college placement offices, or they may be obtained by applying directly to the employment departments of the individual publishers or broadcasting companies. Graduates who previously served internships with these companies often have the advantage of knowing someone who can give them a personal recommendation. Want ads in newspapers and trade journals are another source for jobs. Because of the competition for positions, however, few vacancies are listed with public or private employment agencies.

Employers in the communications field usually are interested in samples of published writing. These are often assembled in an organized portfolio or scrapbook. Bylined or signed articles are more credible (and, as a result, more useful) than stories whose source is not identified.

Beginning positions as a junior writer usually involve library research, preparation of rough drafts for part or all of a report, cataloging, and other related writing tasks. These are generally carried on under the supervision of a senior writer.

Some technical writers have entered the field after working in public relations departments or as technicians or research assistants, then transferring to technical writing as openings occur. Many firms now hire writers directly upon application or recommendation of college professors and placement offices.

ADVANCEMENT
Most writers find their first jobs as editorial or production assistants. Advancement may be more rapid in small companies, where beginners learn by doing a little bit of everything and may be given writing tasks immediately. In large firms, duties are usually more compartmentalized. Assistants in entry-level positions are assigned such tasks as research, fact checking, and copyrighting, but it generally takes much longer to advance to full-scale writing duties.

Promotion into more responsible positions may come with the assignment of more important articles and stories to write, or it may be the result of moving to another company. Mobility among employees in this field is common. An assistant in one publishing house may switch to an executive position in another. Or a writer may switch to a related field as a type of advancement.

A technical writer can be promoted to positions of responsibility by moving from such jobs as writer to technical editor to project leader or documentation manager. Opportunities in specialized positions also are possible.

Freelance or self-employed writers earn advancement in the form of larger fees as they gain exposure and establish their reputations.

EARNINGS
In 2001, median annual earnings for salaried writers and authors were $42,450 a year, according to the Bureau of Labor Statistics. The lowest 10 percent earned less than $20,570, while the highest 10 percent earned $83,180 or more. In book publishing, some specialties pay better than others. Technical writers earned a median salary of $49,370 in 2001.

In addition to their salaries, many writers earn some income from freelance work. Part-time freelancers may earn from $5,000 to $15,000 a year. Freelance earnings vary widely. Full-time established freelance writers may earn up to $75,000 a year.

WORK ENVIRONMENT
Working conditions vary for writers. Although their workweek usually runs 35 to 40 hours, many writers work overtime. A publication

that is issued frequently has more deadlines closer together, creating greater pressures to meet them. The work is especially hectic on newspapers and at broadcasting companies, which operate seven days a week. Writers often work nights and weekends to meet deadlines or to cover a late-developing story.

Most writers work independently, but they often must cooperate with artists, photographers, rewriters, and advertising people who may have widely differing ideas of how the materials should be prepared and presented.

Physical surroundings range from comfortable private offices to noisy, crowded newsrooms filled with other workers typing and talking on the telephone. Some writers must confine their research to the library or telephone interviews, but others may travel to other cities or countries or to local sites, such as theaters, ballparks, airports, factories, or other offices.

The work is arduous, but most writers are seldom bored. Some jobs, such as that of the foreign correspondent, require travel. The most difficult element is the continual pressure of deadlines. People who are the most content as writers enjoy and work well with deadline pressure.

OUTLOOK

The employment of writers is expected to increase faster than the average rate of all occupations over the next several years, according to the U.S. Department of Labor. The demand for writers by newspapers, periodicals, book publishers, and nonprofit organizations is expected to increase. The growth of online publishing on company websites and other online services will also demand many talented writers; those with computer skills will be at an advantage as a result. Advertising and public relations will also provide job opportunities.

The major book and magazine publishers, broadcasting companies, advertising agencies, public relations firms, and the federal government account for the concentration of writers in large cities such as New York, Chicago, Los Angeles, Boston, Philadelphia, San Francisco, and Washington, D.C. Opportunities with small newspapers, corporations, and professional, religious, business, technical, and trade publications can be found throughout the country.

People entering this field should realize that the competition for jobs is extremely keen. Beginners may especially have difficulty finding employment. Of the thousands who graduate each year with degrees in English, journalism, communications, and the liberal arts, intending to establish a career as a writer, many turn to other occupations when they find that applicants far outnumber the job openings available. College students would do well to keep this in mind and prepare for an unrelated alternate career in the event they are unable to obtain a position as writer; another benefit of this approach is that, at the same time, they will become qualified as writers in a specialized field. The practicality of preparing for alternate careers is borne out by the fact that opportunities are best in firms that prepare business and trade publications and in technical writing.

Potential writers who end up working in a different field may be able to earn some income as freelancers, selling articles, stories, books, and possibly TV and movie scripts, but it is usually difficult for anyone to be self-supporting entirely on independent writing.

FOR MORE INFORMATION

For information on writing and editing careers in the field of communications, contact

National Association of Science Writers
PO Box 890
Hedgesville, WV 25427
Tel: 304-754-5077
http://www.nasw.org

This organization offers student memberships for those interested in opinion writing.

National Conference of Editorial Writers
3899 North Front Street
Harrisburg, PA 17110
Tel: 717-703-3015
Email: ncew@pa-news.org
http://www.ncew.org

anthropomorphic: ascribing human traits and characteristics to nonhuman things

antiquities: objects and monuments from ancient times

artifact: an object that was created or changed by a human

archive: a collection of documents and records

autobiography: an individual's account of his or her own life

bill: a proposed law that legislators consider and either pass (as law) or veto

biography: an account of an individual's life, written by someone else

bureaucracy: a group of policy-making officials

campaign: the process of competing, or running, for a government office (in the hopes of being elected)

candidate: an individual who campaigns to be elected to a political office

capitalism: an economic system that involves free trade, private or corporate ownership of goods, and investment decisions that are made by private, not government, concerns

civil rights: the basic rights and freedoms that belong to citizens in a democratic society, especially the right of personal freedom in the United States

communism: a society without class levels where all individuals are entitled to the same benefits (such as health care, education, etc) and all means and demands of production are shared by society

culture: a set of beliefs, traditions, and social forms that signifies the heritage of a group of people

custom: a common practice or action that is often specific to a certain country or culture

dead language: a language that once thrived but is no longer spoken

democracy: a form of government in which the supreme power belongs to the people, and the majority rules

demographics: the statistical data (on age, income, educational level, etc.) of a population

dictatorship: a government controlled by one individual or a small elite group

dissertation: a thorough research paper, usually prepared by a graduate student in a doctorate program and presented in front of an academic board for review

famine: a period of time categorized by an extreme shortage of food

fascism: a belief that one's country or nationality is more important than oneself

fieldwork: research that is done on site at a particular location

history: the study of past events and people

historian: an individual who studies the past

language: a group of words and symbols whose sounds and meanings are combined to form a means of communication among individuals

liberalism: the political philosophy that purports intellectual freedom and progress, in addition to economic equality

modern language: a language that is currently in use

primary sources: reference materials from the period that is being studied, such as diaries, legal notices, or firsthand accounts, and photographs

reference materials: texts, such as dictionaries or encyclopedias that contain facts and information for research

reparations: payments that were made (and often demanded) from one country to another throughout history to cover the costs of war

revolution: a sudden and radical change, such as an overthrown government

secondary sources: reference materials written by an individual removed from the period being studied, such as historical textbooks

social classes: the division of people by their standing in society or income levels

tariff: a tax imposed on imported goods to protect domestic trade

terrorism: using threats or menacing acts to make a social, religious, or political statement; done by a radical group towards another country of group of people

thesis: a research paper written and defended by a student seeking an academic degree; see also **dissertation**

women's (or gender) history: the study of past people and events that have affected the role and place of gender in society

Ambrose, Stephen. *To America: Personal Reflections of an Historian*. New York: Simon & Schuster, 2002.

Gilderhus, Mark. *History and Historians: A Historiographical Introduction*, 5th ed. Upper Saddle River, N.J.: Prentice Hall, 2002.

Gustafson, Melanie. *Becoming a Historian: A Survival Manual*. Washington, D.C.: American Historical Association, 2003.

The History Internship Book. Winston-Salem, N.C.: Career Education Institutes, 2002.

Lukacs, John. *A Student's Guide to History* (ISI Guides to the Major Disciplines). Wilmington, Del.: Intercollegiate Studies Institute, 2000.

Prevenier, Walter, and Martha C. Howell. *From Reliable Sources: An Introduction to Historical Methods*. Ithaca, N.Y.: Cornell University Press, 2001.

Schulz, Constance et al. *Careers for Students of History*. Washington, D.C.: American Historical Association, 2002.

Storey, William Kelleher. *Writing History: A Guide for Students*. New York: Oxford University Press, 1998.

Williams, Robert Chadwell. *The Historian's Toolbox: A Student's Guide to the Theory and Craft of History*. Armonk, N.Y.: M.E. Sharpe, 2003.

Wineburg, Sam. *Historical Thinking and Other Unnatural Acts: Charting the Future of Teaching the Past* (Critical Perspectives on the Past). Philadelphia: Temple University Press, 2001.

Zinn, Howard. *A People's History of the United States: 1492–Present*. New York: HarperCollins, 2003.